SEVEN DEADLY SINS

SEVEN DEADLY SINS

DAVID WALSH

SIMON &
SCHUSTER

London · New York · Sydney · Toronto · New Delhi

A CBS COMPANY

First published in Great Britain by Simon & Schuster UK Ltd, 2012
A CBS COMPANY

1 3 5 7 9 10 8 6 4 2

Simon & Schuster UK Ltd
1st Floor
222 Gray's Inn Road
London
WC1X 8HB

www.simonandschuster.co.uk

Simon & Schuster Australia, Sydney
Simon & Schuster India, New Delhi

A CIP catalogue record for this book is available
from the British Library

HB ISBN: 978-1-47112-753-3
TPB ISBN: 978-1-47112-754-0
Ebook ISBN: 978-1-47112-756-4

Typeset by M Rules
Printed and bound by CPI Group (UK) Ltd, Croydon, CR0 4YY

For John, his brothers, his sisters and mum

I watch the Olympic Games but I don't bother to remember the names of the athletes any more. It's like theatre – but I prefer the theatre because the relationship between actor and spectator is clear. In sport's theatre, both are still pretending it's real.

Sandro Donati

You're no messiah. You're a movie of the week. You're a fucking T-shirt, at best.

Brad Pitt, *Se7en*

Prologue

'Finally, the last thing, I'll say to the people who don't believe in cycling, the cynics and the sceptics: I'm sorry for you. I'm sorry that you can't dream big. I'm sorry you don't believe in miracles.'

Lance Armstrong, 2005 Tour de France victory speech

Le grand depart.

My first conversation with Lance Armstrong was in the garden of the Chateau de la Commanderie hotel about ten miles south of Grenoble. This was late afternoon on Tuesday 13 July 1993, a rest day on the Tour de France, and with its trees and shrubs, its wrought-iron chairs and tables overlooking the swimming pool, the setting couldn't have been much better.

At a nearby table Armstrong's teammate Andy Hampsten sat with some friends. A little further away another journalist interviewed the team's Colombian climber, Álvaro Mejía. Armstrong and I sat in the shade and spoke for more than three hours. He did most of the talking, but then he had much to say and I had a book to write.

1

It was the force of his personality that struck you the most: like a wave crashing forward and carrying you with him. Twenty-one years old but he wasn't like most young men of that age. If he had been, he would have talked about the thrill of riding his first Tour de France. Most young sportsmen know the clichés that we like to see recycled. He didn't mention the thrill or the honour, nothing even close. He'd been told by the team bosses he was at this Tour to learn for the future, but he didn't see the good in that. He wanted to win right now. *I am Lance Armstrong, you're gonna remember my name.* As he machine-gunned his way through his past and speeded into the future, he had me at his side, and on his side.

'You've got to see this kid,' I said over dinner to my friend, fellow journalist and former Tour rider Paul Kimmage, that evening.

'Why?'

'He is different. He's got this desire. He's going to win a lot of races, and he's so open. Wait 'til you meet him.'

'You always get too enthusiastic,' Kimmage said.

Eleven years earlier, I'd turned up at the Tour de France for the first time and fallen in love. The man-crush is a hazard of life for the sportswriter. That debut trip covered just the last two race days in 1982; the boat from Rosslare in the south-east of Ireland to Le Havre, a car drive to pick up the penultimate stage and then on into Paris for the race to the Champs-Élysées. I travelled with four people from Carrick-on-Suir, the home town of Sean Kelly, who was then one of the world's best cyclists. Kelly's fiancée Linda Grant was part of our group, as was her father Dan, and local shopkeeper

Jim O'Keeffe. Professional cycling wasn't big news in Ireland then, and if Kelly managed to win a stage in the Tour de France, the result just about made it onto a sports page. Down in Carrick-on-Suir, O'Keeffe was ahead of the rest of us because he knew how to tune his radio into some French station that gave regular updates from the Tour, and if the local hero did well, the local shopkeeper knew it first.

One afternoon O'Keeffe caught news of Kelly winning a stage at the Tour, it might have been the leg to Thonon in 1981. Beside himself with joy he left his shop and just walked down Main Street hoping to meet someone he could tell. Coming in the opposite direction was Kelly's Uncle Neddy, wheeling his bicycle.

'Neddy,' said O'Keeffe, 'you're not going to believe this. I'm just after hearing Sean won today's stage in the Tour de France.'

Taking a second to digest the news, Neddy replied, 'Why wouldn't he win, he does nothin' else except cycle that bike.'

Telling Irish people that they had produced a world-class athlete called Sean Kelly became my first crusade. But in terms of the Irish attitude to Kelly's prowess, things didn't change quickly, and the following year I could get to the Tour de France only by taking two weeks holidays and the considerable risk of travelling on the back of Tony Kelly's BMW 1000 motorbike. On a clear road Tony could get that baby up to 130 mph, and whatever happened, I knew it wouldn't take long. We saw Kelly take the yellow jersey in Pau, found a cheap restaurant and toasted his achievement with a bottle of wine.

Stephen Roche, our other countryman in the race, had the

white jersey for the 'leading young rider' and that evening in the Basque city we felt proudly Irish, members of a privileged elite. Next day we waited on the Col de Peyresourde and measured the scale of disaster by the minutes Kelly and Roche lost to the new leaders. As hard as it was to see your men wither in the mountains, it was impossible not to be captivated by the great race beyond them. The Tour thrilled me like no other sporting event, and no sooner had Tony returned me to Dublin I was talking to my wife about how good it would be to move to France. So in 1984 Paris became home and I got to follow most of the great races on the cycling calendar.

One experience begot another until, in early 1993, I agreed with the UK publishers Stanley Paul to write a book about the Tour de France, a series of stories from the three-week pilgrimage around France that I envisaged as a Canterbury Tales in lycra. At the beginning would be the story of the rookie, the kid in his first Tour: he'd be starry-eyed and about to have his senses overwhelmed and his body wasted. Armstrong was the obvious choice, the youngest rider in the race but also the newcomer with expectations on his shoulders. Perfect.

I don't know about Lance but I was pumped and ready. He had agreed to do the piece and arranged for me to come to the Motorola team hotel in Bourgenay on the evening after the opening prologue.

I turned up at Les Jardins de l'Atlantique but was met by Jim Ochowicz, his team manager, who told me that Lance felt down after his disappointing ride in that day's prologue. The rider wanted to know if we could do the interview sometime later, perhaps on the Tour's scheduled rest day. I agreed but continued to observe him for my background notes. I watched him in the tented village at Avranches on the sixth morning as an Italian journalist tried to interview him. He wasn't rude, but the moment two attractive French girls passed by in their short skirts it was clear they interested him far more than the questions. Human, I thought.

So here I am in the Chateau de la Commanderie, sitting down with a young man who will be a central part of my life for almost the next twenty years. He doesn't exude the sense that this will be the start of a beautiful friendship, but that's okay. Meanwhile I want to know everything about him.

His biological father?

'I never met him. Ah, I guess I met him but I was a one-year-old at that point. That's when he left.'

The stepfather he never liked?

'When I was young I got along with him all right. You don't know how to dislike somebody at that age, but I tell you, the first day I learned to dislike somebody, I disliked him.'

Phew! Whatever happened to Mom's apple pie and starry-eyed rookies?

He tells about the impact on him of his mum and stepdad splitting up. 'When you're growing up, you're fourteen, fifteen or sixteen and you're in high school, or whatever, your friends' parents are getting divorced and the kids are falling apart. They start crying, they get upset, all of this. And my stepfather has left and I had a party, you know, because it's such a load off my back. I got confused because I thought, "Well, man, what is wrong with you? This tears kids up and yet we're kicking this guy out and you're ecstatic." For a while I thought maybe something's wrong with me.'

5

I wanted to like him. Sportswriters are like this, especially with the young ones, toting pencils through the foothills on their journey to Mount Olympus. We want to say we walked some of the way with them. Knew them before the world knew them. And this Armstrong, you knew he wasn't going to settle for an ordinary life.

He had something inside that made him unlike any other young sportsman I had met. Radioactivity. How did I know this? Because it was obvious.

'I mean when I'm in there, physically I'm not any more gifted than anybody else but it's just this desire, just this rage. I'm on the bike and I go into a rage, when I just shriek for about five seconds. I shake like mad and my eyes kinda bulge out. I swear, I sweat a little more and the heart rate goes like two hundred a minute.'

Then he paused, became more reflective. 'And it's funny, every time I do that I think about my mother, I really do, because if she was there ... she didn't raise a quitter and I would never, I'd never quit. I'd never, just never. And that's heart, man, that's not physical, that's not legs, that's not lungs. That's heart. That's soul. That's just guts.'

I left the Chateau de la Commanderie knowing I'd met a kid with a future. He wasn't going to be another rider in the pack. I couldn't wait to tell Kimmage. To let him know that I'd just got into the lift on the ground floor with a guy who was going up.

1

Breakfast at 10 rue Kléber in Courbevoie, west of Paris, followed a pattern. An early morning walk to the patisserie, a dawdle at the newsagents on the way home and then the luxury of strong coffee, warm croissants and *L'Équipe*. It is August 1984 and sitting across the breakfast table is Paul Kimmage, a young Irish amateur cyclist who my wife and I have rescued from a hovel in Vincennes on the east side of Paris. I've known Paul for four years, since I was a rookie sports reporter covering the bike races he rode. He was moody and headstrong then and still is, but he is also intelligent and honest. It's an easy trade-off.

We became friends quickly. When Paul went to Paris to pursue his dream of being a pro bike rider I followed him soon after. I'd agreed to write a book about my hero, the cyclist Sean Kelly, and I wanted to live in his world. As Paul

7

and I were both in Paris, it was always likely I would bump into him. He had come with his brother Raphael who was also hoping to turn pro and they rode for the best-known Parisian amateur team, ACBB. Raphael fell sick a lot, missed races and then he just got sick of being sick. So he went back to Dublin, leaving his brother alone in Vincennes. It was then Paul came to live with us.

He and I shared a love of cycling; he was born to it while I rode in on the bandwagon fuelled by Kelly's success. But by this point I'd been at the Tour de France three times, covered all the spring classics, Paris–Nice, the Tour of Switzerland and could read the cycling pages of *L'Équipe*. I considered myself virtually French. It was however the minor accomplishment of my literacy that brought tension to the breakfast table on that August morning in 1984.

'Bloody hell! Roche isn't riding the Worlds, an insect bite or something,' I say, speaking of the Irish cyclist Stephen Roche and guessing the meaning of *les mots* that I don't understand.

'Look, I'd rather read the paper myself, after you're done with it,' Paul says.

'What's the difference? I'm telling he's out of the Worlds.'

'I'm telling you, I'd rather read it myself.'

'That's just stupid.'

'Okay, it's stupid.' And we mightn't then talk for an hour or two. And then we would talk for an hour or four. He told stories of the hardship and indignities that came with riding as an amateur and I brought stories back from Hollywood. What Kelly and Roche were up to, what it was like at the Tour de France, what a talent this young American Greg

LeMond was, whether Laurent Fignon was right to taunt his French rival Bernard Hinault, but mostly we talked about Kelly and Roche.

I told Paul about the Saturday afternoon after the Amstel Gold race in Holland when we waited for Roche to finish at drug control so we could get on the road to Paris – they were giving me a ride back home while Kelly's fiancée Linda would drive his car back to their home near Brussels. As we sat around in the car park waiting for Roche, Linda leaned against Sean's immaculately clean Citroën and placed an open palm on the bonnet. After she moved away, Sean sidled over to where she had been, then discreetly took a tissue from his pocket and cleaned away the little hand-stain left by his wife-to-be.

Catching this unspoken reprimand, Linda wasn't impressed. Only half-joking, she said, 'Sean, that's so typical of you. In your life it's the car, the bike and then me.'

Kelly never blinked an eye, nor offered the hint of a smile. 'You got the order wrong, the bike comes first.'

Where we were from defined our allegiances: Kimmage, like Roche, came from Dublin, and was in his camp. I sprang from the south-east of Ireland, no more than 20 miles from Kelly's home town. He was my man. But Kelly's hardness had a universal appeal and there wasn't a Kelly story that Kimmage didn't want to hear.

He was interested in journalism as well, would check what I wrote and say whether he thought it was any good. And he railed against my refusal to speak the little French I had. One day in the kitchen he pursued this theme in front of a few visitors.

'He reads *L'Équipe*, but won't speak French,' he said.

'I don't know enough French to speak it,' I said.

'You know enough to try. Once you start, it gets easier.'

'It's okay for you, you're in a French environment at ACBB, you have to. I'm mixing with English-speaking journalists.'

'No, you've got to try because you do have enough vocabulary. French people like it when you try to speak their language.'

'Do they?'

'Course they do. So look, don't be afraid to just speak it.'

Paul can be persuasive and suddenly I felt emboldened.

'Okay,' I said, 'I'll do it. I'm covering the Blois–Chaville classic on Sunday and I need to get a hotel in Blois for Saturday night. I'll just ring up and book one.'

Picking up the thick Michelin hotel guide in the next room, I rifle through the options and come up with a perfect resting place in Blois: Hotel La Renaissance, 150 francs (£15) for the night. 'Right,' I say to the half-full kitchen. 'I'm ready to go for this.' A respectful hush falls and I dial the number for La Renaissance.

'Hello?' the voice says.

'Hello,' I say, triumphantly.

'*Oui?*

'*Oh . . . je m'appelle David Walsh, je suis journaliste irlandais, je voudrais une chambre avec salle de bains pour une nuit, cette samedi.*'

'This is a fucking private house,' the guy says.

I want to die but I do worse than that.

'How did you know I spoke English?'

He hangs up. And there it ended, my life as a French speaker. From this moment on I will accept only non-speaking parts in French movies.

I got to Blois and followed the race to Chaville, hoping that Kelly might win his third one-day classic of the year, for he'd been the season's dominant rider and, as his biographer, I wanted it to finish well. Paul had ridden the Grand Prix de *L'Équipe* earlier in the day, that race finishing in Chaville, and he waited by the final corner to see the finish to the pros' race. Kelly came around that last corner in 10th or 12th place and Kimmage thought it would be a miracle for him to get in the top three. He won easily.

In the *salle de presse* that evening, there was the now customary procession to where I sat. '*Parlez-vous avec Kellee?*' Everyone knew Kelly spoke to me and because he wasn't always the most forthcoming interviewee, this gave me status. That evening back at rue Kléber, Paul and I sat up talking, about how good Kelly had been, about whether Paul would get to realise his dream of riding with the pros, and no matter how much we talked there was more to say.

That was how much in love with cycling I was back in those days. The truth is that I thought of little else and dreamed of little else. If I read a paper it was for cycling news. Ditto the television. If I thought of a *double entendre* it invariably had to do with bikes rather than sex.

The 1984 World Championships were to be held in Barcelona early in September. Sean Kelly was always conflicted about his preparations for the Worlds. He needed some good three- or four-day stage races, but he preferred to pocket the guaranteed appearance fees earned in small-town criteriums. For Kelly getting paid was important. That's why he did what he did.

So it was that he came to be racing in a small-time mid-week criterium in August in the one-horse town of Chaumeil in Limousin, central France. He was the star. The prize money meant nothing. The appearance money meant a lot. To me, as his Boswell, the criterium was an opportunity. I contacted the various Irish media I was working for and sold their bemused sports editors the idea of me travelling to Chaumeil. I guaranteed that I would have unhindered access to Kelly. And as I was writing a biography about Kelly it was good to combine the needs of the newspapers with my need to get material for the book. Better if the newspapers paid for the trip, which they did.

I agreed with Sean that I would travel down, watch him race and meet up afterwards to do the interview. Apart from material for the book our chat would serve up some preview material for the forthcoming Worlds. Two birds. One stone. All on expenses.

Not surprisingly it was an incredibly hot day. When is central France not hot in early August? I watched the race from a grassy bank out on the course. We Irish have never really learned to handle extreme heat with much grace or dignity. Not being familiar with either performance-enhancing substances or the subsequent work of Bear Grylls, I began to wilt.

I had brought with me the paraphernalia of the Irish survivalist, a packet of Jaffa Cakes and a bottle of Lucozade. I stood in the August sunshine, my skin turning crispy, my mouth turning to sandpaper. All this happened at a time long ago before mankind had invented the screw-off cap. The unreachable contents of the Lucozade bottle were getting warmer the longer I sat there.

Near the end of the race, just as dehydration was bringing me past confusion and towards a coma, I sprang into action. Confusion was fine. A coma would almost certainly impair my interviewing style.

Behind me on a slight hill there was a row of attractive bungalows. The little town of Chaumeil was about a two-mile walk away. So I abandoned my post and walked up the tarmac drive leading towards the first bungalow. The front of the bungalow showed no promise of life. I wandered around the back.

'Hello?'

A woman emerged from the house. Mid-twenties. Very attractive. Friendly. I hit her with my smooth pidgin French, something along the lines that I was *trés desolé* for the trespass but I needed an opener for my Lucozade. I showed her the bottle and simulated the act of taking off the top.

She understood. Told me not to worry. She disappeared into the house and re-emerged with the bottle opener. She watched as I sucked the Lucozade from the bottle with the elegance of a man who had spent too many months in the desert.

'What brings you to Chaumeil?' she asked.

I explained that I was a cycling journalist from Ireland and that I was here to interview Sean Kelly. She seemed oddly unimpressed by these details. She made some more chat. She asked where I lived.

'Paris,' I said.

It always feels good telling somebody that you live in Paris.

Ah, Paris. Her husband worked in Paris. He would leave Chaumeil early on a Monday morning and not return again until Friday.

This was Wednesday.

'I get very lonely,' she said.

I nodded sympathetically. I offered some words along the lines of, '*Oui, oui, c'est tres difficile.*' She said that if I wanted to come in for coffee, I was welcome.

Sacre bleu. She had understood nothing. I was thinking of Kelly and starting to panic. I backed away offering thanks and wondering how long it would take me to walk back into Chaumeil. Kelly was heading on to Limoges where we'd agreed to do the interview. I needed a lift and the one certainty was that Sean Kelly wouldn't hang around waiting for a late reporter, not even his Boswell. This was a lot to convey by means of gesture for a man with Jaffa Cakes in one hand and Lucozade in the other. Missing the lift would be a professional and personal disaster.

It was a year, maybe two years later, when I was telling a friend about the bottle of Lucozade and the interview and how nice the woman had been, that I realised the story could have had another dimension.

'Phew!' said my friend. 'That's like the plot of a porn film. You must have been tempted?'

'How do you mean?'

'The heavy hints. Attractive but lonely French woman. Husband away until Friday. Dead summer heat. What do you think I mean?'

'Oh Jesus, do you really think so?'

Talk about regret: how many nights has that nice woman

of Chaumeil lain awake wondering what might have been with the sunburned Irishman and his Jaffa Cakes?

As for me? Just another innocent abroad.

It was a terrific year, 1984.

Mary loved Paris. We went with two children and came home with three, as Simon was born in a small hospital about a half-mile from rue Kléber. That's another story. On the Saturday night of his arrival, his mum lay on her bed in rue Kléber writing letters and saying there was no need to call the taxi just yet. It would be hours. I did as told until it got close to midnight but then began to worry about getting a taxi so late. Eventually I was given the go-ahead to walk across to the taxi rank outside the Pentahotel in Courbevoie and arrange for one to come round to the house.

When Mary put down her pen and got out of bed to dress for the hospital, she was reminded that things had progressed more than she'd realised. The contractions were serious. From the front door to the cab was perhaps ten metres but my wife had to take the journey in three stages; four metres, contraction; three metres, bigger contraction; three metres, massive contraction. She whispered that it was okay, that her time only seemed closer than it was.

Aghast, the taxi driver watched and then motioned me round to the other side of the car so I could examine the cleanliness of his back seat.

'Monsieur,' he said in French I could easily understand, 'I keep this taxi very clean. Look, see for yourself. It's not possible for me to take your wife.'

I tried to sound nonchalant. I needed to convince him that

I was an expert in this field and that he was just misreading the signs.

'Don't be stupid,' I said. 'The baby will not come for four or five hours and we have an eight-hundred-metre journey to the hospital.'

While the argument went back and forth, Mary stayed upright with support from an open rear door. 'Three minutes and we'll be at the hospital,' I said. He demurred, I insisted, and, reluctantly, he agreed. Every traffic light was green, the ride took maybe two minutes, and a minute and a half after we got there Simon was born.

In mid-September Paul and I went to beautiful Senlis, about twenty miles north of the capital for the start of the Paris–Brussels semi-classic. It was a working assignment for me but we both went there as fans, wanting to savour the atmosphere and hoping to catch up with Kelly before the race left town.

We got to him about thirty minutes before the start and as he sat and chatted with us, we could have been speaking to the lowliest rider in the peloton, not the number one. Through those years people continually asked, 'Kelly, what's he like?' My favourite answer was that he was the kind of fellow that if he found a geyser he wouldn't come back and tell you he'd invented hot water. Paul had grown to love him too.

After shooting the breeze for twenty minutes or so, it was time for Kelly to get himself to the start line. He stood up, hopped on his bike and, as he was wont to do, he bounced the rear wheel off the road a couple of times to check he had the right pressure in his tyre. As he did, there was the unmistakable sound of pills rattling inside a small plastic container in his back pocket. I looked at Paul, silently asking, 'Did you hear that?' He had. Then Kelly was gone and we were silent; kids who had got close to Father Christmas and seen the glue that held his beard in place.

'Could it have been anything else?'

'No, it was definitely the sound of pills.'

'Why would he need those in a race?'

'Don't know.'

'Me neither.'

I wondered if they could be supplements but we knew no rider was going to use supplements during a race. It should have been a seminal moment. We had inadvertently seen the realities of professional cycling, but we weren't ready for that. I had a biography to write, one in which the hero is a farmer's son from Carrick-on-Suir, a man who as a boy had eaten raw turnips when hungry.

He got to the top because he never lost that hunger and he was loved because he remained true to the modest background whence he had come. Pills rattling against plastic didn't fit into the story. When you're a fan, as I was, you don't ask the hero about the sound that came from his pocket. Still, Paul and I could never forget it.

Kelly finished third that day, went to doping control and failed. The banned drug Stimul was found in his urine. What I remember now is how Sean Kelly looked that evening. A small semi-circle of journalists stood around him at Rhode-Saint-Genèse asking about his third-place finish but it was his deathly white face and the enlarged pupils that struck me. He didn't look like himself.

When the news of his positive test was made public, he did what all cyclists did: denied using Stimul and said there had to have been a mix-up in the doping control room. One of his arguments was that there were six or seven people in the room when he was giving his sample as opposed to the stipulated two. If Kelly had used Stimul, he had behaved very stupidly because it was an easily detectable drug and by finishing third he had ensured that he would be tested.

Robert Millar, the Scottish rider, was dismissive of the charge, not on any moral grounds but on the basis that Stimul was passé, a seventies drug no one used any more. Karl McCarthy, international secretary for the Irish Cycling Federation, flew into Brussels to plead on Kelly's behalf, and when the Belgian Federation still insisted he was guilty, the Union Cycliste Internationale (UCI) sent the case back to them and asked them to reconsider.

Sixteen months after the race, the UCI confirmed the original result stood.

Kelly was fined 1000 Swiss francs, which was approximately one sixth of what he earned for showing up at a village race, and given a one-month suspended sentence. When I wrote about the 1984 Paris–Brussels in the biography, I didn't mention the rattle of pills in the morning and I tried to make the case that it was hard to believe Kelly had used a substance so easily detectable. I chose to see the ridiculous leniency of the authorities as proof that, at worst, it was a minor infraction. It wasn't how a proper journalist would have reacted. At the time I knew what I was doing.

Things changed over the following fifteen years.

We returned to Ireland in 1985, reluctantly leaving Paris, and I went back to covering the entire range of major sports.

Paul stayed for a second year on the amateur circuit in France, achieved better results and earned a pro contract. It was a dream for him, something we had talked about over so many teas and coffees at rue Kléber. I couldn't wait to see how his career would turn out. It was to be a bitter-sweet experience for him, a four-year collision with the reality of professional cycling. He experienced the joy of finishing the Tour de France but that, in the end, was overwhelmed by the certainty that if you didn't dope, it was virtually impossible to compete.

In those years we spoke on the telephone a lot and Paul's despair at cycling's doping culture was palpable. He rode the Tour in 1986 and on the day at Alpe d'Huez that Bernard Hinault and Greg LeMond held hands as they rode across the finish line, I interviewed him for a piece commissioned by *Magill*, a current affairs magazine in Dublin.

It was a long interview, almost four hours, as we had so much to talk about. Kimmage wasn't able to speak about doping because if he did he would have been drummed out of the sport the next day, but he spoke about the race like no one I had ever heard speak about the Tour de France. Honest, human, unromantic, but packed with insight. On the Monday morning that the race ended, the magazine editor Fintan O'Toole rang.

'Where's the piece?'

It wouldn't be the last time I would hear that question.

'How much do you need and when do you need it by?'

'Five thousand words and by two-thirty this afternoon.'

It was a little after nine in the morning, and I had yet to listen to the tapes.

'Fintan,' I said, trying to sound authoritative, 'this piece will work as a first-person piece, directly from the mouth of a rookie.'

'That's okay. I will send a bike to your house for two-thirty. Okay?'

'Fine.'

Then the strangest thing happened. I sat down, played the tape and started typing. Every other minute there was something that had to be in the story. Paul had the gift of storytelling; gritty and unromantic but wonderful for that. It was by far the easiest five-thousand-word piece I've ever written: the Tour de France as you had never seen it. I can still remember his description of the pain as he struggled up the Col du Granon. So wasted he could barely keep the pedals turning and in danger of being outside the time limit, his slow progress and tortured face were an unspoken plea, '*Poussez-moi, poussez-moi.*' And the fans did, pushing him forward as they have done for those in difficulty since the Tour began.

Of course it is against cycling's rules to accept a push and in the team support car directly behind, a man known to Paul only as Robert screamed at the fans to stop. Confused, they stepped back, and after this had happened a few times Paul mustered up the energy to turn his head back to the car: 'Robert, for fuck's sake, let them push me.' And Robert, embarrassed by the mistake, then yelled at the fans to help Paul.

After Kimmage's first-person account of the race appeared, Fintan O'Toole called to say that in his time as editor it was the best piece he had ever run. I knew from the ease with which I'd extracted five thousand words from the tape that

Kimmage could be a journalist and told him so. He didn't believe me but that would change.

In 1988, two years after that *Magill* piece, Paul began writing columns about his life as a pro cyclist for the *Sunday Tribune*, the paper where I was working at the time. Given that he had no sports-writing experience, the columns were absurdly good. Vincent Browne was an outstanding editor at the *Tribune* and a man who didn't often doubt his own judgement. He read the Kimmage columns and felt he knew the score: Kimmage told his story to Walsh who dressed it up as journalism.

'Vincent, Paul is doing these columns entirely on his own.'

'Yes, David, but you're editing.'

'I'm not, and if I was I couldn't make them as good as they are.'

'I still don't believe he's doing them on his own.'

'Okay, Vincent, when Paul calls in with his column this week, you go and sit by the copytaker and see what he dictates.'

Vincent stood over Rita Byrne as she tapped out Paul's words on her electric typewriter, scanning each sentence as it appeared on the page. This little exercise didn't last long. Next time Paul was back in Dublin, Vincent offered him a full-time job as sportswriter. Paul's writing was going better than his riding and he was enjoying it far more. We would speak on the phone about pro cycling and I now knew enough about the sport's doping culture to understand he hadn't a hope.

He retired in 1989 and then wrote a masterful account of his life in the peloton, *Rough Ride*. His memoir became the definitive tome on doping in cycling but Paul was vilified for writing it. And the criticism came exclusively from within the cycling family. It was shocking to hear the lies people told, distressing to watch the self-serving assaults on Paul's character. His one-time teammate and friend Roche was one of those complaining the loudest. The other great Irish hero of the roads, Kelly, studiously avoided passing any critique on the book or on Paul.

'I'd like to read the book but I just haven't got round to it yet,' Kelly would say to enquiring journalists for years afterwards.

And the fan who had followed Kelly from race to race in 1984 was having his eyes opened, slowly and painfully. At the 1988 Tour de France, the raceleader Pedro Delgado tested positive for the drug probenecid which was banned by the International Olympic Committee because it masks the use of steroids. Conveniently probenecid wasn't due to be banned by cycling's authorities until ten days after the Tour ended. There was no legitimate reason for any Tour rider to use probenecid and after the news broke the director of the Tour de France Xavier Louy went to Delgado's hotel and asked him to leave the race.

The Spaniard refused, saying he hadn't broken any rule. Technically that was the case.

The following morning I wandered through the corporate village at Limoges still angry that a guy caught using a masking agent was about to win the Tour de France. Standing there alone for a moment was Dutch rider Steven Rooks, second overall and the one who would have won the Tour had Delgado been sanctioned.

'Do you not feel cheated, that you are the true winner of the Tour de France?' I asked, wanting him to agree.

He looked at me as if I was an alien with no understanding of anything human.

'No, not at all. Delgado has been the best rider in the race, he deserves to win. It is okay for me to finish second.'

'But he has used this masking drug?'

'He is still the strongest guy in the race.'

Rooks wanted me to know that doping wasn't any of my business. He resented any line of questioning that suggested he was the legitimate leader of the Tour de France. Effectively, there was an understanding between him and Delgado of what was permissible and his rival hadn't breached that. As for you, the journalist, just stay out of it.

Cycling wasn't the only sport with a drug culture.

Two months later I was in Seoul watching Florence Griffith-Joyner break a world 200m record while decelerating. Though she passed the tests, and said she was clean, the performances didn't make sense. Many of those who wrote of Flo-Jo's brilliance on the track were faking it. Then a couple of nights after the men's 100m final Doug Gillon from the *Herald* in Glasgow knocked on my apartment in Seoul. It was 3.30 in the morning.

'Doug, what's up?'

'Johnson's tested positive. Get dressed.'

I could have kissed that Scot for thinking of me and the rest of the Seoul Olympics passed in a blur with only Johnson in focus. After it was all over I followed the path beaten by so many journalists to Toronto, the gym where Johnson still worked out, the track where he used to train and the office of his then lawyer Morris Chrobotek working to show Ben in the best light.

Chrobotek was funny, sometimes intentionally, sometimes not. At the suggestion that one of of Ben's rivals was clean, he threw his head back, then brought it forward: 'I may be ugly,' he said, 'but I'm not stupid.' Afterwards when doping suspicions arose I tried to apply the Chrobotek principle: it was okay to be ugly, not okay to be stupid.

But there is a choice for the sportswriter and it's not straightforward. Most of us have chosen journalism because we love sport. We say we love our jobs but it is getting paid for going to big sporting events that we love. Enthusiasm for the game is what drives our work. When doubts about the worth of the performance arise, they drain our enthusiasm.

This is why so many refuse to ask the obvious questions.

I was lucky when it came to Lance Armstrong.

Most things are a question of timing. Perhaps if the right questions were asked during the 1980s and '90s, it might have emerged that EPO, which was then in widespread use and undetectable, had changed the sport. I saw many of those Tours and never asked a question.

So why, when Lance Armstrong won the first of his seven in the Tour de France, did I have such a different reaction?

I've always thought of my enthusiasm for sports-writing as existing in a well; you draw from it, it replenishes but not quite at the level that you have drawn from it. This used to be a worry. What if the well went dry? That thought doesn't bother me any more because at the 1999 Tour, when the story of Lance Armstrong first announced itself, my enthusiasm for professional cycling was at a very low ebb.

Lance, Tour champion extraordinaire, came into my journalistic life at precisely the right moment.

2

'The race is everything. It obliterates what isn't racing. Life is the metaphor for the race.'

Donald Antrim

On 25 June 1995, I returned home to Ireland after five weeks covering the Rugby World Cup in South Africa. It was about ten o'clock when the plane landed in Dublin. Mary drove from our home in County Westmeath to pick me up, and Paul and his wife Ann came from their home not far from the airport to meet us for a coffee. We spent a couple of hours catching up before heading in our separate directions.

At home, turning into our drive, it was obvious something was wrong. Neighbours were standing around – not just neighbours but the schoolmaster, the priest – no one sure where to look. Inside the car you felt the certainty that once you opened the door your life was going to change forever. I can't remember who it was told me that John, our 12-year-old son, had been in an accident on his bicycle.

'But is he okay?' I asked.

'No, he broke his neck.'

'Where is he now?'

'He's gone in the ambulance.'

'But how is he? Is he going to be okay?'

'No, he isn't.'

That was it. We knew. Then we were thinking of our other children: Kate, Simon, Daniel, Emily and Conor, who all knew before we did. Where were they? How were they?

The accident had happened an hour earlier. John had played a gaelic football match that morning, his team had lost and he'd passed on the sandwiches and soft drinks provided afterwards. Turning into our driveway on the right-hand side of the road, he was struck by an oncoming car and died instantly. There wasn't a mark on his face or body. It was just the force of the collision and the angle of his fall.

John was the second eldest of our children, a kid with an insatiable appetite for life. He was good at school, fiercely scrupulous about getting his homework done: 'Dad, can't talk, I've got three hours homework and there's Champions League on the television.' You stood to one side and let him get on with it. We played a lot of football on our lawn with the Kilmartin kids from next door and often they ended in fights; John and I, mostly.

'It's our throw.'

'It didn't cross the line.'

And from there all hell would break loose. His passion was forgivable. I should have had more sense.

We went on a holiday to the west of Ireland before the 1987 Tour de France and did the hike to the statue that stands on a hill 300 metres above Kylemore Abbey. To get to the statue you follow a steeply rising trail with countless switch-backs. At the top we were all tired but John just wanted to start running back down. We warned him it was too steep for running but we might as well have told him it would be a blast and to go for it.

Waiting wasn't what John did. He just went; I sprinted after him. He was four, I was 31 and a regular runner at the time. Again I was the one who should have had more sense. Some sense. With his 10-metre start, it should have taken about a minute for me to catch him. I never saw him until I got to the bottom of the hill. He scared the life out of me. It exhilarated him and, even at four, he savoured that victory over his dad.

It didn't matter what the sport was, he loved it. He played gaelic football, loved Liverpool, taped every game that mattered in the 1995 Rugby World Cup knowing I would watch them when I got home. Seeing how he'd indexed them and lined them up on a shelf in my office was heartbreaking.

He could break your heart in others ways too. Once, when Paul came to the house, John ambushed him.

'Paul,' he said. 'You know in your book with Andy Townsend?' (Paul had ghost-written the autobiography of the ex-footballer.)

'Yeah, John?'

'Townsend talks about the night Arsenal beat Liverpool at Anfield to stop them winning the double?'

'Yeah, I remember that.'

'Townsend says in the book he can still see David Seaman bowling the ball out to Lee Dixon, a long, long ball to Alan Smith and then the pass to Michael Thomas for the goal?'

'Yeah?'

'It wasn't Seaman who was in goal for Arsenal that night. It was John Lukic.'

He was 12 and Paul was toast.

In September 1994 I travelled to the All-Ireland gaelic football final with Martin McHugh, who had been a star of the Donegal team that had won the title two years before. McHugh and I were friends and John came with us. Down beat Dublin that day and on the journey home John asked Martin question after question about the game. He never stopped and Martin's patience never wavered.

Next day back in his native Donegal, Martin bought a pair of Patrick football boots for John and had them couriered to our home.

'You didn't need to do that,' I said.

'I've spoken to a lot of kids about football,' he said, 'but never with an eleven-year-old who asked questions like your lad's.'

You may think it impossible to find any comfort when your son is taken but I did. Soon after his death, the school principal Tim Looney told a story of a day in the classroom when some boy had mischievously written on the blackboard.

'Okay, who did this?' Mr Looney asked.

No one owned up.

'Well, we're all going to stay here until I find out who did it.'

The silence and the detention continued into the lunchtime break and with the principal showing not the slightest inclination to back down, someone had to do something. John put up his hand.

'Yes, John?'

Standing up, he turned to his best friend. 'Andrew,' he said, 'you know you did it, we know you did it and you probably won't be even punished if you admit it.' Andrew stood up and said, 'Sir, I did it.'

'Thank you, Andrew, for being honest. Now you can all go on your break.'

Later another teacher, Mrs Twomey, told of reading the Nativity to John's class and getting to the point where she related how Mary and Joseph lived a modest life in Nazareth because Joseph was just a carpenter. John's hand went up.

'If they were so poor, what did they do with the gold they were given by the three wise men?'

Mrs Twomey had been reading the story of the Nativity to children for more than thirty years.

'John, that's the first time anyone's asked me that. I don't know the answer.'

I have held onto all the stories, especially the two from the classroom. If you can, you've got to stand up and be counted. And you have to ask the obvious but sometimes difficult questions. What *did* Mary and Joseph do with the gold?

Sean Kelly came to John's funeral and, finding me on my own, he asked how exactly the accident had happened. From which direction had John been coming; which direction the car? We walked down the garden so he could get a better picture of precisely what had happened. Kelly then asked about my trip from Dublin Airport and whether John might have expected us to be already home as he cycled down the road to the house. I said we should have been back but we had a long coffee with Paul at the airport.

'As John's coming to the house,' he said, 'he's already look-ing to see if your car is in the driveway. He's glancing across while his brain is telling him to turn, but his eyes aren't on the road in front of him. I've done it a few times, turned across a road like that, but was lucky no car was coming against me.'

Though it was hard to have someone talk you through your son's fatal accident, I appreciated Kelly helping me understand how it happened.

A year after John's death, on a sticky summer's night in Atlanta, a small group of us found ourselves in dwindling light in a small garden behind the swimming arena at Georgia Tech University. I was with my old friend Paul, now well into his career as a successful Sunday newspaper journalist and our newer friend Tom Humphries of the *Irish Times*. Tom's humour made us laugh, his talent kept us humble.

Irish swimmer Michelle Smith had just stormed the first day of the Olympic Games, and won a gold medal. It was an incredible achievement from a woman who through her career up to then had seemed destined for much lesser things. The obvious but difficult question was whether her improve-ment was credible? Could she have won this gold without drugs? This was the start of the aftermath.

As we stood under the cicadas and rhododendrons only the lights from the now empty arena illuminated the scene as three of us debated the implications with a group of American journalists and swimming people. We were uneasy. What we had just seen had a bad smell to it.

We didn't know a lot about swimming but there was the

old joke that a good result for Irish swimming was one where no one drowned. Of course, this wasn't fair but we weren't a nation that excelled at swimming, *au contraire*. Jimmy Meagan, my one-time colleague at the *Irish Press*, who is no longer with us, told a swimming story from the Montreal Games in '76. One morning Jimmy wrestled with his conscience about going to a morning session to see an Irish swimmer compete in a heat. There was no chance he would qualify but a sense of duty got the better of Jimmy's common sense. He'd get a quote from the guy for the last edition of the *Evening Press*.

Off went Jimmy with a colleague from the *Irish Independent* and, sure enough, the swimmer finished last in his heat, a long way behind the guy in second last place. Disappointment lay not in being last but in a time that was well outside the swimmer's personal best.

'What happened?' Jimmy and his colleague asked.

'I'm desperately disappointed. I can't believe I've swam that slowly.'

'What went wrong?'

'I ate too big a breakfast,' the freestyler replied.

'Oh!'

From there to here, from Montreal's buffet breakfast to a gold medal at the Georgia Tech was a leap, and we knew our newly minted national heroine was the wrong age (26) to have made the improvements she had made. More than that, she was the wrong shape, the wrong height and she was keeping the wrong company. In a sport where the business of coaching had attained the status of science, Michelle was coached by her husband, Erik de Bruin, a shot putter from the Netherlands who was also, inconveniently, serving a four-year doping ban.

An old interview with Erik had resurfaced in which he discussed doping. His stance was, at best, ambivalent.

Patriotically, we tossed the arguments for Michelle into the night air to see how more knowledgeable people would respond. Suppose she had trained 'smarter'? What if coming up to Atlanta, her third Olympics, she had got more serious about the sport? Maybe Erik's background in athletics was actually an advantage? What if everybody else is wrong and our girl is right? But those who knew the most believed the least. They swatted our arguments away.

Then the various conversations hushed. Having finished some interviews for his native Dutch television, Erik joined us in the garden. He had detected (or anticipated) some scepticism in the Georgia air and had come to spin. He sat on a low wall and we gathered around him. But spin works best when coming from a charmer, and while you might have accused Erik of many things, you couldn't have called him one of nature's charmers.

The exchanges were brief and edgy. First, some soft questions swaddled with compliments about this dream which had just come true. What a romance. Then the conversation moved onto the subject we really wished to speak about.

'People here have said that when you were competing you tested positive for steroids?'

'No. That's not true. There was a problem with a test, but I was reinstated by my own federation and the Dutch courts, but I don't want to get into that right now.'

'But just to be factual?'

'Like I said, this is a happy moment for me, I don't want to ...'

'Are you still competing?'

'No, I coach. You think I can coach and compete?' he said, dismissively and as he got up.

'Always the same,' Erik shouted as he muscled through us and back into the arena. 'Always the fucking same.'

Paul, Tom and I drew away from the main group and began walking slowly towards the media buses. It was late on Saturday night, not long before dawn in Ireland, and many of our compatriots were going to wake up with a smile. Our country didn't often win gold medals, especially not in a sport dominated by the Americans. Tom would have to write a piece for Monday's *Irish Times* while Paul and I were glad to have a week to think about what we would write for our Sunday newspapers.

As we walked and talked there wasn't a chance we would shirk from asking the questions. That wasn't an option. Anybody in the garden a few minutes before knew that the suspicions of the swimming world would become a big part of the story. There was too much simmering anger. Michelle's rise was too weird and too wonderful to go unquestioned.

We knew too, though, what would be going on at home. Mass celebrations. Delirium. People who had never before watched a swim race, seeing our redheaded, Gaelic-speaking Michelle destroying the field to take gold in an Olympic final. In terms of Irish sporting celebration this would be as good as it gets. You ring home and you realise your own family has really 'gotten into the swimming', and you want to say, 'Better get out of it.'

Paul, Tom and I parted company with heavy hearts. Michelle would be racing all week long. She would be standing on podiums every other day. The madness at home would increase with every race. We were going to be asking the nation to sit down and have a cup of tea because we had some bad news.

As it happened, the three of us were the only members of the Irish media who opted to ask any questions. Everywhere else it was a whitewash job: big brush, broad strokes. Let's all drink to Michelle, and none of that old tea, thank you. 'Michelle, how did you feel when they played the national anthem and you saw the flag go up?' Hear no hard questions. Speak no hard questions.

There was an almost funny side to this, if you could see it.

Those in Michelle's corner saw the questioning of her performances as the evil work of jealous Americans trying to steal away Ireland's sunshine. America, after all, had no more bitter rival in the world of sport than Ireland. No sight churned the American gut more severely than that of a red-haired, freckled Irish girl winning races against the odds. They could accept reds from Russia, communists from China, but not this smiling Irish cailín. So they tried to muddy the waters. And spit in our stew.

A lot of journalists chose to sell that story, and back in the homeland there were buyers. Others chose to ignore the story completely. We didn't. Our stories said her victories couldn't be trusted because the improvement was too great to be natural. A small handful made a cottage industry out of attacking the three of us in print and on the airwaves. We were attention-seeking traitors who would get our comeuppance as soon as Michelle got around to suing us for libel. You are going to sue them Michelle, aren't you? Take away their houses and their jobs and their reputations? Soon, please Michelle?

Long before we came home from Atlanta, the three of us were isolated and denounced. The debate over Atlanta took place in two different languages. Paul, Tom and I attempting to lay out the basis for asking questions about how an earnest second-rate swimmer should morph into one of the great Olympians. The other story was glorious: a week-long hallelujah, a fairytale written by journalists whose enthusiasm overwhelmed every critical faculty. Perhaps they also sensed what the Irish public wanted.

I have always been a sucker for wanting to win people round to my point of view. On the Wednesday of this 'special week for Irish sport', I got talking with Anne Cassin, who was then a television news reporter for Ireland's national broadcaster, RTE. She was open to persuasion.

'The thing is, she's been an international swimmer for ten years, been at two Olympic Games before this and no one ever saw her making a final. Now this.'

'You really think the suspicion is justified?'

'Of course it is. Her incredible improvement happens after she falls in love with a discus thrower who later tests positive for a banned drug and gets a four-year ban.'

And on I went. A believer in Smith at the beginning, Anne was pretty convinced of the case against her by the time we finished. She was going to speak with her producer back in Dublin and make the point that they too should be asking questions. It seemed like a little victory. Later that evening, I met Anne at the pool. She had spoken to her producer and he gently dissuaded her. 'We don't really want to interfere with the national mood, do we?' he said. Ireland was *en fête*.

On the day of Smith's last race she had a problem with her goggles and was late to the starting blocks. Not far from where the three of us sat were the nine or ten Irish journalists who had been writing hymns of praise. They didn't much like us that week and we weren't their biggest fans either.

But with Smith's starting block temporarily vacant, six or seven of her journalist fans rose from their seats and headed for the stairs that would take them down to the pool area. As they filed past us, one of them looked up and caught my eye. 'She's been done,' he said quietly, meaning he reckoned Smith had learned of a positive test and that explained her failure to come out with the other seven finalists. She hadn't 'been done', but it was a little insight into the minds of her believers.

The two years that followed were difficult but transformative. 'Daddy, why are you mean to Michelle Smith?' the kids asked when they came home from school. In the end, Michelle would receive a four-year suspension for tampering with a urine sample she provided at her home in Kilkenny in 1998, but until her final hearing in Lausanne everything the three of us published on the topic of her miraculous rise was greeted with hostility and catcalls. Paul and I did okay on Smith, Tom was outstanding.

But asking the obvious questions, like John's simple query in that classroom, 'What did Mary and Joseph do with the gold?' had become an unavoidable duty. The bonus was that it felt like journalism.

*

The following summer Paul, Tom and I were thrown together again. The World Athletic Championships in Athens were an anti-climax media wise. Sonia O'Sullivan, the perennial Irish favourite, had another difficult meet, but on a broader level the people of Athens seemed as indifferent to what was happening on the track as the rest of the world. At one point, the IAAF asked the Greeks if they couldn't fill the empty seats in the stadium with military personnel. It's an old sporting custom, but the Greeks said this wasn't why they maintained an army.

Stories were few and our newspapers weren't overworking us. There was time to enjoy Athens, the Acropolis and all that, but first a round of golf. Paul and I are keen and Tom was dragged along to the splendid Glyfada course in the suburbs. The great and good of Athens had fled to the islands for the hottest weeks of summer and we had the fairways of Glyfada to ourselves. Well, Paul and I had the fairways. Tom preferred the rough.

For once in our lives our press accreditation impressed somebody. We were treated like royalty at Glyfada. The club locker room was thrown open to us and we were permitted to choose our weapons from row after row of members' bags. Each bag was as big as a trailer home and the clubs they housed left us with no excuses.

Something was bothering Tom, however, and it wasn't just his driving. This was unusual because unlike Paul and me, he's not by nature contrary. When he got it off his chest, the three of us fell to arguing passionately and the sightseeing agenda was forgotten about. Tom had listened to a lot of our old Tour de France stories. The day Kelly did this, the day

Kelly said that. Paul and I encouraged Tom to get to the Tour and see for himself.

What Tom couldn't figure was the gap between the affection and the esteem in which myself and Paul still held Sean Kelly and the position we had taken on Michelle Smith.

'Surely a doping offender is a doping offender?' he said. 'And Kelly twice tested positive?'

'But, Tom, the difference between Kelly and Smith is that he was beating the world's best from his first season with the pros. He was a genuine talent from day one; she was nowhere near.'

'There are no degrees of guilt here. No good dopers and no bad dopers,' he said.

'It's not as black and white as that. Cycling is a different sport to swimming. Virtually all the top guys do stuff in cycling.'

'Look, both of you guys have written successful books on cycling. Paul, your book showed how much doping there is in cycling but neither of you has called out Kelly.'

'Tom,' said Paul, 'I wanted to focus on the doping culture and how every rider was forced to make a choice: dope and have a career; don't dope and watch your career go down the drain. If I'd pointed the finger at individuals, people would have missed the more important point. It's the sport that corrupts the individual.'

'But still, you both have had opportunities to remind people that Kelly twice tested positive, but because you like the guy you haven't done it.'

It was true that we liked Kelly and when our questions about him weren't soft, they were non-existent. That morning in Senlis, when he jumped on his bike and sent those pills rattling against the plastic, we knew exactly what we'd heard, and when he later tested positive for the urine sample he gave that day we didn't tell about what we'd heard.

We'd rationalised it in a way that suited us and tried to tell Tom that he didn't understand the context.

'Tom, the people who knew swimming were the loudest in saying they didn't believe Smith. Those inside professional cycling loved Sean Kelly and never expressed any suspicion about his status as champion. So there was no basis for anyone else to be suspicious.'

'Weren't two positive tests basis enough?'

'Eddy Merckx twice tested positive and everyone accepts he was the greatest ever cyclist. So, should we say Merckx wasn't a true champion?'

We told Tom about how the French and Belgians loved Kelly and if anyone knew the sport, it was them. To them he was a legendary hard man. We painted the picture of a world where, yes, most riders took drugs but in a kind of egalitarian way and the outcomes would still have been the same. Kelly would have been one of the *patrons* of the peloton no matter what.

And we told Tom some of our best stories, showing Kelly's insatiable appetite for training, his need to win, the shyness that once made him nod in answer to a question on radio. I told about the times I'd seen him stick 20,000 French francs in small bills down his underpants after being paid for riding a criterium.

'Tom, you're just not getting the context.'

'What I get is the effect. If the strongest guys dope, what effect does that have on guys down the food chain? Don't they then have to dope to remain in the same world? Here is this sport of yours, so beautiful in its simplicity, so inspiring in its stories, and you're telling young riders that in order to survive you need to put this and you need to put that into your body.'

We didn't have an answer.

Paul had been one of those young riders, forced to make that choice.

'Fuck. Fuck you, Tom, you're right. That's what I wrote the book about, the choice, that's the story I told in *Rough Ride*. That culture is why my career got screwed up; where you end up not knowing how good you could have been.'

Paul is rightly proud of *Rough Ride* but, six years after it came out, we both wanted to pretend that Kelly could be separated from this doping culture, almost as if he was somehow different. Tom wasn't buying it. We were blinded by our affection for Kelly. We drove back to Athens in silence.

That was the summer of 1997.

Over the years I've often thought about how my life changed in the years before 1999 and how my attitude to the Tour de France was so different in '99 to what it had been when I first discovered it in 1982. I've wondered, too, about the effect on Armstrong of having life-threatening cancer.

After he came back and questions of doping were raised he would say, 'Do you really think I would put that stuff in my body after what I've been through?' It was a convincing argument. But there was a voice in my head that said, 'Hold on, he's had to deal with the possibility of dying, how scary must that have been? Now maybe nothing scares him.'

Now, in the summer of 1997, Armstrong was turning his thoughts to a comeback.

3

'The greater the suffering, the greater the pleasure.'

Tim Krabbé, *The Rider*

Two weeks before the start of the 1999 Tour de France, race organiser Jean-Marie Leblanc made the journey to Notre-Dame des Cyclistes in Aquitane to say a little prayer. As he settled into his pew beneath the stained glass window depicting the great rivals Coppi and Bartali at peace, Leblanc had good reason for seeking a little serenity himself.

Twelve months earlier, customs and police officers had taken the world inside the Tour de France, revealing a fetid counter-culture fuelled by unimaginable quantities of banned drugs. The tightly knit brotherhood of pro cyclists didn't enjoy sharing the secrets of their private lifestyle with the police and the broader public. Six teams withdrew from the race in protest. Cycling's mass audience was horrified. The '98 Tour might as well have never got on the road for all it had to do with sport.

A year on, Leblanc wanted God on his side and while he visited the cyclists' church he spoke also to the Abbot Massier, though he wouldn't reveal what was said. Leblanc promised the world that the 1999 Tour would be different. He even came up with a catchy sound-bite: the Tour of Renewal. *Le grand boucle* would be cleaner and more credible than '98. Lower, slower, weaker. Leblanc said he didn't mind that the pace of the '99 Tour would be more sedate because that would show everybody there were fewer drugs in circulation.

Not just God, Leblanc wanted the media on his side. He wanted sponsors on his side. He wanted his old life back. He wanted to enjoy the month of July.

I knew Leblanc from back in '84, when he was chief cycling correspondent for *L'Équipe*. We would meet at races and occasionally we would shoot the breeze as he would often ask about Sean Kelly. Having seen him in action one afternoon at a swanky reception, hosted by the Tour de France organisers in the centre of Paris, I had decided he was destined for a life more prestigious than filling *L'Équipe*'s cycling pages.

When I showed up that afternoon he was immersed in conversation with three important-looking corporate types and, as he saw me approach, he quickly averted his gaze, fearing I would come and say hello and he would have to introduce me and a high-powered conversation would drop a few notches.

Nothing personal, *mon ami*, but this isn't the moment. I understood. He would be director of the Tour de France within five years, one in a line of former journalists promoted to one of the most powerful roles in world cycling. I wondered whether a former pro like him believed it possible to have a clean Tour.

I was returning to the '99 Tour after missing '98 and '97 and, in part, my return to the race was down to my colleague John Wilcockson with whom I had travelled on and off at the Tour since 1984. Softly spoken and unfailingly polite, John is the epitome of the reserved Englishman. He qualified as an engineer but his passion, which bubbled well beneath the surface, was cycling: first as a competing amateur and then as a reporter/writer. For cycling he would go out in the midday sun.

The thing about John was that he never grew old; his slim physique didn't gain a pound, his curly hair seemed to twirl itself a little tighter with each year, while his enthusiasm, which started at the summit of Mont Blanc, was now moving on to Everest. He loved talking to cyclists, writing about them, just being in their space, and when I wasn't wondering about the darker side of the sport he and I got on well.

In '98, I would be in France covering the football World Cup as the race unfolded. My sports editor at the *Sunday Times*, Alex Butler, asked who we could get to cover the Tour. 'John Wilcockson,' I said. 'He covered the Tour for us way back, he's reliable and, unlike me, he'll file on time.' Alex thought this a good deal, John agreed and everything was dandy until the Wednesday before the start when Willy Voet, a masseur with the cycling's number one team Festina, was stopped by customs with a bulging cargo of banned drugs in the boot of his car.

John wrote about the drugs bust and the recriminations that followed but his heart wasn't in it. He preferred the romance, heroic breakaways, riders once eloquently described by our old friend Robin Magowan, as 'angels on wheels, Simon Pures somehow immune to the uppers and downers of our own pill-popping society'. In the midst of all the vials of EPO, testosterone patches, rider protests and police interrogations, John could still find the enthusiasm to describe that year's Tour winner, the Italian Marco Pantani, as 'the nine-stone wonder climber from Cesantico'.

'Next year,' Alex said to me, 'you're back on the Tour.'

I returned, but as a different journalist. Michelle Smith was the most recent reminder that fairytales in sport can be just fairytales and the legacy of the '98 Tour was that pro cyclists would now have to prove their innocence.

The Tour started at the theme park Le Puy du Fou in the Vendée in western France and at the end of the race's traditional opening test, a short individual race against the clock for each cyclist, Lance Armstrong became the first winner at the '99 Tour. He stormed round the 6.8km prologue course, 8 seconds faster than runner-up Alex Zülle. This, you thought, must have been what LeBlanc and Abbot Massier were discussing privately at the cyclists' church two weeks before.

For what could have been more uplifting for the Tour than a man who had survived life-threatening testicular cancer returning to his sport to reveal an even more heroic version of himself? And in the Tour of Renewal too? It helped that Armstrong hadn't raced the 1998 Tour and that his four pre-cancer years in the peloton were untainted by suspicion of drug abuse. He seemed what the race needed.

But, of course, for those who had witnessed or followed the parade of drug takers and drug traffickers from the year before, there were questions to ask and the man in the yellow jersey is expected to answer them. Leaner and looking physically harder than before his cancer, Armstrong was ready for doping enquiries. 'I will speak about this now and that's all I will say,' he said at Le Puy du Fou.

'It's been a long year for cycling, and as far as I'm concerned, it's history. Perhaps there was a problem, but problems exist in every facet of life: sport, cycling, politics. We can only do so much. We test [for drugs] as much as possible and at some point we have to realise enough is enough. Journalists, you come to training camps to assume we are all doped. That's bullshit. We're not.

'We have all got to fall back in love with cycling. I wasn't here last year – maybe that was a good thing. I hope cycling renews itself, and we should start now.'

As he spoke I was reminded of the kid I'd interviewed in Grenoble six years before and a story he told about a $1m bonus he'd earned for winning three designated races in the US earlier that season. First the insurers offered twenty annual instalments of $50,000 or $600,000 straight up. Armstrong went for the $600k.

Then he left it to the two most senior riders in the team, Australian Phil Anderson and Englishman Sean Yates, to decide how the money should be divvied up among all the riders. Anderson and Yates couldn't agree and soon Armstrong, 21 years of age and the newest guy on the team, got impatient. 'Hey, it's my money. I'm gonna do it. Leave it to me. I'm gonna be the bad guy here. I'll take care of it.' He took control.

And at Le Puy du Fou, he took care of the doping questions. Perhaps there was a problem but journalists now needed to stop thinking cyclists were dopers, and if only we could all fall back in love with the sport, things would be better. What I heard in Armstrong's words was the sport's old arrogance coming from a new source. Doping is not to be publicly discussed and then only to reassure the public that it's none of their business.

In victory he wasn't as likeable as the kid in Grenoble. Perhaps because doping was now on the agenda and he actually wasn't convincing on the subject. Why would he say something as asinine about the '98 Tour as: '*Perhaps there was a problem?* And when it came to him lecturing journalists on being too suspicious, I wanted to follow him back to his hotel room and introduce him to a little history.

I wanted to tell him that the problems of the more recent past were in part down to journalists being too gullible. And to remind him of the role journalists and newspapers had played in the creation of the Tour de France. The race itself came from the imagination of journalists and has been sustained in no small way by the ability of journalists to convey the distinct wonder and madness of the three-week pilgrimage around France. Journalists are sentimental creatures and the success of the Tour is built on emotion and memory.

And if the history of the race meant anything to him, he would appreciate that the Tour (which once in a rare moment of fancy he described as maybe 'the most gallant athletic endeavour in the world') came about after another endless and bitter debate over the innocence or guilt of one man. Alfred Dreyfus was accused of selling state secrets to the

Germans. *Le Vélo*, then the largest sports paper in France, carried political comment favouring Dreyfus. Some advertisers demurred and formed a rival paper, *L'Auto*, which was a dismal failure until they dreamt up the Tour de France and decided some time later the leader's jersey would be yellow like the paper they printed on. *L'Auto* metamorphosed into *L'Équipe*[1] and the relationship between the paper and the race has been close to the point of being symbiotic for more than half a century.

But journalists are human too and on that Saturday evening of the prologue, the *salle de presse* buzzed with the excitement of journalists feeling they had a good story to tell. Cancer victim returns to take yellow jersey! But from that first answer to the first doping question, I wasn't sure about him. How did the race leader's jersey give him the right to lay down the terms under which he would discuss doping? '*I will speak about this now and that is all I will say*,' as if one ridiculous understatement on the only question that mattered was sufficient.

There were also good reasons too for wondering about his improvement from 1993 to 1999.

Our interview in 1993 was originally scheduled for the evening of the prologue and was rearranged only because he was demoralised after a crushing experience over the same 6.8km course that was now the scene of great triumph.

The numbers took some explaining.

---

1 *L'Auto* was deemed to have been too close to France's wartime puppet president Philippe Pétain and was ordered to be closed after the war. *L'Équipe* was permitted as a successor but one condition of its publication was that it be printed on white paper rather than yellow, which was too closely associated with *L'Auto*.

Back in 1993 Miguel Indurain, stoic and unconquerable in the middle of his run of five Tour victories, devoured the prologue in one mouthful, covering the 6.8km in 8 minutes 12 seconds. He was a specialist against the clock. Lance came into that Tour as a strong one-day rider with a definite game plan. Accepting he wouldn't be fast enough to beat Indurain and other specialists in the prologue, he figured that if he gave it everything, he could finish somewhere in the top 15. From there he could then infiltrate a breakaway group in the first week and be in position to take the yellow jersey.

But he rode a terrible prologue, starting too fast and arriving at the Côte du Fossé 4 kilometres in with nothing left. Eventually, he puttered in at 8.59 putting him 81st in the 189-rider field. He wasn't in much humour for entertaining a journalist. Eighty-first? No Texan had ever been 81st in anything. 'Could we do the interview on the rest day?'

Six years later, same course, same conditions, another massacre but this time Armstrong had inflicted it, not endured it. He rode the course in 8.02, more than 8 seconds per kilometre faster than he had recorded in 1993, and the performance catapulted him to a new level. It was also 10 seconds faster than Indurain's winning time in '93. Inside the race and around its margins, people wondered how he'd become so good in this short race against the clock.[2]

2 The 1999 Tour de France opened with the prologue on 3 July. Armstrong won the prologue, but within days received notice of a positive test for a banned substance for which he did not have medical authorisation. A cover story was concocted backdating a prescription for cortisone cream and suggesting that the prescribed medication was to treat saddle sores. We hailed this as 'the butt-cream defence'. UCI bought it though.

In the press centre, some eyebrows were raised but most of the eyebrows were still receiving physio for the lingering fatigue of the Festina wars. The easy rationalisation was that this was just a prologue, one tiny leg of a three-week marathon: a neat story, for sure, but it wasn't like Armstrong was going to go on and win it. Reporters at the Tour also found that when they spoke with their sports editors, they realised that the further one's distance from this story, the more believable it seemed.

'This is the guy who had cancer, right?'

'Yeah, testicular, only given a fifty-fifty chance of pulling through.'

'Yeah, good story. It's amazing, isn't it? Cancer survivor with a chance of winning the most gruelling race in sport!'

Any suggestion the prologue victory was a one-off was quickly dismissed. As soon as the race left Le Puy du Fou it was clear Armstrong was very strong, as was his US Postal team, and their strategy was exemplary. They allowed Jaan Kirsipuu from Estonia take the yellow jersey at the end of the first stage, putting the onus on Kirsipuu's French team Casino to control the race. US Postal then sat back and saved their energy for the mountains, by which point Kirsipuu would be back in the pack.

My travelling companions on the Tour were my old buddy Wilcockson, his colleague from *Velo News* magazine Charles Pelkey and the Australian journalist Rupert Guinness whom I knew from way back.

Our routine at the Tour was to leave our hotel early in the morning so we could mosey around the cordoned-off corpo-rate village to which sponsors brought their guests and journalists mingled in the hope of bumping into a cyclist. Sometimes you got lucky but mostly you picked up a newspaper, had a coffee and gossiped with other journalists.

During that first week a 25-year-old French competitor in the Tour wrote a column for *Le Parisien* which was easily the most arresting written about the race. Christophe Bassons poured cold water all over the Tour of Renewal.

'We are racing at an average speed of more than 50 kilometres per hour, as if the roads of France are nothing more than one gigantic descent.'

Le Parisien ran Bassons' column beneath a strap-line that said, 'Bassons rides the Tour on pure water, that is to say without doping products.'

Bassons also said he didn't think it possible for anyone to be in the top ten and ride clean.

In the car, we talked about the race. Charles was our driver, on his third Tour; tall, thin, always ready to laugh but with an enquiring mind. He came with the American's enthusiasm for a country and a race that had a lot of history, and though he loved bicycle racing he was the one paying most attention when I began expressing scepticism.

Rupert was an experienced cycling writer and an enthusiastic wearer of Hawaiian shirts. Like me he had once moved to France to experience the sport first hand before returning to Australia to settle down, but he never lost his love for the Tour. We would run together in the mornings and he had the grinder's diesel engine.

Once, 50 minutes into our run, he stopped to help an old lady who needed directions. I didn't wait. It was the only time I beat him. Cyclists liked Rupert because he was a good bloke and though he didn't disagree with the questions I was asking, he also didn't want to become too sceptical.

John, the eternal enthusiast, rarely engaged in any conversation that questioned Armstrong.

In that first week, we discussed Bassons's view that you couldn't be in the top ten without doping.

'I believe this guy. Why would he say it if it wasn't true?' I said.

'I kind of agree,' said Charles. 'And I definitely agree that Bassons believes this to be true.'

'The thing about Bassons is that he's inside that peloton and he feels how fast everyone is going. And we know from the average speed of the race so far, this Tour's going to be faster than last year's, when we know doping was pervasive.'

'But if it's a tiny bit faster, how much does that prove?' Charles would ask.

'Not a lot but Leblanc said he looked forward to a slower tour, proving that fewer drugs were being used.'

On and on we went, Charles trying to offer counter-arguments but mostly coming down on the side of scepticism. I sensed Rupert thinking we were probably right. Without uttering a word, John emitted sound that expressed displeasure. He didn't have much time for our debate.

His reluctance to engage irritated me far more than if he'd attacked our arguments. The obvious counter was that I was basing too much on hunch and not coming up with any evidence of Armstrong doing wrong. It would have been better if he said Armstrong was clean but he just didn't want that debate. His silence meant my taunting went on, like a matador flashing the red cape and the bull just sucking the air in through his nostrils, squeezing it out of his mouth, his hoof scraping the ground.

In the press room, there was widespread indifference to Bassons. Armstrong was a better story and any reporting of Bassons' complaints would lessen the feel-good effect of the back-from-cancer hero. More attention was paid to the French rider by his fellow professionals.

'You've got to stop your bullshit,' Pascal Chanteur, a rider with another French team, told Bassons one day. 'You're on your own; you've turned everybody against you. What you're doing is wrong. Journalists are idiots.'

Thierry Bourguignon, a veteran French rider, was one of the few riders in the peloton to speak with Bassons and he gently suggested the journalists were using him to further their own agendas. 'I know that but I am also using them to say what I have to say,' said Bassons.

Bourguignon was concerned at the consequences of being associated with the young rebel.

'Why do you always mention me in your columns?'

'Because you are the only one who continues to speak with me,' Bassons replied.

Through my friend Pierre Ballester, I'd been introduced to an exercise physiologist/coach called Antoine Vayer, who lived at Laval in the Vendée. Thirty-six years old, Vayer had been a physical trainer with the world's number one team Festina but refused to be involved with the team's systematic doping programme. Bassons was one of three Festina riders from a squad of twenty-three who rode clean and he and Vayer became friends.

Their friendship and coach–rider relationship survived the disintegration of the Festina squad.

On the fourth day of the '99 race, the Tour de France rolled into Laval, and Vayer thought it a good opportunity to bring some like-minded journalists together for an informal gathering at the Gobelen bar. Invitation was by word of mouth and the rendezvous had a clandestine feel to it as only journalists known to be openly anti-doping were going to be present, and the group wasn't more than twenty strong.

As soon as I walk into the Gobelen, the owner nods discreetly. He knows who I've come to see and points his head towards the small garden at the back. Outside, charcoal smoke climbs into the night air and the man standing over the barbecue is a giant with a two-foot fork.

Around the tables are the revolutionaries, the ones who don't believe the Tour of Renewal is what it's meant to be and understand the need for a more radical journalism. Pierre Ballester is here, so too Stéphane Mandard from *Le Monde* and there are one or two others whose faces I recognise, but the evening is held together by the balding Vayer around whom everyone loosely sits.

They know more than I do, they have lived in this country, breathed the Tour de France and among them Vayer is the most interesting because he has worked with a doping team, tested their riders and seen for himself the effects of doping. Towards the end of the evening I coral him and we talk in English. What was it like for him being at Festina?

'Of course I was marginalised. I had no credibility. I was not allowed to go to team meetings and when I was around, the riders would not speak openly. But I came to the team with my integrity and I left with it.'

He could see some improvement from 1998 but not a lot.

'Before last year, pro cycling was a junkie sport – not because of what people took but because of the mindset of the rider. Things have improved a little but, really, the culture is still the same. For example, the use of corticosteroids: riders take them when they are stressed, they take them when they are down, they take them if they mess up. For them, life must be without stress. It's a junkie mentality.'

Speaking about pro cyclists, Antoine's lack of reverence set him apart from the majority of those who worked in teams, and virtually everyone in the press tent. He saw them as human beings sucked into a doping culture and desperately in need of help. 'I met Hein Verbruggen [UCI president] the other day and we spoke for an hour. He said he was head of 171 federations and I said, "Stop your shit, your only duty is to stop doping. That's all you have to do."'

Antoine's passion came with empathy; his belief was that doping didn't just damage health but also had dehumanising effects. 'Many of the best riders have become psychotic. They want to win money, to screw others because, compared to them, everybody else is small. They want to have a nice house, a nice wife, a nice car and they will do whatever to get these things. They have no more emotion, no more thinking, no more feeling, no internal life. Everything they are is down to their success and they would kill to hold on to that.'[3]

We talked about Bassons and the trainer said how good he'd been as an amateur and how he'd then made a successful

3 When Vayer made this case for the top cyclists being psychotic he was not thinking of Lance Armstrong, who at this point was just another contender in what seemed a wide-open race. In hindsight, much of what he did say would prove to be applicable to Armstrong.

transition to the pros. Word went out that he had ridden clean through his first two seasons in the professional peloton and it was also known he had a naturally low haematocrit which made him more valuable because when he started using EPO, he would be able to use a lot without exceeding the 50 per cent maximum put in place by the UCI.[4]

Antoine spoke about Bassons as a father might speak about a son. On one occasion Christophe received a cortisone injection for a painful knee and, as his doctor had prescribed the treatment, he was free to race. But feeling the cortisone was enabling him to perform better, he voluntarily withdrew from the competition.

Results were never what they should have been and many advised him to get real and commit to a doping programme; even his parents said they would understand if he felt he had to. He discussed it with Pascale, his fiancée, and she said she would not want to marry a man who used banned drugs. Pascale was more important to him than winning bike races and he never seriously considered doping.

Everything Antoine said about Christophe endeared him to me.

His Festina teammates accepted he wasn't one of them and made the best of it. He was useful when the testers showed up for he would be sent down first to stall them while his

---

4 Haematocrit is the amount of red cells in blood expressed as a percentage of total blood volume. Because UCI allowed riders to have a haematocrit up to 51 per cent in 1999, this meant a rider with a naturally low haematocrit like Bassons was deemed to have a natural advantage. Because of his low haematocrit, he could use a lot of EPO to generate extra red cells without pushing beyond the 51 limit. Bassons refused to dope and therefore his 'natural advantage' was irrelevant.

teammates got hooked up to the saline drip that would dilute their blood and keep them safely below 50.

Then the '98 Tour happened, the Festina team was caught with its hand in the pharmaceutical sack, so too many other teams, and Bassons thought this the ill wind that would blow some good his way. Greater scrutiny would lead to lesser doping, and in this new world his career would be better.

This is not how it worked out. From the early part of the season the average speed in races was such that Bassons knew doping was still rife. By the time he got to the Tour he was despairing, and then to see the peloton riding much faster again was too much. He offered forthright honesty to every journalist who asked, and within the peloton he became a pariah.

In my mind he was being screwed by his own sport. After four days of the race, he was the only rider I was sure about.

Excited by the subversive atmosphere in that back garden and energised by Antoine's passion for greater fairness in the sport, I left the Gobelen feeling I'd joined an underground movement committed to fighting doping in professional cycling. Slipping back unnoticed into the hotel I shared with John, Rupert and Charles, I thought about the twenty or so journalists who had turned up to the meeting and knew them as some of the finest, most intelligent journalists on the race.

My faith in the Tour of Renewal was diminishing by the day but my evening at the Gobelen was a reminder that you had to keep trying. And if you didn't support Christophe Bassons, how could you call yourself a journalist?

Most times the Tour de France runs to a plot determined by what happens in the first individual time trial eight or nine days into the three-week race. If one of the contenders for overall victory wins that, he will generally take the yellow jersey, and it is then his to lose. Soon after that time trial the race goes into the mountains, and often that first venture into the Alps or Pyrenees is the favourite's greatest test.

Over a 56.6km circuit in the eastern city of Metz, Armstrong won the time trial and regained the yellow jersey he had claimed on the first day but then given up on the second. His victory in the race against the clock was emphatic and it gave him a lead of 2 minutes and 20 seconds over second-placed Christophe Moreau. From being a contender, Armstrong became everyone's idea of the Tour winner.

To me, the time-trial performance was puzzling at best, downright suspicious at worst. He had ridden the Tour de France four times before falling ill with cancer in '96 and recorded remarkably consistent results the three times he rode it.[5] In '93 he finished 6.03 minutes down on the winner, 6.23 minutes in '94 and 6.24 minutes in '95. He wasn't bad but nowhere near the best. To go from there to being the best was a staggering leap.

But two days later, Armstrong would go into the mountains for the first time and tell us whether he was going to win the Tour or be an adornment. The mountains shouldn't have been his favoured landscape by any means. The form sheet was there. In his previous Tours Armstrong's best placing on a mountain stage was 39th on the Saint Etienne to Mende leg of the 1995 Tour. In the other eight mountainous

5 Armstrong got sick early in the 1996 Tour de France and had pulled out before the first time trial.

races he'd ridden, his placings were much worse and the deficits far greater.

Yet in the press room in '99 there is an expectation among his growing number of disciples that this new edition Armstrong will be different as he'd ridden well in the previous year's Tour of Spain and, post-cancer, he was much stronger. From being a man who might finish 8 or 28 minutes behind, he has become the peloton's mountain goat. The way is being prepared for Clark Kent's next deed. No need to wonder, folks, it can all be logically explained.

Me?

My instinct says, 'Don't believe it. This is all about as logical as the Tour being led by a lobster on a bike. A lobster complete with helmet and a moving backstory about a last-minute escape from a pot of boiling water.'

The first mountain stage is a brutally tough 213-kilometre race to Sestriere over the border in Italy. Sestriere is an iconic climb of both the Giro d'Italia and the Tour de France. Taken alone it is not an especially long ascent, nor a particularly hard and punishing one, but it is beloved because of its location and its history and because of the style of the men who've conquered it.

It was here that the charismatic Fausto Coppi broke clear and stole almost 12 minutes on his eternal rival Gino Bartali on his way to the 1949 Giro. Coppi also won the Tour that year. His first double.

Three years later, Sestriere first appeared on the Tour route. Sestriere was stage eleven but stage ten, two days earlier, was the first stage to finish at the summit of Alpe d'Huez. Coppi, on his way to another Giro–Tour double, took the yellow jersey on Alpe d'Huez and then came out and massacred the field with a heroic solo ride through wind and rain to the summit finish at Sestriere.

For those present on this day, there was a memory for life. Coppi was a character and stories about him were once told around the fireplace or at the foot of a bed and they created a romance that wrapped itself around the Tour and kept it warm.

One of the Coppi stories goes back to when he was a prisoner of war in 1943, having been captured by the British in Tunisia. In captivity he shared his food bowl with another prisoner, an amateur racer called Arduino Chiappucci. Coppi had gone to war as a great hero of Italian sport and such was the affection in which he was held that the Italian army tried to keep him away from danger for as long as possible.

In captivity Chiappucci grew close to his idol Coppi and often gave him his own food in order to keep up the great man's strength and morale. When the war ended Coppi and Chiappucci went their separate ways. Coppi rode part of the way home on his bike and then hitched a lift with a lorry-load of former detainees.[6]

---

6 Coppi is one of the great figures of cycling, but no saint. Gino Bartali, his old rival, watched him like a hawk when they competed together. In their retirement the pair often appeared on television together. Bartali, who as a racer had been in the habit of searching his rival's room after he left a hotel, looking for traces of what had been consumed, would tease Coppi, crooning at him about 'the drugs you used to take'. One famous exchange tells us much about the culture of a time when doping had been invented but not yet banned:
Bartali: 'Do cyclists take *la bomba* [amphetamine]?'
Coppi: 'Yes, and those who claim otherwise, it's not worth talking to them about cycling.'
Bartali: 'And you, did you take *la bomba*?'
Coppi: 'Yes. Whenever it was necessary.'
Bartali: 'And when was it necessary?'
Coppi: 'Almost all the time!'

Chiappucci went home and raised a son, Claudio, whose head he filled with tales of his time with the great Coppi, whose most wondrous deeds were still to come.

Forty years after Coppi's lonely ride to Sestriere, Arduino Chiappucci's son won on the same mountain. I was there on that day in 1992 and this was a classic ride straight out of the book of Coppi mythology. A Saturday afternoon and 254 kilometres worth of attrition, stretching from St Gervais to Sestriere. Just 12 kilometres in, Claudio Chiappucci attacked, which seemed much too early, but we knew not what was about to unfold.[7] All we saw was daredevil ambition. No strategy, just attack, attack, attack; scorching off into the land of pain.

First he got rid of his fellow escapees but behind, the monster in the yellow jersey, Miguel Indurain had him in his sights. Chiappucci's pace was too much for Indurain's teammates, however, so the leader had to make his own pursuit, which evened things up. I loved the style and recklessness of Chiappucci, his Italian need to win on the day the race crossed into his country. This was bravura. This was the Tour offering us a late-twentieth-century epic. This was sport. This was why we came.

In cycling you cheer for the guy who, in the French expression, 'makes the race'. But Chiappucci had been out there so damn long that we became fatalistic. These guys always get hauled in. The romance of the Tour is that there is no romance. It's hard and it's cruel and it's crushing. On the

7 Later we learnt Chiappucci had worn a heart monitor for the stage to Sestriere, which was unheard of at the time.

climb to Sestrierre, Indurain was close enough to know that he could take Chiappucci. Whenever he wished.

In his pomp Indurain was as relentless and uncharismatic as one of the riders of the apocalypse.

His shadow would catch Chiappucci any second. And we knew that Chiappucci and his dream were dead. Indurain was going faster. Chiappucci had been hanging on for too long and Indurain knew what would happen when he bore down on an opponent. He would devour him like a python coming off a Lenten fast. *Ciao* Claudio.

And then this half-crazy Italian resurrected himself. Strength returned to his legs like a river undammed. The dreamer in you imagined that this was strength leased from his great Italian heart. He went again. There would be a happy ending after all. Chiappucci forged a small gap, increased it and got away from the monster through the last gruelling kilometres.

He won by 1.45 on a day so brutal that eighteen riders who finished outside of the time limit were eliminated. Victory wouldn't be enough to win Chiappucci the Tour but his breakaway wasn't about a place high on overall classification but about glory, a thing of beauty in itself. That day he gave us as grand and swashbuckling a race as we could ever hope to see. As sweet as it gets. Romance.

It sounds embarrassing now but I cried in the press room when Chiappucci found the strength to hold off Indurain. I couldn't help myself as it was the most beautiful, romantic, heroic thing I'd ever covered. Courage beat calculation, as an athlete driven by the need to perform before his own people, transcended himself.

EPO and the weary cynicism it generates weren't on our

radar. I stood there and wept. Not alone either. This was why we loved the Tour. Why July in France could be the best month of your year, any year.

Four years later Chiappucci told an Italian judge Vincenzo Scolastico he had been using EPO since 1993 and, older, wiser, more cynical, I thought, 'That's convenient, Chiappa, your greatest ever performance happened just before you started doing EPO. Yeah, right.' Chiappucci would later retract that admission, but what did it matter, he failed an EPO test before the 1997 Giro d'Italia and later that year was kicked off the Italian team for the World Championships because of an excessively high haematocrit, indicating EPO use.

And I could never see that late surge away from Indurain with the eyes that had originally seen it. That second wind, is that what EPO can do? Was that the first great EPO ride? The circus had turned us into the rubes and the dupes, the suckers and the mooks. And the romance of Fausto and Arduino was chemically shrunk. Happy tears in the *salle de presse* would be no more. Question everything. Ask what Mary and Joseph did with the gold.

4

'A boo is louder than a cheer.'

Lance Armstrong

In 1999 Sestriere became a fork in the road for the press corps. Those who wanted to do journalism went one way; their old comrades took the other route. Things wouldn't be the same for a long time.

Survey this 213km toil through the Alps. We begin at the ski station in Le Grande Bornand and then hit the climbs through the Col du Télégraphe laurelled already by storm clouds, onto the mighty Galibier (in 1911 when the Galibier was introduced to the Tour only three of the peloton didn't get off their bike and walk), through the Maurienne Valley and then up the climb of Montgenèvre, before we finish with the 11km ascent to Sestriere.

Early in the day Armstrong's US Postal teammates hauled the pack after them on the Col du Télégraphe, allowing their leader to focus on nothing but the wheel in front of him as they took care of the rest before hurtling down into the town of Valloire, recovering and going again on the early slopes of the Galibier.[8]

It is raining now. The peaks are dressed with freezing mist. Few things sap the morale of the pack quite like rain and mist and freezing cold. A shivering peloton rolls on. The lead group is down to ten, pursued by twelve more desperadoes a minute behind. Armstrong is with the front group. Comfortable.

Onto Montgenèvre and now only the strong survive. One from Armstrong, Alex Zulle, Fernando Escartin, Ivan Gotti and Richard Virenque will win. Armstrong still looks comfortable but, with his teammates no longer around him, you guess he will be happy to hang in there. As they descend from Montgènevre, Gotti and Escartin make their move. They get to Sestriere 25 seconds ahead of the rest.

Before them, above them, the picturesque ski resort freckled with chalets marks the last great challenge. Armstrong is in that second group but all he has to do is keep his one

8 Funny thing. In a hospital in Indiana in 1996 Betsy Andreu heard Lance Armstrong tell a physician that he had used performance-enhancing drugs. Betsy made her husband Frankie swear to her that he would never do the same. Betsy watched the first two weeks of the 1999 Tour on TV at home in Dearborn, Michigan. She saw Frankie lead his friend Lance up the early climbs that day and shook her head. 'It was the first mountain stage, the one to Sestriere, and as they began the climb Frankie was at the front of a line of Postal riders. Frankie is about as much a climber as the Pope is an atheist. "What the hell is this about?" I said.' She called her husband and said she didn't believe he was clean any more. He was too tired to argue, but Lance's troubles were just beginning. Betsy would later recall that one night at a late dinner in Nice some months before the 1999 race Pepe Marti, the US Postal Service team trainer, arrived to provide what she was told was EPO to Armstrong. The dinner was late because Marti was travelling from Spain and considered it 'safer to cross the border at night'. Armstrong took a brown paper bag from Marti, held it up and pronounced it, 'liquid gold'.

dangerous rival, Zulle, within his sights. After five and a half hours in the worst conditions, he's just got to stay there. Hold onto what he's got.

The final skirmishes that day were breathtaking but not in the manner of Chiappucci. You can't walk into the same river twice because neither you nor the river is the same. Eight kilometres from the summit, Armstrong rose out of the saddle and let the juice flow. In the space of a kilometre he closed 21 seconds to Gotti and Escartin who were both shattered.[9]

His rhythm never dropped and Zulle, his rival, was left behind. Armstrong, with a new yellow jersey on his back, had done his post-race interviews and was back in the US Postal team bus while most of the field was still labouring up Sestriere.

I had watched the final climb to Sestriere on a big screen in the *salle de presse*. At the moment of Armstrong's acceleration there was a collective and audible intake of breath and, as he rode clear, there was ironic laughter and shaking of heads. Not every journalist was overcome with scepticism, not even the majority, but there were enough to form a platoon of sceptics. This wasn't everyone's Tour of Renewal.

That evening I called Alex Butler, my sports editor at the *Sunday Times*.

'Hell of a stage today,' he said. 'Armstrong's got it now, hasn't he?'

'He will win the Tour, no doubt about that.'

---

9 In his autobiography *It's Not About the Bike*, Armstrong wrote of almost bumping into the pillion passengers of the escort motorbikes in front of him, of how it felt 'effortless'.

'You're not convinced about him?'

I can hear disappointment in his voice.

'Afraid not. Actually, I think it stinks. This guy has ridden the Tour de France four times before now, ridden nine mountain stages and not been anywhere near. Suddenly he's an outstanding climber.'

'David, if we are going to cast doubt on him, a lot of readers are going to be upset.'

'I know that but I don't believe we can applaud. There's a young guy in the race, Bassons, and I would like to write a shorter piece about him. He's talking about doping, saying it's still a big problem. The other riders have turned against him.'

'But back to Armstrong for a minute, David. Do you believe he's doping?'

'Yeah, I do. Of course I can't prove it. I'm going to talk to people, see what others are saying.'

'Well, make sure you give it to us in time for the lawyers to see.'

This was the first time Alex said this to me. It wouldn't be the last. In fairness he didn't flinch.

Covering the Tour de France means spending considerable time in the company of the journalists with whom you travel. Not quite Brian Keenan and John McCarthy chained together in Beirut, but close. With these guys you co-ordinate hotel accommodation, eat evening meals at the same table, breakfast the next morning and also drive to the start of the stage, before undertaking the five- or six-hour journey to the finish, day after day for twenty-three days.

Rupert, our itinerant Aussie, shared the back seat with me,

his ever-dazzling selection of shirts bringing a little piece of Caribbean sunshine with him every day. His dress code reflected an easy and sweet nature. He could cheer up mourners at a funeral just by appearing. In the driver's seat Charles' freshness was a joy, as he wanted to know again and again why I couldn't warm to Armstrong, and why I was so unconvinced about the Tour of Renewal. John would keep his head down, writing down the name of every escapee in the breakaway even though we all knew they would be reeled in in no time.

Day after day in the car, evening after evening over dinner, we spoke about the race and what we were seeing. Frequently we would discuss my refusal to accept it was possible without doping to make the leap Armstrong had made.

'I don't understand how a guy can ride the Tour de France four times and show nothing that indicates he will one day be a contender to suddenly riding like one of the great Tour riders.'

'Was he that bad in those four Tours?' Charles asked, lobbing the balls up for me to smash home.

'Well, he was always capable of winning one of the flat stages but he didn't even enter the race for the final yellow jersey. His usual was six minutes behind in the long trial, anything from seven to thirty in the mountains.'

'David, he was only twenty-one when he first rode the Tour,' Charles would say.

'But Anquetil, Merckx and Hinault, who all won five Tours, won the first one they rode. LeMond was third in his first, second in his second when he should have won, and then he did win his third. Armstrong went into his third Tour in ninety-five on the back of good form and got his best ever placing, thirty-sixth. The bottom line was he couldn't time trial well enough and couldn't survive in the mountains.'

Occasionally I would aim a question straight at John.

'You were here last year, saw how much drugs the police found. And here we are a year later and the average speed is higher. Just doesn't make sense?'

And once, he engaged: 'The speed of the race now has a lot to do with the improved road surfaces, the lighter-framed bikes, and this year the meteorological conditions have been favourable.'

But mostly when I said something directly to John, he would turn his head a little to the side so the words could flow in one ear and out the other. Perhaps he was so focused on the race itself that he didn't want to look underneath it all.

So it was back to Charles.

'This is mad. Clean guy goes faster than the EPO generation? So what do you think, Charles? Smoother road surfaces? Tail winds every day? Lighter bikes? Or these leaders are doping, as Bassons says?'[10]

'I can't argue with your logic,' Charles said, 'but I find it really hard to believe that a guy who has had cancer, pretty serious cancer too, would come back and put that shit in his body.'

'I know, that's the bit that's hard to believe. But, on the other hand, what drug do they give you when you're recovering from

---

10 We now know that during first two weeks of the Tour, Armstrong, Tyler Hamilton and Kevin Livingston used EPO every third or fourth day, injecting themselves quickly then placing the syringes into Coke cans which they would crush till flat. Dr Luis del Moral would then dispose of the cans containing the syringes as quickly as possible.

cancer? EPO. Side-effects? Seemingly far less than for most drugs. The bottom line is that you can't go faster without EPO than with it, and we're being asked to believe you can.'

I had shared a car with John as far back as the Tour of 1984, but Sestriere was the fork in our relationship. He couldn't live on this race without access to certain riders; namely the top Americans and Lance. He would do the bread-and-butter job of reporting better than most, but for him the cream came in the team hotel in the evening, when you might snatch a fifteen- or twenty-minute interview with one of your favourites.

His enthusiasm for the company of the stars irked me, because it was never balanced by any expression of concern for the lesser-known riders who might be having their careers destroyed by the doping of others. I never heard him wonder about Christophe Bassons and the possibility that he was having his career stolen. Just as I never heard him empathise with the injustice Paul had exposed in his book *Rough Ride*.

And I was tired of the duplicity. The tests were useless because there was no test for the drug of choice, EPO. Instead the UCI tried to control its abuse by withdrawing from races those riders whose haematocrit exceeded 50, which was considered dangerous to a rider's health but not proof of doping. It wasn't proof but everyone knew that haematrocrits generally got to 50 because of EPO abuse.

Charles was curious and spoke to Dr Leon Schattenberg, who was on UCI's medical committee and believed the haematocrit limit ensured those riding clean didn't have to compete against riders with ridiculously high haematocrits, and that this was better than nothing. Encouraged by Charles' industry, I too spoke with Schattenberg.

'From the blood tests you do, you know the haematocrit of every rider in the Tour de France?'

'That's right,' he said.

'I'm not going to ask for the haematocrits of each rider because I know you will say that is private medical information. I'm not going to ask for the average for each team, but can you say what, according to your blood tests, is the average haematocrit for riders in the Tour de France this year? No names, just the overall average?'

'I'm sorry,' he said, 'I can't give you that information.'

'Why not?'

'Because it is not information I am allowed to give.'

'The reason you don't give out this information is that if you did the public would see the average was much higher than it should be, and realise a lot of guys in this race are using EPO.'

Schattenberg wasn't responsible for what was effectively a cover-up and the UCI would argue that without a test for EPO their hands were tied. But they could have done more, even if it was to publicly say that haematocrits were unusually high (especially in some teams), because the governing body was well aware that it wasn't a clean Tour.[11]

Some of the more thoughtful practitioners of our trade like

11 In his book *The Secret Race*, Tyler Hamilton wrote that UCI's pre-race blood tests showed most of the US Postal riders had haematocrits just below or above 50 (in 1999 up to 51 was okay). The high numbers were cause by using EPO. UCI privately expressed their dissatisfaction to the team but that was it. The governing body could hardly have been unaware that most riders in the team were using EPO.

to say that if you are to be a sportswriter it's better to love the writing more than the sport. I loved the sport. I loved the role that sportswriters could play in sport: afflicting the comfortable, comforting the afflicted, as news reporters used to say. No longer did I see it as our role to smile up at the dais for a press conference, reassuring the organisers and competitors that 'there ain't nobody here but us chickens'.

French police and customs had forced us to open our eyes in '98 and I wasn't going to close them again. I didn't want to be a fool just because of my love for sport. And I didn't want to act as an agent in making fools of readers and fans on behalf of the UCI. This was supposed to be the Tour of Renewal! So far there were plenty of questions but no answers.

Two days after Armstrong's dominant performance at Sestriere I wandered through the *salle de presse* feeling nothing but sadness at the unfolding story. The scepticism felt by many as he soared like an eagle on that first mountain stage was less apparent now as the realisation dawned that Armstrong was going to win, and it was better to accept, even embrace, his performance.

There were a few whom I knew would not be so easily turned, guys who didn't want to be peddling the fantasy. There was Philippe Bouvet, now the chief cycling writer at *L'Équipe*, the son of a former professional and a man who had grown up with the sport. Philippe had written questioningly of Armstrong and the sport through the first two weeks.

He believed the Tour was racing at '*deux vitesses*' [two speeds], caused by the fact of many but not all riders using EPO. Armstrong, he described as 'an extraterrestrial'. It didn't

71

take genius to work out where exactly Philippe was coming from, and it wasn't from the same upbeat rose-tinted place that the organisers wished him to be.

'What do you make of it?' I asked.

'There is a new kind of cycling,' he replied. 'You see things you don't understand. Doping is an old story in cycling, but over the past few years the manipulation of riders' blood has changed the nature of competition. What we are getting is a caricature of competition. It is killing the sport. I can still write about cycling, but not in the same way, not with the old passion. Cycling has to change.'

Philippe's belief about EPO killing the sport is important. Almost always the first line of the dopers' defence, when a question is asked about their affairs, is to point out that to pose the question is to hurt the sport. For many years the former president of the UCI, Hein Verbruggen, would berate journalists for 'talking too much about doping'.

Through the eyes of too many riders and administrators, doping was always yesterday's problem. 'Perhaps there was a problem . . . I hope cycling renews itself and we should start now,' Armstrong had said on the first day. He wanted us to forget when the imperative was not to forget. In fact the first task of anybody who cared about the sport, let alone dusty abstracts like journalism and truth, was to be standing up and shouting, 'Stop!'

Among the journalists who cared for the sport more than a three-week carnival around France in July, it was common to find sadness and a reluctance to celebrate. Jean-Michel Rouet's daily column in *L'Équipe* expressed disbelief at Armstrong's resurgence and the idea of this as a Tour of

Renewal. His approach was based on bitter experience. 'What we learned last year was that everybody in this sport can fuck us,' he said.

Rouet held onto his disbelief, as did another strong-minded French journalist, Jean-François Quénet, writing then for *Ouest-France*. 'I haven't written an enthusiastic line about Armstrong,' he said to me. 'They told us cycling would change but it hasn't. After all the drugs last year, they said this would be slower because there would be no dope. This year's race will be the fastest in history.'

Professional cycling has always exercised an *omerta* and it has played a significant role in the endurance of a drug culture. But more than a code of silence is at work here and it is not coincidental that the Sicilian word has become so associated with the peloton, because when a rider breaks the code, he can expect a mafia-like response.

After his individual time trial at Metz earlier in the day, Christophe Bassons watched television coverage of the leaders in his hotel room. They travelled at a speed he couldn't believe, for the race against the clock had once been his own speciality. He was especially interested in Armstrong's performance because their physiological profiles weren't that different: same height, same weight, Armstrong's VO2 Max was 83 to Bassons' 85. Regarded as a key barometer of athletic potential, the VO2 Max is the maximum capacity of an individual's body to transport and use oxygen. Yet when Antoine Vayer did the maths afterwards, he told Bassons that he would have finished 6 kilometres behind Armstrong if they'd started at the same time.

On the night of Sestriere, Bassons and his teammates watched highlights of the American riding away from his rivals on the mountain and they were stunned by the ease with which he outdistanced them. They didn't believe it. Bassons continued to tell every journalist who crossed his path that the doping culture had not gone away.

His refusal to observe the code of silence was a challenge to the leaders in the peloton, especially the rider in the yellow jersey. Armstrong was more than happy to deal with the upstart.

On the morning after his win at Sestriere, the yellow jersey decided the following day's race should be sedate until the approach to the first climb. The *patron* has the right to do this and normally such decrees are strictly observed. But Bassons thought, 'What the hell, I'm the black sheep anyway,' and he launched his breakaway in defiance of the informal truce.

With Bassons gone, Armstrong gave the nod to his US Postal teammates and they immediately pursued. It didn't take long for them to recapture the breakaway and as they joined him Armstrong put his hand on Bassons' shoulder indicating he had something important to say, as a mafia boss might when deciding to personally deliver the punishment.

'What are you doing?' asked Armstrong.

'I'm making the race. I attack.'

'You know what you're saying to the journalists, it's not good for cycling.'

'I'm simply saying what I think. I have said there is still doping.'

'If that's what you're here for, it would be better if you returned home and found some other kind of work.'

'I am not going to leave when I haven't changed anything. If I've things to say, I will say them.'

'Ah, fuck you.'

By this point Bassons' own team had turned against him, believing they were being victimised by the peloton for his speaking out of turn. They told him he had to stop, he said he wouldn't, but the pressure was beginning to tell. Two days after the dressing down, he left the team hotel in Saint-Galmier and abandoned the race.

So that morning we left Saint-Galmier and the news that Bassons had abandoned was delivered on Radio Tour. The previous evening he'd cracked and, despite his fiancée Pascale and his friend Antoine pleading with him to remain, he couldn't cope with the hostility coming from his fellow professionals. In the car I railed against the treatment he'd been subjected to, especially by Armstrong. Charles and Rupert agreed. John remained silent.

Somewhere along the way to Saint-Flour we passed under a banner draped high across the road: FOR A CLEAN TOUR, YOU MUST HAVE BASSONS. Seeing that was the high point of my day.

Before his bullying of Bassons, I considered Armstrong nothing more than a likely, almost certain cheater, one of a great number of professional cyclists still hooked up to the old doping drip. His treatment of Bassons revealed a nasty, almost sociopathic side to his nature.

On the morning after Bassons left, there were various reports that quoted his fellow professionals. Sympathy for the departed one was virtually non-existent. 'He wasn't injured, so why did he go home?' said one, and the general view was that he had behaved unprofessionally. It was an important moment for the Tour. The new *patron* had sent out a message: anyone who broke the law of silence would be dealt with.

'Would a clean rider, one committed to sport without drugs, have treated Bassons as Armstrong has treated him?' I asked in another car debate.

'I don't believe so,' said Charles, in that measured way of his.

We could hear the gentle flow of air up John's nose.

After successfully defending the yellow jersey through the Alps, Armstrong's position seemed unassailable even with two days in the Pyrenees to come. With Bassons banished there would be no dissent from within, but the French newspapers were still holding back. *Le Monde* and *Libération*, perhaps the two most thoughtful, were derisive when not dismissive and *L'Équipe*'s most important writers – Bouvet, Rouet and Ballester – clearly didn't believe.

Because *L'Équipe* is part of the organisation that owns the Tour de France and because it gives so many pages each day to its coverage of the race, its refusal to warm to the champion-elect was significant. It was almost as if official recognition was being denied to the race leader. Armstrong felt it and a week before the end of the race he saw to Ballester in Saint-Gaudens, the last staging post before the Pyrenees.

They knew each other as Ballester had been to Austin to interview Armstrong during his recovery from cancer. That friendship didn't count for much in Saint-Gaudens as the rider held Ballester's arm to draw him closer and then, loud enough for others to hear, said, 'This journalist isn't professional.' Ballester was flabbergasted. 'Hey, Lance, you can't leave it at that. What's this about?' But Armstrong had disappeared into the US Postal team bus.

That evening Armstrong called Ballester on his mobile phone, complaining that *L'Équipe* wasn't being fair to him, and, like any good journalist, Ballester convinced the rider the best way to express his sense of injustice was in a one-on-one with the newspaper. They arranged it for the following day. Armstrong began by expressing his disappointment about what he saw as unfair treatment in the press. Ballester thought, 'Fine, that's part of the story,' but he had some doping-related questions that would give the rider an opportunity to end the speculation.

'Are you using any medical certificates?'

'None,' said Armstrong.

'None at all? Not for corticosteroids or EPO?'

'Nothing.'

'Did you ever use this product to cure your cancer?'

'No, never.'

'Are you taking any medication to stop any return of your cancer?'

'No, absolutely nothing. I just have to consult my oncologist, Dr Einhorn, once every four months.'

Ballester is a tough, straight-to-the-point interviewer, utterly unfazed by the reputation of his interview subject. His piece on Armstrong wasn't the hymn of praise normally sung to athletes on the cusp of their greatest triumph. Armstrong's denials were convincing enough except for his insistence he had not been treated with EPO during his recovery from cancer, when he had. Under pressure, it seemed he couldn't admit using EPO even when it was legal and proper to do so, and a normal part of cancer treatment.

Jean-Marie Leblanc, the Tour de France organiser, was furious with Ballester for what he saw as unfair and overly aggressive questioning. Leblanc let Ballester know what he thought, complaining the interview read like a 'police interrogation'. He also arranged a meeting with Rouet, the newspaper's cycling editor.

The following morning I met Rouet and he mentioned how upset Leblanc was with *L'Équipe*'s coverage of the race, especially its treatment of Armstrong. Had Rouet been working for a newspaper that was totally independent of the race, he might have listened to Leblanc's complaints but they wouldn't have got past his interior walls. This was different.

He and Leblanc had once been colleagues and they were now still branches of the same tree. On a commercial level, the Tour is a godsend for the newspaper, as circulation and advertising rise during the month of July. And within the organisation, the Tour de France organiser was further up the food chain than the newspaper's cycling editor.

Sensing that Rouet had been shaken by his conversation with Leblanc, I read every piece in the newspaper through the remaining five days and it wasn't difficult to detect a shift in *L'Équipe*'s position. They were softer on Armstrong, more accepting of him as the Tour de France champion.

I don't know how much influence the Tour de France organiser was able to exercise over what appeared in *L'Équipe*, or what consequences (if any) were threatened or hinted at; but the questions were no longer phrased in headlines and the newspaper somehow seemed to suspend its disbelief. They never descended to cheerleading, and Bouvet, Rouet and Ballester stayed true to their disbelief, but no longer could you say, '*L'Équipe* doesn't believe Armstrong.'

I was learning lessons, and the first was that with a drugs story you know you are onto something when somebody in control warns you to stop and perhaps gently suggests you remember who puts the butter on your croissant.

Almost ten years earlier, when Paul had quit the peloton and written *Rough Ride*, the chorus of disapproval from his old comrades was loud and aggressive. One of his old team-mates tried to physically assault him. He had spat in the soup. Many of his new colleagues in the press tent weren't a lot better. They were sipping from the same bowl.

Armstrong's last important challenge in the race didn't come in the Pyrenees or in the individual time trial at Futuroscope on the penultimate day, but from an investigation by the journalist Benoît Hopquin of *Le Monde* that showed he had tested positive for a banned corticosteroid earlier in the race. Such drugs can be permitted under prescription, but Armstrong didn't mention he had one when signing his doping control form. At a press conference in Saint-Gaudens, Hopquin asked what had happened.

Without so much as a quiver of doubt, Armstrong pressed the 'attack' button and called *Le Monde* 'the gutter press' and then, turning on Hopquin, said, 'Mr *Le Monde*, are you calling me a doper or a liar?' The journalist was taken aback by Armstrong's aggression, and every other journalist in the room remained silent, instinctively fearing any intervention would draw the wrath of Armstrong upon them.

Le Monde would run the cortisone story saying he had tested positive, but the UCI quickly released a statement saying it was not a positive test, clarifying that it had received a prescription for the drug found in Armstrong's urine and reminding journalists to exercise caution before writing about this story. In its communiqué, the UCI did not specify when it received the prescription from the US Postal team.[12]

The Tour rolled on to Paris. And Lance Armstrong, for whom the years since his last Tour had been spent in part having a testicle, lung cysts and brain lesions removed from his body, showed not a hint of vulnerability. On the morning of the final stage, riders transferred by train from Futuroscope to Arpajan, south of Paris. Only three of us made that journey in the car as John got a one-on-one interview with Lance and travelled as his guest on the train.

Already the story had divided the *salle de presse*, even split our little group of four. A Dutch journalist complained to me of the French: 'There is no evidence and in Holland everyone gives Armstrong credit.' I asked what if the suspicions of doping turned out to be true. He looked at me with pity. 'Everyone knows Tour de France riders are doped. If you don't accept that you shouldn't be covering the sport.' And we, the guys asking the questions, were the cynics?

Armstrong's control of the race was absolute and for a

---

12 Emma O'Reilly, Armstrong's masseuse at the time, explained in *L.A. Confidentiel – les secrets de Lance Armstrong*, that she was present on the night Armstrong and two team officials decided to get team doctor Luis del Moral to write and backdate a medical prescription to get round the problem. Much later, in an affidavit to the United States Anti-Doping Agency, Jonathan Vaughters said he had heard from within the team that Armstrong had used the banned corticosteroid Kenacort before the Tour and that this was what the test detected.

diminishing few in the press tent this was disturbing. For others their sense of admiration made any suspicions or questions a trespass. Some of those who knew the most about what we were seeing said the least.

In my mind the pro-Lance masses were cheerleading a great sport all the way to the hospice. Close to Paris Jean-Marie Leblanc, God bless his commercial soul, declared that the Tour 'has been saved'.

On the day that the race entered the Avenue des Champs-Elysées, the headline on the story I wrote for the *Sunday Times* said, FLAWED FAIRYTALE. I was proud of that because, written back in London, it offered support that was hard to find on the race.

'This has been no renaissance Tour,' I wrote in the second paragraph of that *Sunday Times* story, 'rather a retreat into the old ways of the peloton where doping is their business, not ours. Where the law of silence supersedes all others.'

For the piece I had spoken to Dr Armand Mégret, head of the French cycling federation's medical commission, and asked if he believed the Tour was racing at '*deux vitesses*'? 'If by this expression you mean there are clean riders and others who are not clean, then the answer is yes, this is cycling at two speeds. Doping has not been eradicated.'

In Gilles Delion I saw another Kimmage, an older Bassons. A 32-year-old veteran at the time, his innocence was taken a long time before but he had once been a young, talented and ambitious rider. In his first Tour he finished 15th, 21 places higher than Armstrong's best in his first four, but Delion wouldn't dope and his career meandered downhill.

He was asked about the Tour of Renewal: 'That makes me

laugh. The renewal affects just one part of the peloton,' he said. Writing about Delion, Kimmage or Bassons, I felt a lot better about my job as a sportswriter.

As for readers of the *Sunday Times*, I hoped they would think a little before loving this new hero. 'For too long sportswriting has been unrestrained cheerleading, suspending legitimate doubts and settling for stories of sporting heroism. Of course there are times when it is right to celebrate, but there are other occasions when it is equally correct to keep your hands by your sides.'

That afternoon on the Champs-Élysées I had no desire to applaud the winner of the Tour de France.

5

'He's not the messiah, he's a very naughty boy.'
Monty Python, *The Life of Brian*

Americans who characterise the French as a nation of cheese-eating surrender monkeys have never met Pierre Ballester. If every one of us press-room trolls could be like Pierre I think that even Lance would respect us. He's an impressive guy. We've done a lot of work together, a lot of work that I am proud of, but anybody who winds up working with Pierre feels like Garfunkel to his Simon.

I liked the guy from the start: his sense of humour, his take on what journalism was about. We met during the 1993 Tour de France when he was working for *L'Équipe* and hit it off from the start. He's serious about work, quick to serve up the *scoop du jour*, but less serious about life. He's good fun over lunch, as a Frenchman should be, but then sharp and focused once he's dialled into a story. What threw us closer as journalists was the fear and loathing on the 1999 Tour and our shared allergy to the official version of the Lance Armstrong story. The more spoonfuls of good news we were force fed by the UCI, Jean-Marie Leblanc and many of our friends in the media, the more prickly we became.

At the centre of our difficulties was the enigma that was Lance Armstrong. There was a curious contradiction in the other riders' view of Armstrong. Many in the peloton chain gang didn't appreciate his Texan arrogance or his view of himself as a natural leader among men. Most, though, reckoned Lance to be a good thing for a sport that was still in intensive care after the Festina scandal. Just a year before, as Festina unfolded in all its Technicolor squalor, Armstrong was commentating on the Tour as many of the riders felt hounded by the police and alienated from their public. Now he was among them again, a good news story without the stain of '98 upon him. The riders enjoyed the warmth from his halo as they rode in his slipstream.

This view of him being good for the sport, a tonic for the Tour, became orthodox and was propagated by Tour organiser Leblanc, the sponsors, the UCI and the majority of the journalists. There was a moratorium on questions as the vested interests of cycling implored Lance to redeem the Tour and cleanse everybody with the sparkling pure waters of his urine samples.

Lance was the saviour with additional feature benefits. He would blaze a trail towards El Dorado, the lucrative US market, and like filings to a magnet the public would be pulled back to cycling. They'd realise how much they loved the sport and how they'd missed it. And they'd want to be part of this era because, well, Lance Armstrong was a damn good story.

All of this was evident and many in the press room, as well as in the steamy world of cycling administration, were relieved that it was business as usual again. Cometh the hour, cometh the man, etc.

Yet Pierre and I in our conversations found that we held the same view, borrowed from Monty Python's *Life of Brian*. We wanted to tell the world, 'He's not the messiah, he's a very naughty boy.' Maybe it was a contrarian instinct in the face of so much hype, but I think that your visceral response remains yours, no matter what you are being told. That gut feeling is the only thing left after so much else has been taken. Journalists should always listen to what their gut is saying. Like me, Pierre didn't believe in Armstrong. He'd had his doubts from way back. He could recall how uneasy he first felt after visiting Lance in Austin, Texas in November 1996, during his recovery from stage four testicular cancer. Now, on the 1999 Tour, Pierre's gut was aching from too much *déjà vu*.

Pierre is an especially fearless interviewer. He suffers from some sort of deference deficiency. He's not arrogant but nobody impresses or intimidates him. The question-and-answer session with Armstrong that Tour organiser Jean-Marie Leblanc had depicted as 'a police interrogation' was a fine piece of journalism. What Leblanc disliked was what I liked. Pierre didn't genuflect before the champion-elect. He didn't coat the difficult questions with sugary moral cowardice.

'Your critics claim that . . .' blah, blah, blah.

'How do you respond to those who . . .' blah, blah, blah.

'Is this experience being diminished for you by . . .' blah, blah, blah.

Pierre asked Armstrong if he'd used EPO. Straight question: yes or no? Pierre Ballester wanted to know. By virtue of asking that question, Pierre would put himself in Armstrong's bad books, the library from which there is no escape. By proxy, Leblanc was infuriated. *An injury to Lance is an injury to us all* was the war cry of those who would protect the soup from journalistic expectorations.

That disapproval wouldn't have bothered Pierre one whit. It was more like winning an award. His Lance interview was a text-book example of how we should all get up off our knees and approach stars with a level gaze and honest questions. I drank it in and felt better, stronger.

Pierre had asked the questions and because Armstrong wasn't open and honest in his answers, there was a strong sense that we were looking at a young man whose obituary would one day state that he could ride but he just couldn't hide. Pierre had merely done his job, but in a press tent crammed to dangerous levels with sycophants and time servers you wanted to hand over the Pulitzer there and then.

We knew that the '99 Tour de France was ushering in the reign of a great pretender but were powerless to do much about it. It wasn't just the feeling that Armstrong had doped and won, what most rankled was the confederacy of cheerleaders which protected him: the UCI bosses who knew about the uniformly elevated haematocrit values, especially in the US Postal team, and decided that was a part of the story best kept secret; the journalists who saw poor Bassons being bullied out of the race and thought, 'That's okay, he's only a small rider'; and the Tour de France organiser who decreed that Armstrong had 'saved' the Tour.

Poor old Jean-Marie Leblanc. He had gone to Notre-Dame des Cyclistes to say a prayer for a saviour to appear on the 1999 Tour. He'd forgot to ask for the extra miracle he needed to persuade every agnostic in the house. Leblanc would need to do some pretty charismatic preaching to get Pierre and me to buy what he was selling.

Pierre was so tired of the dishonesty that in one of our final conversations at the '99 Tour he said that he would continue covering cycling but not like before. Every story from then on would in one way or another deal with doping, and if his newspaper didn't allow him to do this, he would turn his hand to something more fulfilling.

(I was reminded of the possibly apocryphal story of the journalist at the *New York Times* who went to his bosses and argued that he would only continue to cover the Olympic Games if every report bearing his byline concluded with an asterisk and the words, 'None of the above reflects the beliefs of the writer.')

If you'd said to Pierre that doing only doping stories in cycling would hurt his career at *L'Équipe*, he would have shrugged and said, 'Yeah and so what?'

As for Pierre's stubbornness, I loved him for it and felt a similar desire to do more investigating, to start writing more about doping. I went to a mirror and practised shrugging like a Frenchman.

Linford Christie, the 100m Olympic champion from Barcelona, empathised with my situation. He reached out to me. Six months before, the previous February, he had competed at an indoor meeting in Dortmund, Germany, and had been randomly selected for dope control. His sample contained a level of the banned steroid nandrolone that was almost 100 times over the limit. At the time he was two months short of his 39th birthday. Those in Linford's corner scoffed at the ludicrousness of it. 'Do you really think that, with his career virtually over, he would endanger his reputation by taking nandrolone?'

This was another version of the seemingly irrefutable Armstrong defence: 'Do you really believe that after what he's been through he would put banned drugs into his body?' In both cases I thought, 'Yes, actually, it's entirely possible.'

Christie was 38 but not running like an old man. Three weeks before the positive test, he'd done 6.57secs for 60m in Karlsruhe, his best start to the indoor season for six years. 'It was the performance of runner-up Linford Christie which was really sensational,' said the reporter for *Athletics International* at the meet. Such was his form that Christie struck a bet with a friend that he would run 6.5secs before the end of the season, something only three Europeans had done before, Christie being one of the three.

After suffering through a Tour de France in which most of the leading contenders filled their tanks with undetectable EPO, this was a reminder that testing can sometimes work. Often just by dumb luck. But even when athletes test positive, it is startling to see a little cottage industry spring up manufacturing excuses for the offender. Search parties are sent out to scour the countryside for a loophole through which their man can escape. Doping is the great scourge; more testing is needed. Meanwhile it seems that only the innocent get caught.

There were plenty of people in the UK athletics community who didn't want to believe Christie had taken nandrolone. He was that most attractive of stars: half man, half media. His colleagues on the BBC's panel of athletics experts, Roger Black, Steve Cram and Sally Gunnell, all supported him. Perhaps they should have spoken with Professor Wilhelm Schanzer, head of the IOC-accredited laboratory in Cologne, who had dealt with Christie's sample.

'I did not have to think too much about this case after I made the analysis,' he said. 'It was a very clear finding. If the concentration of the banned substance is low we have to do additional work to make sure what we estimate is correct. In this case there was no need for this. It is nearly correct to say the result was one hundred times greater than the permitted level. It was a clear, clear result.'

It was good to write the Christie story and to ask why it took six months for the story to be made public. The tale only saw the light of day when an IAAF source leaked the information to *L'Équipe*. UK Athletics, who had been informed of Christie's positive test in March, denied they had covered it up, saying they had to allow their disciplinary process to run its course. Their hand was forced by the leak. UK Athletics banned the former Olympic and World champion for two years.

For the sportswriter determined to be more journalist than fan (and, let's face it, keen to finish ahead of Sally Gunnell in the Sports Journalist of the Year Awards), the difficulty comes when you measure the toll that doping question takes on your enthusiasm.

Armstrong wins the Tour de France but you're sure he's

cheated, so that's not much fun. The world goes all happy clappy and you stand there with a face like a slapped backside, shaking your head slowly. But if you observed closely, you weren't alone. As the stampede to turn the water of *maillot jaune* into the wine of sporting salvation passed by in a cloud of dust and cheering, the Italian Vincenzo Santini also stood to one side: 'I hope that the governments and the cycling authorities can find a way out of the mess that cycling is in. Until that happens we can forget the joy of the victory.'

Back in England an ageing Olympic champion sprinter can also forget the joy of victory because he is due to take receipt of a two-year suspension.

As for me I'm off to sunny Spain, to beautiful Seville for the World Athletics Championships. I'm hoping that this will re-energise me. Give me back the old enthusiasm, restore some belief. Lately I've found myself sitting morosely in the corner of bars as people celebrate and snog and sing. I have a little sign in front of me, beside my drink. It says Beware. Man With Too Many Questions.

Sadly, when I hit Seville there is only one story in town: Merlene Ottey's exclusion following a recent drug test, another nandrolone positive, has got there before me. It's so tiring carrying a head full of questions everywhere. Especially questions about Merlene Ottey, the queen of Jamaica, who will one day become the Queen of Slovenia. She is glamorous, beautifully athletic and at this point in her career, she is a 39-year-old with eight Olympic medals and still competing at the very highest level. She is immensely likeable. And four days before the start of Seville, she has announced that she has tested positive for nandrolone. Oh, say it ain't so, Merlene, say it ain't so.

So, in the same month, two 39-year-old sprinters, one an Olympic gold medallist in the 100m and the other an eight-time medallist at the Olympics, are dealing with the fall-out from positive drug tests.

And no matter how many times you tell people that you are a sportswriter the response is the same, 'Oooh, I would love to do your job.' And it feels churlish to argue. When everybody is celebrating it feels odd sometimes to be wondering if it's natural for a sprinter to be so competitive when he or she is crowding forty?[13] The easy choice would be to suspend the disbelief and go with the flow. Let this be mere entertainment, not sport. Release sport of all the burdens you place on it just by loving sport and believing in sport and wanting to be inspired by sport. In Seville this means trying not to remember that the new women's 200m world champion Inger Miller has knocked 0.3secs off her best time in the final. Better to forget too that earlier in the year Miller tested positive for caffeine.

In the midst of the debate over Ottey's positive, Marion Jones came to her rival's defence. With friends like Marion . . .

'I don't think I'm one hundred per cent sure that it's the correct testing procedure. Over the last couple of weeks our beautiful and lovely sport has been marred by all of this.'[14]

13 Ottey claimed her positive test was the result of a 'mistake' and, after being given a two-year ban by the IAAF, she appealed to the Court of Arbitration for Sport. Her appeal was upheld on a technicality and the suspension was lifted. She now lives in Slovenia and competed at last summer's European Championships at the ripe old age of 52.
14 At the Sydney Olympics a year later, Marion Jones won four gold medals. In 2007 she admitted she had used banned performance-enhancing drugs as far back as those 2000 Olympics. Her Olympic medals were returned and Jones was given a six-month prison sentence a year later for lying under oath before a Grand Jury investigation into doping in sport.

Thanks Marion. See you at the drive for five.

I watched Michael Johnson run majestically in the 400m, Hicham El Guerrouj's brilliance in the 1500m and Maurice Greene winning the 100m, but I was no longer the kid enraptured by the Kip Keino–Jim Ryun rivalry or the young man once riveted by Steve Ovett and Seb Coe. After the men's 1500m final in Seville my poor brain was boiling with questions. I wondered why third, fourth and fifth were all Spaniards and all had run 3.32. Was I dreaming? Were they making drugs now that didn't just make people run faster but made them all run precisely the same time?

Encountering an IAAF official, I mentioned how unlikely this was.

'Do you think I believe it?' he asked.

So I settled for writing about Paula Radcliffe with her bobbing head, her grimacing face, and the plucky red ribbon pinned to her GB vest. The ribbon was a call for more anti-doping action from the authorities, namely the introduction of blood tests, but my attraction to Radcliffe was down to the sense that she could be trusted. She ran her heart out to finish second to the Ethiopian Gete Wami and collapsed a few yards beyond the finish line. Radcliffe's exhaustion recalled the athletics of our childhood, sport more human and easier to identify with.

I asked her about the decision to wear the ribbon. 'It was building up inside me,' she said. 'I was training my guts out, making all the sacrifices and asking myself, "Do I want to be doing this if I am getting nowhere?" I didn't accuse anybody but I sensed women were following the men into using drugs. And I hated the idea that people might be asking, "What's she on?"'

In January 2000, separate investigations into doping in sport were taking place in the Italian cities of Turin, Bologna, Ferrara, Venice, Trento and Brescia. Two of the investigations involved athletes that interested me. In the inquiry into the Ferrara-based doctor, Professor Francesco Conconi, Ireland's Tour de France winner Stephen Roche was listed among twenty-three riders in what would be called 'the EPO file'.

Equally intriguing was Kevin Livingston's involvement with another Ferrara-based doctor, Michele Ferrari, who was being investigated on suspicion of doping cyclists. Livingston was Lance Armstrong's most trusted lieutenant on the US Postal team in the 1999 Tour and his involvement with Ferrari raised important questions.

The *Sunday Times* agreed I should go to Italy and see what I could find out. It was a good trip, made memorable by an interview with Fulvio Gori, a likeable Italian policeman who worked for NAS, the Italian anti-drug squad, in Florence. Gori sat behind a big desk in an office that was more like a small warehouse, with floors covered with boxes of files. He was a portly, amiable man who laughed at the slightest excuse and kept a photo on the wall of the amateur football team he coached. Trying to get a handle on doping in cycling was the worst part of his life.

'In this investigation,' he said, 'I have interviewed almost thirty cyclists, brought them into this office, sat them down and not from one of them did I get co-operation. They tell nothing about what they do.'

In May 1996, the Carabinieri discovered that a pharmacy in Tuscany had been selling large quantities of EPO to professional cyclists. They didn't need Sherlock Holmes to figure that the riders were re-stocking their supplies for the Giro d'Italia later in the month. So the Carabinieri in Florence decided they would pay a surprise visit to the Giro to see if they could find some of that EPO.

That year the Giro began in Greece, spent three days there before making a ferry crossing to Brindisi, and the police plan was to arrive as the team cars were coming off the ferry. 'Here we were,' said Gori, 'driving from here to Brindisi, eight hundred kilometres. I am reading *La Gazzetta*, my feet up on the dashboard, and I come across a tiny story on one of the cycling pages. It says, "The police are planning a surprise visit to the race in Brindisi where they will check the team cars for drugs." I struck the dashboard with my fist. I was so angry, angry, angry.

'How did they know? Why was it printed in the newspaper? It made us more determined. I swore from then on we would never let them go.'

Knowing the Carabinieri were coming, some team cars came the long way home, overland through Albania, Montenegro and Croatia before re-entering Italy from the north. Other teams opted to dump their stashes of drugs into the sea. After Gori and his partner made the long journey back to Florence, not having found even a trace of a banned substance anywhere, their office-bound colleagues were waiting for them: 'We hear there are enormously big fish, with great stamina, swimming across the Adriatic Sea.' Gori wasn't amused.

Bike riders not telling journalists about their doping is to be expected, but it was a surprise to learn from Gori that the Italian riders felt they could bring their *omerta* into a Florence police station. At the time doping was not a crime in Italy and they could stonewall Gori and his colleagues with impunity. Somehow they had come to think of themselves and their secret culture as separate from the outside world, beyond the reach of the law.

Rather than be mindful that the doctors who advised them to take banned substances and the pharmacies who sold them were both breaking the law, they felt honour-bound to protect their suppliers.

Fulvio Gori was a relatively young man, early 40s, married, no kids. Thirteen months later he died from cancer. Partly because he was taken so prematurely, the time spent with him remains a vivid memory.

Stephen Roche's involvement with Conconi was a difficult story as Roche and I went back a long way. He'd retired six years before but the files related to the last two years of his career. He was in the file under his own name but also under aliases, two of which were Rocchi and Roncati.

Roche's career had been highly successful and in 1987 he won the Giro d'Italia, Tour de France and World Championships, a treble previously achieved only by the legendary Eddy Merckx. Before this connection with Conconi, Roche had never been linked with doping. I had written his official autobiography, *The Agony and the Ecstasy*, in 1987, and though we were not close friends we had remained very friendly.

While writing his book, I had stayed at his home in Paris, and at his then in-laws' holiday home in south-west France; we'd spent a lot of time in each other's company. Ringing him about this story wasn't an easy call. He was relatively calm: 'I met Conconi once; after that I did all my blood tests for our team doctor, Giovanni Grazzi. I know Grazzi was based at the

University of Ferrara [as was Conconi] and it's possible that's how we ended up in Conconi's files.'

He was trying to say it was all a mix-up. 'My haematocrit was forty-six or forty-seven when I raced; forty-four when I rested, and it never went above those levels,' he said, perhaps unaware that haematocrit drops when one races, rises during periods of rest.

I asked Roche why Conconi had used aliases. 'I asked Grazzi the same question and he told me it wasn't that unusual for code-names to be used for high-profile athletes.'

But why?

As Roche had once been a national treasure in Ireland and remained a high-profile former champion, the story that he may have doped caused a stir. I knew there would be blow-back. Just not how much.

Let me explain something.

There are only two types of people in Ireland, though at this stage it would be hard to tell which is in the minority. There are those who watch *The Late Late Show*. And there are those who have been on *The Late Late Show*. In 2002 I was promoted to the latter group.

The Late Late Show has been the crucible for many of the debates which have shaped Irish society down through the years, but as the presenters have changed and become more wooden so the format has had to be adjusted to something more safe and predictable. Still, the programme has always retained some of the cachet of its heyday. It still tries to mix the responsibilities of being a national forum with the require-ments of light entertainment. The show still has a 'here comes everybody' feel to it.

The call to appear on *The Late Late Show* isn't unlike an invitation to Buckingham Palace. It is expected that you be undemanding and a little awestruck. You should dress nicely, arrive sober and try to fit in with the royals no matter what they suggest. Here was what *The Late Late Show* suggested to me as the format for a 'debate' with Stephen Roche on the issue of drugs following my disclosure of his name on the Conconi files. It would be a production starring Stephen Roche as the wronged party. Stephen would come out first to sit and be interviewed with respectful stiffness by our host Pat Kenny. After a while the subject of drugs would be introduced and, lo, the camera would swing around and there, sitting in the audience like a malevolent stalker, would be *me*.

And I would have to account for myself and the things that I had written about a man who wasn't in the audience, a man who had attained sufficient celebrity within Irish society as to be an actual guest on *The Late Late Show*. And Pat Kenny and Stephen Roche would face me down and people in the seats either side of me would look uncomfortable being seen in the company of such a kook. So I declined that invitation.

Exasperated by my ingratitude, *The Late Late Show* conceded that I could sit on a grown-up's chair beside Pat and Stephen for the debate, but I couldn't come out and sit on the chair until Stephen had been given a good fifteen minutes' headstart out there, doing a tender one-on-one with Pat. Stephen does beatific very well; he gives great piety. He would remind everybody that butter wouldn't melt in his lycras. Then I'd come out. Boo!

I accepted the deal reluctantly. On the night, Stephen wore a dark suit, dark shirt and dark tie and slicked-back hair, and if it wasn't for that madly camp half-French, half-Dublin accent of his, he could have passed for an unctuous undertaker to an accident-prone mafia family. He duly spoke with Pat Kenny about his life and career for fifteen minutes or so. Then with a shout of 'unchain the gimp' the journalist was sent in. The early exchanges were civil and a little on the dull side. We reassured everybody that there would be no bloodshed, that we had known each other for many years, and had the utmost respect for each other.

Stephen was doing his wounded soul routine. 'Daveeed, I accept what you are zaying but I never told you a lie.'

I, like any experienced parent, was making the point that I wasn't cross with Stephen about his name(s) turning up on the Conconi files; no, not cross, just a little disappointed. I was attempting to remain controlled and get my message across. Roche was unsure as to whether he could be seen to be trying to land a knockout punch, so he either acted baffled or was actually baffled by the evidence.

To demonstrate bafflement Stephen had brought with him a sheet that he held up to the camera. It listed the various aliases that Francesco Conconi had given him during tests carried out in Italy. There were all sorts of notations and great swathes of dayglo highlighter which made the document look like a schoolchild's study schedule. The dates and the results of various tests sat alongside the letters s or n (for *si* or *no*) which Conconi had filled in depending on what levels he found. It was all meaningless and there was enough bafflement for everyone in the audience.

When Stephen was asked if he had dealt with Conconi, he replied helpfully that Conconi wasn't the team doctor, implying that he, Stephen, was strictly a one-doctor sort of guy. The debate was flagging, the details of the chart were confusing for everybody and the discussion was about to fizzle out when Pat Kenny produced his trump card.

In the audience, possibly in the seat once earmarked for myself, Pat had planted some help: Dr Bill 'that's entertainment' Tormey from Beaumont Hospital in Dublin. Now in TV terms if you scrape the barrel long enough and then reach down for what is under the barrel and then go on some more you end up with Bill Tormey in your audience. He's the man who once called a female hospital colleague a 'right geebag' and who would later become famous for his primitive views on gay marriage and for calling for missionaries returning from Africa to be Aids tested.

Now he was here to play to the gallery. And he felt the gallery should be grateful. To paraphrase Wilde: Bill, if you had to do it all again, would you still fall in love with yourself? He began by reciting a litany of Irish sporting stars and then announced that, 'Stephen Roche is right up there.'

Without further ado he hopped to the science bit. Stop reading if you lack a Nobel Prize in either physics or chemistry. 'Now, Pat, as you know, I am a cynic. The only reason I am out here tonight is because of what they are doing to this man. I wouldn't come out otherwise, even though you're a good bloke yourself [*crowd all cheer ecstatically*].

'I tell you this. Stephen Roche is a great bloke. [*Shit. Pat and Stephen Roche are both blokes within the good to great range. I feel isolated and unworthy.*] To hammer a guy like Stephen Roche who, in 1987, won the Tour de France, the Giro d'Italia and the World Championship, and I am grateful to

Jimmy Magee for actually showing it to us on TV [*for the uninitiated Jimmy Magee is a commentator, not an actual TV channel*] and I must say one thing about Stephen, to do that when EPO wasn't even on the market? Everybody here should realise that you couldn't inject EPO into yourself in 1987 because it wasn't available in 1987. That's the first thing. That's very relevant. So Stephen won this stuff clean because at the time, if he was taking amphetamines, remember what happened to Tommy Simpson taking amphetamines [*he died, but, as Lance Armstrong himself has pointed out, he didn't test positive*], Stephen would have been caught taking amphetamines, the only other thing that's worth a damn in terms of endurance testing for something like cycling, to the best of my knowledge, anyway, at the moment . . .'

I was starting to think that this was actually a skit, a piece of light entertainment, the heavyweight expert as buffoon. Then Tormey inflated a little further and finally started speaking of himself in the third person. He addressed Stephen Roche personally, great bloke to great bloke.

'I am going to assume that the hangman, judge and jury that is sitting up there beside you from the *Sunset Times*, Murdoch's organ, is correct. Tormey is now the court of appeal judge and I am going to go through this . . .'

And he proceeded to demonstrate that he had not only the specific doping expertise of a bright seven-year-old but the legal knowledge of a dim six-year-old to boot. He held a little mock appeal hearing in monologue, and grandly pronounced a verdict of not proven for Roche. And to the stockade of shame for the *Sunset Times* (*comedy gold by the way! Sunset Times!*).

And then up on stage we went back to our chat for a few minutes, ploughing on to the end of the stage and an advertisement break: Bill Tormey and Pat Kenny drafting Stephen Roche all the way to the line; me a *domestique* in the media peloton suddenly realising what it must have felt like to be Christophe Bassons on a bad day.

On the way out of RTE's television centre that night, one of the staffers at the station said they had taken almost 400 telephone calls from viewers and they had broken down evenly: half supported Stephen, half were for me. To me that sounded like a result.[15]

Being more confident when he has the scent of a story, Pierre would have handled Roche and Tormey better than I did that night.

Like me, Pierre went back quite a way with Lance Armstrong. They had met in a nightclub in Oslo on the night in 1993 that the Texan had become the youngest ever winner of the World Championships.

The new world road race champion had yet to discover that all us journalists were, as he would later say, snakes with

---

15 The question of whether or not Roche and his fellow riders in the Conconi file doped would be answered by Judge Franca Oliva in a summary delivery some time after the end of the case against the accused doctors, Conconi, Grazzi and Ilario Casoni: 'The accused have, for several years and with systematic continuity, aided and abetted the athletes named in the court indictment in their consumption of erythropoietin, supporting them and de facto encouraging them in that consumption with reassuring series of checks on the state of their health, with examinations, analysis and tests designed to assess and maximise the impact of that consumption with regard to sports performances. Therefore, on a point of law, the crime as originally charged against the defendant still stands.'

arms. He sipped a beer, talked candidly with a small group of journalists and, according to his media companions, was good company. He laughed easily and never let the conversation slow.

Given the beer, the celebration, the noise and the relaxed atmosphere this was a different Lance to the one we would come to know. Nothing was taboo that evening. No boundaries. He talked a lot. Pierre could see that he enjoyed talking and would have sat trading stories until sunrise if Armstrong's friends hadn't hauled him away.

They had an early start the next morning. Four hours after leaving the nightclub they were on the plane to a criterium in Châteaulin, but Pierre and Lance had established a relationship. They spoke again for interview purposes in the spring of 1996. Lance said that he had been acting like a jerk around the time of La Flèche Wallonne and then in Liège. Pierre wrote it as he heard it. The next time he met Armstrong he braced himself for an earful of Texan but Lance just shrugged the shoulders. 'It's okay; it's true. That's what I said to you.'

Pierre felt there was some mutual respect. When Lance fell ill later that year, his agent Bill Stapleton was snowed under with interview requests. He showed them all to Lance, who picked two: veteran Sam Abt, who for many years has written for the *New York Times* and the *Herald Tribune*, and Pierre.

Flying to Austin in November 1996, Pierre was greeted by a thin and frail-looking Lance. A cap was pulled down tight over his bald head. There was a weak Texan sun in the sky but Armstrong didn't look like a man feeling its warmth when he greeted Pierre on the doorstep of his Mediterranean-style villa tight by a branch of the Colorado River.

Abt and Pierre arrived at the same time and Lance brought them to his kitchen where they passed the time in small talk as he made himself a vegetable smoothie. The two journalists offered to interview him simultaneously, but Lance said he'd rather do them separately.

Sportswriters always prefer one-on-ones and Ballester and Apt were quietly pleased that Lance decided on two interviews. He also decreed that Abt would go first. At a loose end, Pierre wandered around the huge house. Armstrong has always been a fan of paintings and Pierre studied what was on the walls. In the garage he ran his hands slowly over the five bikes which hung there. He leaned down to peer in at the speedometer of the black Porsche. Things had changed hugely in this young man's life since that night in Oslo three years earlier.

Rambling on, Pierre arrived in a hallway that led to a bedroom. He sensed somebody behind him. 'Are you looking for something?' said Armstrong.

'Something? No, nothing special. I didn't want to disturb your interview with Sam so I'm walking around, that's all. A newspaper article needs a sense of atmosphere, as you well know.'

'But there's nothing in my bedroom.'

'Nothing? How do you mean? Nothing? At all?'

'If you think you're going to find a bag of dope . . .'

'A bag of . . .? What are you talking about? Excuse me, but I don't understand.'

Armstrong abruptly ended the exchange and grinned. It was a strange episode but now it was closed.

When Pierre sat down for the interview some time later, he encountered the other Lance, the one who could speak movingly about coming face to face with death. Pierre liked this Lance.

Their relationship changed at the 1999 Tour de France. Lance thought *L'Équipe* treated him unfairly but doing a one-on-one interview with Pierre only made a difficult relationship between Tour leader and newspaper worse. Pierre had changed since that nightclub encounter in Oslo, too.

Lance would have preferred the early-model Pierre.

Next time they met was at US Postal's pre-season camp in 2000 at San Luis Obispo, California. It was January. The team had, for promotional purposes, invited thirty international journalists to their camp. Pierre didn't think the press conference was much good to a man who had flown 6000 miles to be there. He collared Lance afterwards.

'Well, what do you want?'

'Not this.'

'What do you mean "not this"?'

'Not this quarter hour devoted to the press. Some people travelled six thousand miles to see you, and I'm one of them.'

'I know. I saw your name on the list.'

'As interesting as your press conference was, you can understand that my newspaper and I want to spend a little more time with you.'

Lance turned around. He was playing with the room key in his hands, pretending to think about it. He cracked a little smile.

'If I didn't want you to come, you wouldn't have been allowed. How much time do you want?'

'Three quarters of an hour would be good. Tomorrow, does that work for you?'

'Tomorrow. Okay for tomorrow. A half hour.'

'Thanks, Lance.'

The interview the following day took thirty minutes precisely. Not one minute more. Pierre asked that John Wilcockson be allowed sit in. Lance declined. The answers were short and terse. Nothing he heard allayed Pierre's suspicions but he came away thinking that Lance Armstrong scarcely cared any more. Pierre had been banished to that world where Lance Armstrong sends people he has no more use for.

A month or so before the 2000 Tour de France, Lance Armstrong's autobiography, *It's Not About the Bike: My Journey Back to Life*, was published. Ghost written by the *Washington Post* columnist Sally Jenkins, the story of the cancer survivor who came back from the brink to win the Tour de France was quite brilliantly told. Jenkins' skill is apparent throughout and the book would become a worldwide bestseller. More than that, it would become a source of inspiration to many stricken with serious illness, especially those with cancer. As well as earning millions of dollars for Armstrong, the book did more than anything to make him a global icon.

I read the book and was carried along by Jenkins' storytelling which was remarkable, as a source from inside Armstrong's world had said that Lance had not been as available to Jenkins as both would have liked and that she'd had to rely on interviews with friends and family, especially his close friend John 'Collidge' Korioth. What did it matter? The story was gripping, inspiring and hugely entertaining and the public loved it.

There were, though, a couple of contradictions. In the book Armstrong was portrayed as a sympathetic character, one who would never have turned on Christophe Bassons as he did during the 1999 Tour and, naturally, there was no mention of his contretemps with the French rider in the book.

The second element that didn't stack up was the hostility to drug testing expressed in the book, which he described as 'demeaning': 'Right after I finished a stage I was whisked away to an open tent, where I sat in a chair while a doctor wrapped a piece of rubber tubing around my arm, jabbed me with a needle and drew blood. As I lay there a battery of photographers flashed their cameras at me.'

He went on to add: 'The drug tests became my best friend, because they proved I was clean. I had been tested and checked and retested.'

This portrayal of the drug-testing operation at the Tour de France was so confused and inaccurate it wasn't worth bothering about except in that it gave one a sense of Armstrong's antipathy towards the system. Would it not be more demeaning to ride clean and have to compete against forty or fifty doped-up riders? It was also a bad joke to suggest the tests proved Armstrong rode clean. How could they when the most important drug EPO was undetectable?

The 2000 Tour began at another theme park, Futuroscope, and it was there that Bill Stapleton entered my life. I'd never met him before; he didn't introduce himself and I didn't recognise him. But he knew me and perhaps thought I would know him. Halfway through our conversation, it twigged.

'David, I just want to have a word?'

'Yeah, fine.'

'Look, we're aware of what you wrote about Lance last year, what you've been writing this year.'

'Yeah?'

'Well, we could have a better relationship, things could be better between you and Lance.'

'What do you mean?'

'What I mean is that if you were more balanced in what you wrote, we could help with access.'

'I believe I've been fair.'

'We are going to be watching what you write very closely and we will not be afraid to take action if that is necessary?'

'Bill, is that a threat?'

'It is a threat.'

Bill Stapleton, agent to Lance Armstrong and attorney at law, had delivered his message.

6

'No tears in the writer, no tears in the reader. No surprise in the writer, no surprise in the reader.'

Robert Frost

A media tale.

After the 1999 Tour de France, Pierre Ballester sat down with his cycling editor and friend Jean-Michel Rouet and spoke softly about hard things. Pierre explained that he no longer had the stomach for writing about the sport. At least he couldn't write as he had for much of the previous decade. Reporting races, interviewing victors, presenting winners as heroes, he couldn't do this any more. Jean-Michel empathised with Pierre's dilemma and was happy for him to concentrate on the doping side of the sport.

'It wasn't possible for me to cover cycling in any other way. No longer could I do the touchy feely stories because I didn't believe in these guys. I wasn't sure how *L'Équipe* would react and I was aware that covering doping could harm my career and even put my job at risk but, at the time, they thought they needed me and they wanted to keep me happy.'

L'Équipe is a serious operation. The newspaper has 380 journalists. Pierre was the only one to ask if he could concentrate his work on doping, surely the biggest ongoing sports story of our time. For a while the newspaper saw Pierre as their moral conscience made flesh. And doping was becoming a bigger story, and doping investigations were good for selling newspapers. Perhaps this was the right idea at the right time. In October 1999 doping was a story. The Festina trial was beginning at Lille in the north of the country.

This was the official inquiry into the widespread doping revealed by customs and police at the 1998 Tour de France. Pierre enjoyed every moment of his time in Lille, sifting through the wreckage of the 1998 Tour. For once he felt that he was able to report the realities of professional cycling. Witness after witness came forward, each telling a story more wretched than the previous one. The scandal of the previous summer had left a lingering bad taste and the French people demanded some honesty and contrition from the cycling community.

Pascal Hervé, a rider with the Festina team, said he would have told the truth earlier but for the fact 'just us nine idiots [Festina's team at the '98 Tour] were caught'. Laurent Brochard, another Festina rider, told how he won the World Championship road race in 1997, subsequently tested positive but an official from the UCI informed his team manager that a backdated medical certificate would get him off. Thomas Davy, who rode alongside five-time Tour winner Miguel Indurain at the Banesto team in Spain, said: 'There was a systematic doping programme, under medical supervision, at the team.'

Richard Virenque, who had lied incessantly for eighteen months about his doping, was told by Judge Daniel Delegove to tell the truth. And at last he did. 'Even though I doped,' Virenque added, 'I did not have an advantage over my rivals.'

Antoine Vayer, the exercise physiologist who refused to play any part in doping while working at Festina, was called as an expert witness. 'Armstrong rides at fifty-four kph,' he said. 'I find it scandalous. It's nonsense. Indirectly, it proves he is doping.' A second expert said Vayer's analysis made perfect sense. And Pierre Ballester was in his element, writing the pieces that might help cycling to face its problems.

His work from the Festina trial was praised by his bosses at *L'Équipe* but, while there was no shortage of doping stories, *L'Équipe*'s enthusiasm for the subject wasn't anywhere close to Pierre's. The newspaper's bosses would praise him for the work he did in Lille, but his fellow reporters in the cycling department weren't so impressed.

Each of the major sports at *L'Équipe* has a separate department. Cycling, for example, had its editor, Rouet, his number two (Philippe Bouvet) and then nine reporters. 'I'd known Jean-Michel and Philippe for a long time and they're good guys. But when I concentrated on doping, I knew some of the others wouldn't like it very much. They didn't think my writing about doping was good for the newspaper, and at least two of them, Philippe Le Gars and Manuel Martinez, believed my writing was making it harder for them to get access to the riders.'

One of the bosses spoke with Pierre about his concerns.

'He said that he didn't think I was in harmony with the newspaper and I replied, "Am I the problem or are you the problem?" They wanted me to write some things about doping, but there were just too many doping affairs for their liking.'

While working exclusively on doping, Pierre discovered something unexpected. Always, the message came back to him that riders and everyone else complained about his work but whenever he sat down one to one with a rider and looked him in the eye, the reaction from the other side of the table was positive. 'The ones who would actually talk had a lot of respect for what I was doing and many of them wanted me to keep doing it.'

Tensions increased on *L'Équipe*'s cycling desk.

At first some of the other journalists were suspicious, then they refused to speak with Pierre, and in time he became a pariah, totally alone within that group of nine. He was Monsieur Propre. His presence made people uneasy. It was a terrible time for Pierre. Philippe Le Gars and Manuel Martinez were particularly unhappy about his work. It was clear that they would have been happy if Pierre was fired.

Pierre knew that Le Gars and Martinez were friends with some of the top cyclists and liked to socialise with them. This was the time when partying bike riders would swap their per-formance-enhancing drugs for recreational drugs and inject pot belge, a lethal mixture of recreational drugs including heroin, cocaine and amphetamine.

People gossiped about Le Gars and Martinez. There were rumours that they had been present at some of these pot belge parties. Sensing that these same two journalists were

111

undermining his position at the newspaper, Pierre decided to make enquiries about the social habits of his colleagues.

He spoke with Bruno Roussel, the former Festina team director; Willy Voet, the former masseur; and Jerome Chiotti, a former Festina rider. They told Pierre they knew Le Gars and Martinez had been at some of those parties, had gotten drunk with the riders and injected pot belge, sharing needles with the riders. A Festina car had been damaged on the way back from a party.

Pierre asked each his contacts to write down what they knew about the journalists, as if they were writing witness statements, and to sign them at the bottom. They knew these statements would be shown to senior people at *L'Équipe* and still they all agreed to make formal statements about the involvement of Le Gars and Martinez .

At first Pierre tried to work things out through Jean-Michel, but after showing the cycling editor the three damning testimonials, he realised his friend didn't want to deal with the discovery that two of his reporters had engaged in recreational drug use with professional cyclists. Pierre believed *L'Équipe*'s reputation as a serious newspaper was compromised by the journalists' behaviour.

'I didn't want them to lose their jobs but I wanted to say to them, "You've gone too far here, you can't behave like this." I thought they should be disciplined and reminded of their responsibilities as journalists and representatives of *L'Équipe*.'

Jean-Michel Rouet and Philippe Bouvet are fine journalists and good men but they are not by nature confrontational. They didn't want to have anything to do with the three testimonials. Pierre thought, 'That's okay, I'll take them higher.'

He spoke about what he'd learned to the newspaper's editor Jérôme Bureau and his right-hand man Claude Droussent.

In February 2001, Bureau, Droussent, Ballester, Le Gars and Martinez met in a room at *L'Équipe*'s offices. Bureau read the statements of Roussel, Voet and Chiotti, and his anger towards Le Gars and Martinez was made clear. Though Pierre could feel the hostility of his fellow journalists, he wasn't bothered. They thought he was the problem. He thought they were problem. Bureau and Droussent could decide.

A week or so later, Bureau arranged a meeting with Pierre. Le Gars and Martinez had received a warning about their future behaviour. Pierre wasn't sure how the newspaper would deal with him. 'If I had any worries it was because I felt they weren't enthusiastic about the role I wanted for myself at the newspaper.'

Pierre wanted to be the doping correspondent on a paper that had 379 other journalists out there selling the illusion. He was savvy enough to realise that *L'Équipe* sells an image of sport that is about role models and heroes, great victories and heartbreaking losses, triumph and emotion, and it didn't want to look at the backside of this. He knew he wasn't in tune with what his bosses saw as the editorial needs of the paper.

'For the previous six months I wasn't able to get as many doping stories in as I wanted, so I said to Jean-Michel, "Just let me do doping and editing, I don't mind sitting at a desk editing the work of the guys at the races, but please don't send me any more." When I met Jérôme I thought I would be placated and allowed to continue doing this.'

That wasn't how it turned out. 'I met Jérôme and he spoke

to me about how people working for the same department needed to be a team and I hadn't been a team player. He said I was wrong to have got the evidence against my colleagues and I would have to go.'

Pierre was fired a fortnight later.

L'Équipe's view was that he had behaved improperly and they were entitled to dismiss him without any compensation. Pierre was convinced they couldn't do this, but different people had warned that *L'Équipe* might try to justify sacking him and insist he wasn't entitled to a pay-off. Pierre's situation was complicated by the fact that his wife, Liliane Trevisan, was a basketball writer at the newspaper. Still, he wasn't going to allow *L'Équipe* to get away with what he considered a totally unjust sacking.

Pierre knew a Parisian lawyer, Thibault de Montbrial, a young man who once encountered is not easily forgotten. When you get past the good looks, charm and supreme confidence, what strikes you about Thibault is his intellect and his natural affinity with journalists who challenge institutions.

Thibault knew the kind of journalist Pierre was and he liked him. When he heard the story of Pierre's dismissal, he was staggered. He wanted Pierre not to treat this as a simple employer– employee case but as something more serious which he would take before an industrial tribunal. His professional opinion was that Pierre would be awarded a substantial sum of money as a result of the damage done to his reputation by an unjustifiable decision.

'It was a difficult situation for me because Liliane liked her job at *L'Équipe* and it was going to be bad for her if I took up a big legal case against the paper. I did not want her to be affected by my situation with *L'Équipe*. If we'd gone before the tribunal, I don't think she would have been able to stay there. So I decided not to go that route.

'Thibault said it was certain we would win and the pay-off would be far greater than normal. I said to him, "Look, I just want them to pay what they should have paid when they were letting me go." He said that wouldn't be a problem and in the end he made them write a pretty good cheque. It was the right thing for Liliane and me because she wanted to continue working there.'

Liliane Trevisan continues to work the basketball beat for *L'Équipe*. Philippe Le Gars and Manuel Martinez remain reporters in the cycling department.

7

'As you get older it is harder to have heroes, but it is sort of necessary.'

Ernest Hemingway

If you take the decision as a journalist to spit into the soup which is the peloton's favourite nourishment, it's best to understand why you're doing it and to know more about the subject than those who will tell you it's none of your business. This usually means going back to the beginning, unearthing good sources, putting together a chain of events. If there is someone who has been there before you, cleared the ground and made it easier for you to follow, so much the better.

Let me introduce Sandro Donati.

I'd heard of the work that Sandro had been doing as an anti-doping campaigner in his native Italy before I headed to a Copenhagen conference organised by a Danish organisation Play the Game in November 2000. Sandro was meant to speak early in the week but his employers, the Italian Olympic Committee (CONI), refused at the last minute to give him time off. They don't emerge without bruising when Sandro recalls his fight against doping. They don't like that.

Political strings were pulled, pressure was put on CONI and three days later than expected Sandro Donati landed in Copenhagen. Perhaps it was because an official arm of Italian sport had tried to prevent him from speaking, perhaps it was his natural charisma, but Sandro drew the biggest audience of the week. He didn't come armed with slides or power-points or catchy phrases, he just told the story of his struggle against doping and against corruption in Italy. A man with his finger in the dyke. It was more than enough. We listened and we heard how sport had been poisoned. Sandro reminded us of the difficulty of exposing well-connected wrongdoers. With his eye-witness accounts from the front line, Sandro held us captive for an hour and a half.

His passion was for everything we believed that sport should be.

At the end everyone stood and applauded. They continued to clap for what seemed an eternity and there were a few tears. It was about the most inspiring sports story I'd ever heard. 'Who's your hero in sport?' Since that afternoon, I've had an answer.

Smallish and with the light frame of the 3000m steeple-chaser he once was, Sandro is a charming and sympathetic man. In the war against doping, against cheating of any sort, he is gritty and fearless. But there is a human side to his hard-ness: he doesn't want to demonise the athlete but he will do what he can to have his doctor jailed. How he has persevered for so many years is something beyond my comprehension, but I know that if you spend an hour in his company, your complacency is shaken, your faith renewed.

He comes from the wine-producing region of Frascati, outside Rome, and welcomes you with such warmth that it changes the feel of your day.

'*Ciao, Daveeeed!*' he will say, throwing his arms open.

Imagine this when you think of Donati: while a national athletics coach for Italy during the 1987 World Championships in Rome, he noticed that one of the jumps credited to Olympic bronze medallist Giovanni Evangelisti looked highly suspicious. To Sandro's eye it was a poor jump, Evangelisti's reaction confirmed as much, but the electronic scoreboard proclaimed it a good jump. Donati spent hours scrutinising video tapes and eventually found the evidence. A distance that the Italian hadn't jumped was already in the system, ready for an official to press the button. Donati blew the whistle. Long and loud.

The fix had been in for Evangelisti to take the bronze. Sandro could have looked the other way, kept his nose out of what didn't directly concern him, but that would have been a betrayal. It wasn't Evangelisti's fault but officials in high places had thought that 'another medal for Italy' would make the championships a success. The trail led to the top of Italian and world athletics and Sandro followed it. He called foul on a beloved Italian winner right there in the Stadio Olimpico in Rome. Men have been slaughtered by gladiators for less but our anti-doper merely lost his job.

Too tenacious to be out in the cold for long, Sandro recovered. He had to be strong because no matter how many times you chop the head off the beast, the beast returns. Nowadays you hear Tour de France champion Bradley

Wiggins say it disappoints him to have to talk about doping because it's a sin of the past and you want to sit him down in front of Sandro, let him know that doping can never be in the past.

Knowing that the beast always regenerates never deterred him: in 1989 Sandro published a book on doping with the wonderful title, *Worthless Champions*. If you can locate a copy, hold onto it. A fortnight after the book was published it vanished. The publishers, it is said, were paid to withdraw it, pile them up and have a bonfire. It was lost for ever.

Still Sandro Donati kept on swinging his axe at the neck of the beast. Five years later he was head of research for CONI when he began a study on the abuse of EPO in professional cycling. In terms of the lag between cutting-edge cheating and official sport's realisation of what's going on, Sandro's study was prescient. Only two years previously Claudio Chiappucci had outduelled Miguel Indurain on Sestriere in what may have been the first great EPO *mano-a-mano*.

Quietly Sandro went about his work. Anonymity was offered in exchange for information. The riders he spoke to wanted him to know how bad things were. The trail led to an old adversary, Professor Francesco Conconi. Their blades first crossed when Sandro became Italian middle-distance coach in the early eighties and was told early on that he should meet Conconi, a biochemist, based at the University of Ferrara.

For Sandro that meeting was a first taste of disillusion. Conconi spoke enthusiastically about a blood-doping programme which he said already had the backing of the Italian Athletics Federation and CONI. Blood transfusions weren't specifically banned at the time, and Sandro was invited to

offer up some of his runners for participation in the programme.

Sandro quickly surmised Conconi saw coaching as subor-
dinate to his transfusions. He spoke to his athletes outlining
the choice they faced. None of them wanted to become part
of Conconi's master plan. Sandro had made an enemy. A
powerful one. Pressure came from above and didn't stop.

Sandro wasn't playing the game. He was out of step with
every other athletics coach and coaches from all sports.
Conconi was treating athletes from cycling, canoeing, rowing,
long-distance skiing, speed skating, swimming, wrestling and
athletics. Sandro kept shaking his head. No. 'He was convinced I would be interested. He said, "We can take between
thirty and forty seconds off the ten thousand metres, we can
slice fifteen to twenty seconds from the five thousand metres
and maybe another five seconds over fifteen hundred metres."'

This was the future, but Sandro Donati didn't like how it
smelt. It took him until 1985 to figure out a solution. A helpful politician, a new law; and in Italy blood transfusions were
deemed to be doping. The rest of the world would follow. A
small victory but the beast never dies.

Now it is 1994 and Sandro is back on the front line, this
time fighting the linear descendant of transfusions, EPO. It is
like a sequel to an original film: the same bad guy but with
more sophisticated weaponry. An injection of recombinant erythropoietin, EPO, takes seconds to administer and within
minutes the athlete's population of red cells begins to increase
and multiply. Ta da! Sandro knew this drug could destroy sport.

Dr Mario Pescante, then the President of CONI, took *The
Epo Dossier* (as it became known) from Donati's hands with

thanks, but nothing happened afterwards. A couple of years later the report found its way into *La Gazzetta dello Sport*, then *L'Équipe* (to make this happen Donati had basically to steal it back and leak it) and Pescante lost his job as head of CONI.

The beast can't be slain though. These days Pescante is a vice-president of the IOC and Italy's minister for sport. Conconi proved equally indestructible. Committed to blood doping in the eighties, he became involved in assisting athletes in the abuse of EPO in the nineties, and yet he has largely been seen as being on the side of sport's authorities. He possessed a strange talent for walking on both sides of the street.

So in the surreal world of Italian sports politics it came about that the IOC itself asked a German pharmaceutical company to supply Conconi with EPO, so that he could carry out the research which might lead to an EPO test. This generosity would see the creation of Conconi's infamous EPO file, his 'study group of 23 amateurs' who were in fact 22 professional athletes and himself. That EPO, courtesy of the IOC, was used to cheat. Welcome to the brave new world and its Orwellian dialect of doublespeak. Only a figure like Donati could have kept wading through that swamp.

Sandro and I first met in Rome in 2000. He took me to his favourite little pizzeria and I realised that in the world of anti-doping I was yomping in the foothills while Sandro had climbed to the point where he could see the general landscape. What he saw depressed him without defeating him.

Sandro told me something important: going after Lance Armstrong couldn't be what it was all about because the bigger picture was what mattered. Cycling was far more important than one competitor and if you pursue one and become too associated with that pursuit, that is not good. What he said made sense, but I still felt Armstrong was a particular case. No other sports figure exercised as much influence in his or her discipline as Armstrong did within the peloton.

After '98 and the Festina scandal, cycling had a renewed responsibility to tackle the doping epidemic but hadn't done that. The biggest battleground was the 1999 Tour and Armstrong's victory sent a message through the peloton saying, 'Carry on as before, nothing has changed.' And once the authorities declared the race a coronation for the saviour of the Tour de France, the sport's immediate future became bleak.

Sandro understood Armstrong's significance but he had become generally disillusioned with professional sport. 'I watch the Olympic Games,' he said, 'but I don't bother to remember the names of the athletes any more. It's like theatre, but I prefer the theatre because the relationship between actor and spectator is clear. In sport's theatre, both are still pretending it's real.'

Sadly, it is we sportswriters who are often the most willing promoters of that pretence.

From about that time, Sandro started to devote more time to educating young athletes and their coaches about sport's ethics. I don't doubt he can achieve more in education than in fire-fighting.[16]

---

16 On the night in February 2004 that the '98 Tour de France winner Marco Pantani was found dead in a hotel room I spoke with Sandro Donati, who was saddened by the tragedy and angry with those who had helped to bring it about, especially the doctors who helped him to dope. 'I have just watched pictures on the Italian news of him winning in the Tour de France, the Giro d'Italia, and it was pornography, nothing else. There is meaning in Pantani's life and death but we cannot find it in those pictures.'

As we became friendly, trust grew and he helped me find a way through Italy's doping corridors. It was through Sandro that I met the good-humoured policeman, Fulvio Gori, in Florence and I better understood the measure of what we face when we examine doping in any sport. It isn't just the perversion of sport, the abuse of the health of athletes, the duping of spectators: it is a business.

When I hear journalists moan about there being no point in asking questions or digging into the background of events which don't feel or look right, my sympathy is short. Not because I see myself as some sort of super ferret digging and digging, but because usually the answers aren't buried that deep. And usually somebody has been there before you, asking the right questions.

While I was still young and in love with Sean Kelly and the mythology of the peloton, Sandro was there at the beginning of the events which now make up a perfect timeline for modern, privatised cheating. At one stage we liked to think that doping programmes were something which ambitious nation states carried out along with five-year plans and mass military manoeuvres. Thirty years ago though, we freed the world so that anybody could stake out their own private piece of duplicity.

When Sandro met Francesco Conconi for that chat back in 1981 (his introduction to the doping cave, as he called it), the world was a more innocent place. There were men like Conconi out there, however, who were willing to change that. Pioneers you might say.

For a warning about the possible complicity of the authorities in any organised scheme of cheating, you just have to look at the names and administrators who were too close to Conconi. Mario Pescante, one of the world's top sports administrators, failed to act on the first EPO dossier. The late Primo Nebiolo, who went on to become the head of world athletics, badgered Sandro Donati to go along with Conconi's blood-doping programme.

Prince Alexandre de Mérode, once the IOC's doping czar, appointed Conconi to the IOC medical committee and helped fund Conconi's supposed research into a test to detect the use of EPO. The IOC-accredited Anti-Doping Laboratory in Rome was working to establish just how long it took traces of banned drugs to disappear from the urine samples of the individual athletes.

This information and more was all out there. All you had to do was draw your finger along the line and marvel at how Sandro Donati had stayed sane while travelling through the bizarre landscape of corrupted sport. He laughs when recalling the pleasure of being drawn back into the fold in the early nineties to become head of CONI's research department (Settore Ricerca e Sperimentazione). Now, Sandro, we'd like you to join our most earnest and high-powered scientific anti-doping committee. And, best of all, among your colleagues will be the eminent Prof. Conconi, whom we believe you already know. There it was all the time. Whatever we talked about, Sandro had been there, done that, bought the T-shirt and caught the reprimand.

Digging? It was more a case of following the line of money and cheats and incompetents. We just had to go out and round up the usual suspects: sports run by confederations of dunces, athletes and agents on the make, doctors who had gone to the dark side. Sandro had already done the hard work in the trenches. He wasn't bitter, but by the time I belatedly made his acquaintance he had become a little sceptical of journalistic enthusiasms.

Still, a little company in the trenches was better than none. He offered guidance and encouragement. He made a wise point about the conflict of interests involved in media organisations becoming financially involved in the sports which they then cover. Cycling is the obvious example: the Giro d'Italia is run by the company that owns *La Gazzetta dello Sport*; the Tour de France by the company that owns *L'Équipe*; even Team Sky is sponsored by BSkyB which is part of News Corp, the ultimate owner of the *Sunday Times*. For the media to extract itself from that type of marriage would be difficult.

But he finished our meal with some warm words of encouragement, a reminder that striving for an ideal didn't have to be embarrassing in this jaded, irony-sated world. If you were a journalist you had a professional obligation to be honest and to keep the public fully and correctly informed.

That was a chastening thing to hear, but encouraging too. The next step was to go and pick up the trail where Conconi had left off and his prize student Michele Ferrari had stepped in.

Ferrari, I knew, worked with Lance Armstrong's best friend and team-mate Kevin Livingston. It just seemed too unlikely that Livingston, one of life's followers, would have gone to Ferrari of his own volition.

I was a few steps behind Donati. Victor Frankenstein's monster had a decent sense of humour. When he appeared before his creator he would introduce himself along the lines of, 'Good evening, I am the Adam of your labours.' When I think of Lance Armstrong and how he became the greatest pharmaceutical panata the peloton had ever seen, I see Michele Ferrari as Frankenstein. I'm not sure either would object.

'Yo, Michele, I'm Lance, the Adam of your labours, dude.'

Imagine then the poignant scene unfolding early one morning on the doorstep of an understated villa amid a copse of trees just outside the dusty but elegant university town of Ferrara, in the moments after a parcel courier raps on the oak door. It's June 2000 and Michele Ferrari, still in his dressing gown, signs for the package with a smile. Amazon, bless their .com hearts, have sent him the advance copy he had ordered of Lance Armstrong's groundbreaking book, *It's Not About the Bike*. Gleefully he tears the sturdy cardboard wrapping apart, gazes for a fond instant at the familiar handsome face leaning toward him on the front cover. And though Michele Ferrari is not a man who needs the roar of the crowd, he has wondered how he will be listed in the index.

Under the Fs? Probably. **Ferrari**, Michele, debt to, genius of, teachings of, etc.

Maybe the Ks. **Kahuna**, the Big, wisdom of.

Or maybe the Ms. **Michele**, friend, trainer, go-to man.

Possibly the Ss. **Schumi**, affectionate name for Michele.

He doesn't usually allow himself to be disappointed by people, but right now Michele Ferrari is deflated. A book about his greatest creation and it contains no index. Lance, I didn't just tell you what EPO would do, how you'd beat the tests, I gave you the numbers. No index. So he must scan the book chapter by chapter, his eyes sprinting from page to page, seeking Ferrari, Michele or even Schumi. But there is nothing. *Rien! Nichts! Nada! NIENTE!*

You work with a guy for five years, making him. And now this? Nothing from the Adam of your labours. In a book specifically titled, *It's Not About the Bike*?

It's a lonely world on the dark side of doping.

In the peloton, Michele Ferrari is much spoken about and seldom seen. From time to time he will ghost in and out of a team's hotel, but it is said he disguises himself. Mostly his work is done in his nondescript camper-van when a stage has finished and his clients slip in a car, pull shades over their eyes and their baseball hat right down. We know that sometimes he will take a call from Lance's *directeur sportif*, Johan Bruyneel, wondering if the rival who's broken clear in the mountains can maintain his current pace.

We know if a rider is Italian he may refer to Ferrari as *Il Mito*, The Myth. Or, if the rider is American, he may use the name which Armstrong himself minted: Schumi. As in Michael Schumacher and the Italian car he once drove, Ferrari. We know too that Ferrari is important in the timeline. Or bloodline. Conconi begat Ferrari. Ferrari begat Lance. And Lance can be the creator of a new generation of dopers.

Everything we know is stuff that Michele Ferrari would prefer for us not to know. Ferrari rarely, rarely, gives interviews. He works largely in secret. When we speak about doping and all the shades of morality, hypocrisy, piety and fear surrounding the subject, Ferrari is the riddle at the centre of it. We wonder about Michele Ferrari and men like him, the accommodations they have made. He stands on the far

David Walsh

shore of the philosophical argument on doping, gazing across at us, perplexed at our concerns. Crazed zealots all hopped up with what Philip Roth called the 'ecstasy of sanctimony'.

Ecstasy never comes into it. It's not about the sanctimony. Back when Sandro Donati educated me as to the chronology of serious privatised doping, he showed me the starting point as being the moment in the early eighties when Francesco Conconi decided that he would take the Finnish invention of blood doping and create a Mediterranean version.

To examine how Lance became all that he would become, I would have to go back to my own starting point in his story. The kid I met in Grenoble in 1993 was brash and arrogant, certainly, but I doubt he had thought too much about needles and pills. A couple of hard, sobering years changed that. The 1994 season in particular provided a difficult education for all in Armstrong's Motorola team.

Who killed Lance in the Flèche Wallonne on that midweek afternoon in Belgium? The Gewiss boys: Argentin, Furlan and Berzin. And who created them? Ferrari. If you want to be the best you work with the best, and after that day there was one more Texan out there who was tired of having his ass kicked.

It was Eddy Merckx, the old cannibal of the roads, who introduced them. Eddy's son Axel had turned in a decent ride for Motorola in the Milan–San Remo classic in that spring of 1995. The only member of the team not embarrassed, he finished 21st. Axel wasn't Eddy and 21st wasn't bad. The guys knew that Axel was working with Ferrari.

So Armstrong and Eddy spoke about Ferrari and Eddy made the call. Could Michele take a new client? Strong kid.

You know, world champion in 1993. Ferrari resisted but, finally, in November 1995 Armstrong drove to the medieval town of Ferrara and met with Michele Ferrari. The meeting would change both their lives.

Ferrari didn't swoon when first presented with Armstrong. He was a strong physical specimen but too heavy. Those swimmers' shoulders carried too much useless muscle. Yeah, maybe, he could snaffle the odd win in the one-day classics but that body wouldn't survive a long tour.

Still, when Ferrari put Armstrong through the tests he was encouraged. Not because he was anything special physiologically (he wasn't), but he had a good attitude, he could deal with pain and, when they stopped testing, Armstrong asked the right questions. The best pupils are the ones who know how to learn. This one wanted to learn everything.

Ferrari told Armstrong he could come back again. From then on they worked closely, with Armstrong regularly making the three-hour trip from Como to Ferrara. They had a training camp in San Diego early the following year. Ferrari came from Italy for that, and when Armstrong was struck down by cancer later in the year, they stayed in touch.

With Livingston, Bobby Julich and Frankie Andreu, Armstrong returned to Europe in January 1997 for the annual launch of Cofidis, the French team for which he had signed. He also had a quiet visit with Ferrari, for they were friends now. Lance was declared clear of cancer in February 1997 and soon after began the long and slow climb back towards a career. Michele Ferrari had found the perfect canvas for the expression of his life's work.

Ferrari grew up in the traditional university town of

Ferrara, a place of venerable old buildings and quiet piazzas transfused with the life students bring. Ferrari was a decent runner in his teenage years and won a 1000m national championship while still in school. He was good enough to have to make a choice. Academia or sports? He opted for education and stayed at home to study medicine at the local university.

One of his professors was a man of similar interests. Dr Francesco Conconi and Ferrari would often run together before returning to work shoulder by shoulder in the laboratory. In 1981 Ferrari assisted as Conconi developed a simple field test, now known as the Conconi Test. The test permitted endurance athletes to determine their anaerobic threshold, essentially their maximum cruising speed.

With the athlete on a treadmill, Conconi could measure his or her heart rate at varying rates of stress, recording on a data graph the heart rate on one axis and the speed on the other. The heart rate would increase in a roughly linear fashion until it hit a plateau. This point was called the anabolic threshold. The test would continue while the athlete went well past the threshold.

The Conconi Test was considered a useful tool in better understanding the potential of endurance athletes, but far more exciting developments were afoot. Knowing a man's capabilities is one thing, but having the means to take him well beyond that is quite another. Blood transfusions and later EPO were the way of the future and a group of doctors at the University of Ferrara were leading the way.

They had to decide which side of the coming war they were going to be on. Ingeniously, Conconi opted to be on one side while pretending to be on the other. Ferrari was a different kettle of fish, with no wish to ever be seen on the side of the Establishment.

By 1984 the sedate pace of university life had begun to pall with Ferrari. He'd enjoyed working with the Italian cyclist Francesco Moser, who set the world hour record in Mexico City in '84. Everyone knew Moser was a friend and client of Conconi's but they didn't appreciate how involved Ferrari had been. It was then through Moser's influence that he became team doctor for his Gis Tuc Lu.

He continued to work as a team doctor until 1994, by which time he was with the Gewiss-Ballon team and making quite a name for himself. He saw himself more as a '*prepatore*' (sports training coach) than as a medical doctor.[17] Ferrari has spoken affectionately of those early days and his involvement with riders like Moser and the Swiss star Tony Rominger.[18]

---

17 Ferrari was speaking some years later to *Cycling News*, which in an amusingly tender and sometimes awestruck interview elicited exchanges along the lines of:

Dr M.F.: 'If you asked me "define your methods" beyond that point, there are the specific scientific aspects and values that are found in the riders' tests and are quite complex. I'd need a lot of time to explain these to you . . .'

Cycling News: 'But I understand from some riders that you have trained that you have a special way to work with riders, a humanistic approach that these riders found quite easy to deal with.'

Not exactly the Spanish Inquisition.

18 Rominger in particular may wish that Ferrari might be a little less effusive. Late in 2012 newspapers reported that Rominger had 'denied accusations that his management company has links to what Italian investigators believe is a network designed to finance doping, aid tax evasion and launder money'. *La Gazzetta dello Sport* had reported in October 2012 that a large-scale Italian investigation into Ferrari's activities had opened a 'Pandora's Box' of dubious business practices involving money-laundering through various European countries. Riders were also among the individuals at the centre of the investigation.

Moser and Rominger were strong characters, Ferrari's preferred type, and he would recognise even more of this quality in Armstrong.

By the early nineties, Ferrari had established himself as a high priest of performance enhancement. His reputation depended on who you were speaking to. Pro clients flocked to him and passed the word on quietly.[19] Beyond this circle of riders who happily paid Ferrari a percentage of their salary was a world of whispers and rumours about exactly what type of bang the boys were getting for their buck.[20]

Something had to give. And it did. On 12 August 1998, the Carabinieri launched a raid on Ferrari's villa, seizing

19 It would be six years after he started that some of Armstrong's teammates first realised he was working with Ferrari. One assumes ghostwriter Sally Jenkins didn't know either, for there was no mention of the maestro in *It's Not About the Bike*.

20 And it was quite an amount of bucks. Transactions between Armstrong and Ferrari as uncovered by USADA in 2012 report:

2/21/1996: $14,089.65 CREDITO SWIFT NATIONSBANK NA 1, NATIONS HEADQUA O-LANCE ARMSTRONG AC- XXXXXXX RE F. XXXXXXXX USD 13615 – LESS CO USD 14'089.65 (bank record)

5/9/1996: $28,582.33 CREDITO SWIFT LANCE ARMSTRONG AC/XXXXXXX ./.SPESEN/SKA US 7.32 USD 28'582.33 (bank record)

7/24/1996: $42,082.33 CREDITO SWIFT LANCE ARMSTRONG . LINDA WALLING/RFB/XXXXXXXX/ CABLE ADV AT NOC USD 42'082.33 (bank record)

5/6/2002: $75,000.00 Armstrong L. – US$ 75'000. - (Journal entry)

8/29/2002: $75,000.00 Armstrong L. – US$ 75'000. - (Journal entry)

6/5/2003: $100,000.00 Lance Armstrong US$ 100'000. - (Journal entry)

9/10/2003: $75,000.00 Lance Armstrong US$ 75'000. - (Journal entry)

10/6/2003: $300,000.00 Lance Armstrong US$ 300'000. - (Journal entry)

7/2/2004: $110,000.00 AVIS DE CREDIT DONNEUR D'ORDRE: /LANCE ARMSTRONG XXXXXXXXX AUSTIN TEXAS 78703 USD 110,000.00 (bank record)

3/29/2005: $100,000.00 Avviso di accredito D'ORDINE DI LANCE ARMSTRONG USD 100 000.00 (bank record)

12/31/2006: $110,000.00 Lance Armstrong US$ 110'000. - (Journal entry)

Total **$1,029,754.31**

mainly computer discs containing files and records. These included the training diaries of his clients. It was Lance Armstrong's good fortune that what was seized were the records for 1997, the year he spent recuperating in America. He had contact with Ferrari during that year but was not a regular visitor and as he was not racing he would have had no need for doping.

Ferrari later told an interviewer from *Cycling News* that he asked the lead officer on the raid what exactly they were looking for. The policeman said, 'We want to see what you do.'

Among the riders whose files came to light were Claudio Chiappucci, Axel Merckx, Gianluca Bortolami (whose Festina team were at the centre of the previous month's scandal storm) and Kevin Livingston.

I was convinced from early on that Armstrong had to be working with Ferrari, and conversations with Sandro Donati hardened the idea in my head. In September 2001, Michele Ferrari was going to stand trial in Bologna. It wouldn't be his last such experience. Earlier that year Sandro directed me towards contacts of his within the Carabinieri drug squad in Florence. Documents seized from Ferrari's computer were made available to me solely because I was a friend of Sandro Donati's. I scanned the pages for Livingston's numbers.[21] The

---

21 This was the material referenced many years later in USADA's 2012 report. 'Multiple handwritten training plans for Kevin Livingston were found in Dr Ferrari's files during a search of his residence in the first investigation of Dr Ferrari. The cyclists who have worked with Dr Ferrari describe handwritten training plans prepared by Dr Ferrari, and have testified that he placed notations on their plans to indicate the dates on which they were supposed to use performance-enhancing drugs. Multiple asterisks are an evident feature on all of the training plans in the file for Kevin Livingston,' USADA stated.

huge fluctuations in his haematrocrit, from very low 40s to very high 40s, were indicative of EPO use.

This was fascinating. Livingston was a good *equipier*, a popular member of the team, but a follower rather than a leader. His involvement with Ferrari had to have followed on from Armstrong, not preceded it. He looked up to Armstrong.[22] Livingston's connection to Ferrari raised obvious questions.

22 Livingston's relationship with Armstrong is one of the few to have endured, as he runs a fitness centre, Pedal Hard, alongside Armstrong's bike shop in Austin, Mellow Johnny's. Apart from Armstrong, Livingston was the only other American rider to refuse to co-operate with USADA in their investigation into the US Postal team.

8

'We have to distrust each other, it is our only defence against betrayal.'

Tennessee Williams

In April 2001 Bill Stapleton called me. A grey, dry morning in England, and I had just pulled into my dentist's car park, so obviously it was all very exciting.

In this life you remember two key things. One: where you were when Kennedy got shot. Two: where you were when Stapleton called. On the previous year's Tour, it was Bill who had leaned close to me in the press centre and politely offered me a choice in life. If I didn't get with the programme, well, Lance's people would be coming after me. But if I chose to let things lie there might be some pretty good access down the line.

Stick or carrot? My call.

Though I tried not to show it, I had been flattered by this sign that the Armstrong camp wasn't completely indifferent to my existence. We hadn't spoken since, though, and I was beginning to think that perhaps they didn't care about me after all. Now, as before, Bill presented himself as an emissary coming in peace. He mentioned that he and Lance were aware of some people whom I'd had been speaking to and some questions that I had been asking.

He paused, drew in a breath and made his pitch. 'David, I know things have not been good between you and Lance, but Lance would be prepared to do an interview with you.'

'When?'

'As soon as you can get to France.'

I wanted to blurt out the word yes. I wanted to say, 'Bill, you had me at, "Hello".' The words wouldn't come. I realised that I wasn't keen on Bill reporting back to Lance that, yes, the plan was working: 'Walsh just gushed and jumped into my arms telephonically at the mention of an interview. What did I tell you, dude?'

I told Bill I would call him back later. And then I went and sat in a dentist's chair for an hour of contemplation and wholly legal injections.

An audience with Lance. The idea was interesting. The fact that the offer had come from the Lance camp was intriguing. Most newspapers are suckers for access. An interview, no matter how bland, with a big star is cheaper and easier to sell than a long investigation with lawyers circling like vultures in the sky above. This was a major break because there were so many doping-related questions I wanted to put to Armstrong.

'Alex,' I said to the *Sunday Times* sports editor in a phone call that afternoon, 'allow me to make your day.'

'Go on.'

'Got an interview lined up for this week.'

'With whom?'

'Armstrong.'

'No?'

'Yes. His lawyer/agent Bill Stapleton called. They want me to come to France later this week.'

I got a little star to wear on my suit and my picture went up on the employee of the week board. Second place. To Alex.

My thoughts turned to Lance. Or the Frost–Nixon interview, as I was fast coming to see it. Maybe Lance thought this interview would be the first chapter in a friendship renewed for tactical reasons. Maybe all this drug stuff was a misunderstanding. Or maybe he just thought that he could crush me.

If he recalled our conversation in 1993, he would know that I wasn't a single-issue obsessive. Back then we'd spoken for three hours without one mention of doping. We had talked as two passionate men might: I was passionate about cycling, he was passionate about winning and about seizing the opportunity of his career. Perhaps he wanted to show me that the man I warmed to that evening hadn't gone away.

Two days later I sat down to interview Lance Armstrong in the Hotel La Fauvelaie near the village of Saint-Sylvain-d'Aanjou in the east of France. We sat in the lobby of the virtually deserted hotel. Lance wore casual team gear and an air of slight indifference. It was the first time we had sat together since that afternoon in Grenoble eight years earlier.

Much had changed. Lance had lost the muscular square shoulders of the swimmer and, although he was thinner, he somehow looked stronger. Hard bodied. And of course he was already a two-time Tour winner. His earnings from being in the saddle were estimated at $8 million a year. It's not all about the bike, though. Endorsements were bringing in another $5 million. Donald Trump had turned up to listen in on a press conference Lance gave in New York. People mentioned this as if it was a good thing.

The 2001 edition of Lance Armstrong came with pretty much all the things that the 1993 edition had lacked and wanted. He could now ride time trials better than anyone, he was the strongest in the mountains and he enjoyed the backing of the best equipped and most organised team in the peloton. What these things gave him was what he most wanted: the power to control his destiny.

He got cancer.

He got well.

He came back.

He saw.

He kicked ass.

And if he was describing it all in a word he would have said, 'neat'.

So why doesn't he seem happy as he sits on the fake leather sofa opposite me?

Perhaps this is because everything in the Garden of Eden isn't blooming. He knows that at the very least I and many other snakes with arms suspect that he is doping. He brings me here to find out what I know and on the off chance that I might be bought with the illusion of friendship and promises of access.

Travelling from London, I'd told myself the interview would work best if my mind stayed open and he got the fullest chance to answer the questions. But the legacy of the 1998 Tour was that there could no longer be a presumption of innocence. The line from my friend Jean-Michel Rouet had stayed with me: 'What we discovered [from the Festina Affair] was that everyone in this sport can fuck us.'

It was true. A guy in a yellow jersey had only to say, 'Chook, chook, chook, chook,' and we the chickens gathered round to have scraps dropped at our feet.

The first thing Lance asked was if I minded Bill Stapleton sitting in on the interview. As it happened I wasn't keen on Bill inserting himself into proceedings, but Lance's body language suggested that he wasn't actually asking a question. So Bill Stapleton sat down and placed a tape recorder on the table. I put my tape recorder down beside Bill's.

I then put my cards on the table.[23]

'Here's how I am going to approach this, Lance. I am only going to ask you questions about doping because that is all that is relevant to me. If I don't believe you're clean there is no point in asking you about your next races. I have no interest. This will give you the opportunity to maybe convince people that you are clean.'

I was quite calm. Surprisingly so in retrospect. I don't enjoy confrontation and in the years since then anecdotes about Lance's ability to bully people have given him the reputation of a sociopath. Perhaps I was shielded by a little self-righteousness. Or maybe this confrontation was easier because we had met

23 The tapes of the interview would become a contentious issue in later legal proceedings. Despite Bill Stapleton having taped the conversation himself, the Armstrong legal team pressed for me to produce a direct transcript of what had been said.

eight years earlier when we were both different people. I'm not known for being a tough guy, but I didn't find Lance remotely intimidating. I almost wanted to say, 'Hey, hold on, I knew you when you were kid and I liked the way you'd closed the door when walking into cycling's living room, so hard the walls shook.' Meeting him now, I wondered how he had developed, what had changed. I was convinced he was doping but it wasn't like he was going to admit it.

What would be interesting was how he dealt with aggressive questioning. And for me the interview was a chance to get some on-the-record answers on issues he didn't usually have to address.

'That's fine,' he replied. 'Ask all the doping questions you like.'

My tactic was to begin with broad, general questions which suggested I didn't know too much. Lance would have comfortable answers to these questions. Later we would move on to the specifics.

I asked about the 1994 Flèche Wallonne classic, famous for being the race that made Michele Ferrari famous. We all knew the story. Riders whom Ferrari prepared, finished first, second and third. Lance Armstrong was strong that day, he chased the three breakaways but he couldn't latch onto them. Like all the Motorola riders, he was finally blown away. They hadn't one guy in the top ten. Doping in any sport isn't always a gradual evolution. There are great leaps forward. This was one. Three riders from the same team breaking away from the pack in a classic – well that's pretty much unheard of.

Moreno Argentin was first. Giorgio Furlan and Evgeni

Berzin came in second and third. Too much. Every journalist had questions. Where better to start but at the court of Dr Michele Ferrari. This was so outrageous, the usual niceties were dispensed with.

What about this drug, EPO? 'EPO is not dangerous,' the good doctor memorably said, 'it's the abuse that is. It's also dangerous to drink ten litres of orange juice.'

Gewiss sacked him, but Flèche Wallonne and the orange juice quote made Ferrari's reputation. If he had hung out a shingle announcing his services to the world he couldn't have been clearer about what he had to offer.

It was one of the landmark moments in doping history. Except to Lance Armstrong.

'Their doctor, Michele Ferrari, made his famous statement on the evening of that race about r-EPO being no more dangerous than orange juice. Do you remember your reaction to that?'

(Long pause) 'Ahmm, no.'

'You didn't even wonder what r-EPO was?'

'I think that sometimes quotes can get taken out of context and I think that even at the time I recognised that.'

So it went.

By the mid-nineties it was well known that EPO had become a staple for many Tour riders. How conscious of this phenomenon were Lance and his teammates in Motorola?[24]

24 A 2010 study in the *Journal of Sports Sciences* noted that between 1989 and 1997, the average length of the Tour de France rose from 3,285km to 3,944km (2,040–2,450 miles) and featured 17,000m (55,770 feet) of additional climbing. Average speeds should have slowed by 11.3% during this time. They improved by 4.5%.

'We didn't think about it. It wasn't an issue for us. It wasn't an option . . .'[25]

On and on. The Lance version of *omerta*.

'Did you know that Kevin [Livingston, a fellow US Postal rider] was linked with the [police] investigation into Michele Ferrari in Italy?'

'Yes.'

'Did you discuss it with him?'

'No.'

'Never?'

(Nods his head.)

'A guy who is your best friend?'

'In an indirect way, you are trying to implicate our sport again.'

Classic! Never ask a cyclist a hard question! Never *crache dans le soupe*. You are damaging the sport. Spoiling it for everybody.

As we talked, Michele Ferrari hovered over us like Banquo's ghost. It was Ferrari's name that produced the most tortuous circumlocutions from Lance.

'Did you ever visit Michele Ferrari?'

'I did know Michele Ferrari.'[26]

'How did you get to know him?'

25 In testimony in the subsequent SCA case Stephen Swart, the New Zealander who rode with Motorola in the mid-nineties, said that top riders on the team discussed EPO in 1995. He testified that Armstrong told teammates that there was 'only one road to take' to be competitive. I was aware of Swart's claims at the time of the Armstrong interview. We soon learned that Armstrong had begun working with Ferrari as far back as 1995.
26 I would learn later that Lance had actually spent a few days with Ferrari not long before the interview. As well as ten days in three separate visits the previous season.

'In cycling when you go to races, you see people. There's trainers, doctors; I know every team's doctor. It's a small community.'

'Did you ever visit him?'

'Have I been tested by him, gone and been there and consulted on certain things? Perhaps.'

'You did?'

(Nods in the affirmative.)

'He's going to be tried for criminal conspiracy.'

'I think the prosecutors and judges should pursue everybody regardless of who it is. It is their job to do that.'

Looking back, I attribute the odd nature of these responses (and the Sean Kelly-like gesture of nodding into a tape recorder) to some anxiety on Lance's part that perhaps I knew more at that time than I actually did. He was aware, certainly, that I had been asking about the Ferrari connection, that I had been to the police station in Florence, the basement of which housed the many, many boxes of files seized by the NAS (Nucleo Antisofisticazioni Sanità) in raids on doctors with alleged links to doping.

Not knowing precisely what I knew, though, Lance chose neither to deny nor to affirm the issue of visits to Ferrari. As it happened, I wouldn't be able to confirm the pattern of Lance's visits until just before the Tour in 2001.

In the year since then, as Lance's status as an icon grew bigger and bigger, people would often say to me how clever he was in terms of dealing with and manipulating the media. I never found that. Saying, for example, that he and Kevin had never ever discussed Ferrari, even though Kevin was involved in the case, was just plain stupid.

One thing for sure, he was different.

In *Breaking Away*, the classic cycling/coming-of-age movie made back in the seventies, four young guys in an Indiana town brought colour to their lives by sucking in the romance of pro cycling. Some part of the writer in me would love it if Lance, with his screwed-up background, had enjoyed the refuge of the same dreams back in Plano, Texas.

But that wasn't his past. He has no sepia days. He hadn't time to dream, going from shop to shop looking for a sponsor to fund his teenage triathlon career, and when no one stumped up, he bought a tank top and had I LOVE MY MOM printed where the sponsor's name would have been.

'I know nothing of the history of the sport,' he says. I look at him and realise that what he is saying is true. This isn't Hollywood, dude. This thing, this Tour de France, it is a mountain. Everybody can see it. You need a plan, and you need to see yourself standing at the summit. Lance Armstrong from Plano in Texas. Somebody.

So I thought of another mountain. Ventoux. Threw its legend out there.

'So you've never heard of Tommy Simpson? C'mon, surely you've heard of Tommy Simpson?'

He had heard but his answer is bizarre.

'I did, but Tommy Simpson never tested positive.'

I've never met a cycling person who doesn't automatically shake his head in sadness at the fate of Tommy Simpson and what his death told us about cycling. The sadness isn't just borne out of the knowledge of what happened that day but from knowing that after the tragedy the peloton decided to carry on doping. And here we were in 2001, post-Simpson, post-Festina, in a world where a champion rider reaches for a response delivered in legalese when a subject related to doping is mentioned. Here was a wall between the peloton and the broader world.

Tommy Simpson's death on the Tour of 1967 was a tragedy.[27] Amphetamines were in his bloodstream, alcohol too; amphetamines were found in his back pocket. The medical view held that he had contributed to his own death but Simpson was also a victim of cycling's drug culture.[28]

But hey, he never had a positive test.

Lance's response was true but without meaning. Simpson had drugs in his blood, drugs in his jersey, drugs in his suitcase.

27 The aftermath of Ventoux produced mixed results in terms of coverage. Simpson's famously heroic last words, 'Put me back on my bike!' were never uttered. They were invented by Sid Saltmarsh, who was covering the event for the *Sun* and *Cycling*. Saltmarsh, however, wasn't present at the time. In fact he was even in a reception blackspot for live radio accounts of the Tour.

28 Some honour accrued to the fourth estate. Another British reporter, J.L. Manning of the *Daily Mail*, dealt with the news in a rather more honourable way. Manning was a serious character who performed his job well. His exposure marked the first time that a real connection had been made between drugs and Simpson's death, and, happily, he inspired a wave of good reporting among his colleagues. Manning wrote that 'Tommy Simpson rode to his death in the Tour de France so doped that he did not know he had reached the limit of his endurance. He died in the saddle, slowly asphyxiated by intense effort in a heat-wave after taking methylamphetamine drugs and alcoholic stimulants.' One consequence of Manning's work, and of those journalists who supported him, would be familiar to those of us who worked the Tour (of Renewal) in 1999. After Tommy Simpson's death there were promises: 'Dear Tom Simpson,' said Tour organiser, Jacques Goddet, 'you will not have fallen in vain on the stony desert of the Ventoux,' as there would be promises after the Festina scandal in 1998. The reality? *Plus ça change, plus c'est la même chose.*

Lance's answer was instructive though, as it was the reflex response of riders and athletes for decades. It tells us nothing. It tells us plenty. Bernard Hinault used to say it every time.

'Well, *Le Blaireau*, did you take drugs?'

'I passed every test.'

Lance had learned. The tests he'd taken and the tests he'd passed didn't prove anything, but there would always be a constituency out there happy to defend him by parroting the old line about being the most tested athlete on the planet and never having failed once.

In 1993 he had been a kid unimpressed or unaware of the romance of the Tour but determined to use the opportunity to make something of himself. Eight years on he was some-body and wanted me to know whatever methods he and his team deployed ... well, that was insider stuff. Nothing for you to see here.

Journalists were there to sell the myth in return for lim-ited access. The rest was business; theirs not ours. You don't see the greedy calculations going on behind the walls of mirrors in Las Vegas casinos. Lance felt that what went on behind the walls of mirrors in pro cycling was private business too. The absence of romance, the hardness, the steely arrogance, it all diminished him but he never saw this.

Frankie Andreu or one of the other riders told me he'd heard that Lance was furious when he came back upstairs after the interview. Fuming. The impression the other riders got was that Armstrong was shocked by what I seemed to know. For my part I was amazed by what Lance pretended not to know. The news of his anger made me smile. In our game of huffing and bluffing Lance and I had just played out a draw.

In the spring when I had interviewed Lance in person I put the Livingston situation to him, and in keeping with the tone of the interview he was vague to the point of absurdity. How can best friends not discuss the fact that one of them has been dragged into a criminal investigation? The point that I missed was his sense of not having to answer to anyone. So what if it's a dumb answer? What are you going to do about it?

There was only one thing I could do. I went back to Sandro Donati and asked if there wasn't some evidence of Armstrong's presence in Ferrara. Next time I got an audience with Stapleton or Armstrong, I wanted to have something. I asked Sandro to check if the Carabinieri were absolutely sure Lance hadn't been to Ferrara. Donati first got back to me and said he couldn't come up with evidence that Armstrong had been there. But my friend was nothing if not dogged. Soon he came back to me with information from local hotels. The information had come from the Carabinieri, through Sandro to me.

He'd been there.

Lance had been to Ferrara for two days in March 1999, three days in May 2000, two days in August 2000, one day in September 2000 and three days in late April/early May of 2001, the last visit shortly after our interview at La Fauvelaie. The visits came at key points, for Tour preparation and just before the 2000 Olympics, where Armstrong had wanted a medal. In Ferrara he had stayed at the five-star Hotel Duchessa Isabella and at the four-star Hotel Annunziata.

During our interview, he feared I knew more than I was letting on. Now I did.[29]

I'd travelled to the US, to Rome, to Florence in the previous year. I was getting a better picture of the world I was trying to understand. I'd been disappointed with the outcome of the Lance interview in the spring. I'd travelled with a decent stock of evidence but I hadn't even rattled his cage.

There was his coach. If Ferrari was the genius behind the story then Chris Carmichael, Lance's coach and mentor, was the presentable face of things. Carmichael had kept himself out of an odd doping case taken by a former US amateur, Greg Strock, who claimed he had been injected with cortisone against his will and had his career ruined. To extricate himself from the case, Carmichael had made an out-of-court payment to Strock.

I'd asked Armstrong how he felt about his long-time coach paying money to stay out of a doping case. He said it was matter between Chris and Greg.

---

29 In his 2004 pow-wow with *Cycling News*, Ferrari gave a mildly self-pitying version of these events.

Cycling News: 'In the past, didn't investigative journalists come to Ferrara and obtain information about Lance Armstrong's hotel stays during his visits to your clinic?'

Dr M.F.: 'No, that's not how things went; this sports reporter for a British newspaper didn't come to Ferrara, he went to Firenze and spoke to the N.A.S. [National Drug Squad] Carabinieri. They called the Ferrara police station and asked them to check their hotel records for Lance Armstrong. And that information was then put in the paper.'

Cycling News: 'How did you react to that information?'

Dr M.F.: 'It's not normal! This was an excessive use of the power of the Carabinieri: they are not supposed to give a journalist this type of information. But we had nothing to hide regarding Lance; he came here to do his tests and we never denied it at all! It wasn't hidden at all. I don't know this journalist; I've never met him at all.'

'If Chris had paid money to keep his name out of a doping case, it would imply he had something to hide?'

'It's a hypothesis.'

'But it wouldn't look good, would it?'

'At the same time, does it look good that Greg Strock just takes the money? Let's flip it around. Is this about money or is this about principle.'

I had the work of Hugues Huet, a journalist with French TV, who the previous summer had tailed an unmarked US Postal car, filming the two occupants disposing of five plastic bags of rubbish. The bags contained 160 syringe wrappers, bloodied compresses and discarded packaging that indicated the use of a legal but right-on-the-limit product called Actovegin.

Then there was Kevin Livingston, the skinny on what he'd been doing.

A little mountain of evidence was forming. As Lance would say, it didn't look good. Yet when I'd put it all to Lance he had shrugged it away. In the interview he'd pulled a draw out from the jaws of defeat. Champions only need to draw.

This news from Ferrara was different though. This was a game changer. I felt that we had something concrete. We were talking about sixteen days spent in Ferrara over two years. That excluded any visits made in the other direction by Ferrari, which we now know occurred both when Lance lived in Nice (Ferrari liked to test Armstrong on the Col de la Madone climb just outside town) and in Girona, where Armstrong moved in 2001.

All this time spent in Ferrara and Lance had made a point of not mentioning it. Not in his autobiography, not in his press conferences, not in his interview.

Now I have all this information. It hasn't involved hacking computer files or breaking into buildings or meeting anonymous sources in underground car parks. It has just been simple journalism. Questions. I can't believe that Lance has produced his autobiography, it's come out maybe a year before, and the name Michele Ferrari hasn't appeared in the pages. Ferrari is being investigated for doping, soon he will be charged and sent to trial.

We had a hard story.

So it came to pass that on the first day of the 2001 Tour de France, we in the *Sunday Times* revealed that Lance Armstrong, winner of the first two Tours in the period of renewal, was working with a doctor about to stand trial for doping. And Armstrong had never mentioned this once. Never mentioned a connection to the man who had once said 'it doesn't scandalise me', when asked if he would mind if his riders went to Switzerland to buy EPO over the counter.

When I look back at that article, it was one of the worst I've written: too much information too poorly organised. So much good was spoiled by the end product. And I was so naive in my dealings with the Armstrong camp. Having discovered that Lance was going to Ferrari through my Italian police sources, I had trip-wired the alarms in LanceWorld.

I was in Australia at the time, working on the British and Irish Lions rugby tour, as we prepared the article for press. Wanting to give Lance the opportunity to respond to the Ferrari link, I called Bill Stapleton on the Thursday, three days before publication.

'Bill, some questions to ask you.'

'Would you mind sending us what information you've got, and we will respond then.'

I banged off an email telling everything that I knew. I may have thought about adding the word checkmate at the end:

'My information is that Lance was with Ferrari and that these are the dates. These are the names of the hotels. These are the dates on which he was there. This indicates that he has a very serious relationship with Michele Ferrari. Can you or Lance get back to me with a response?'

A reply.

'David, I'll put these to Lance and get back.'

Next, I hear nothing. I call again. Bill says that he's in France for the Tour and having trouble with his email. I feel like I'm getting the run-around, a boy trying to play with bigger boys. So I call again, leave another message. Nothing. Bill Stapleton goes underground, takes his mobile phone with him. I hear nothing more from Bill. Shoot off more emails. Make more calls. No response. Of course Armstrong, combative and spiky as ever, had decided to beat me to my own exclusive.

The next day, Pier Bergonzi, the respected cycling correspondent at *La Gazzetta dello Sport* in Italy, arrived by invitation at the US Postal team hotel to interview Lance Armstrong. Pier had been promised some time with Lance on the Tour, but an interview right before *le grand depart* was a surprise. Bergonzi had been covering cycling for many years and he and Armstrong were comfortable with each other. The interview wasn't confrontational and ran along the predictable lines of an eve-of-race preview.

At the end of the interview, Lance said to Pier, 'You haven't asked me about Michele Ferrari.'

And Pier said, 'Why would I ask you about Ferrari?'

Ta da!

Have I got news for you, Pier! Lance had news!

'He and I are now working together, because we're going to make an attack on the world hour record.'

So that was the front-page story on the following day's *La Gazzetta dello Sport*. It was Lance and Stapleton's way of taking the sting out of what would come on Sunday. By Sunday the Ferrari connection would already have been dealt with, even if the explanation was a blatant lie. Lance succeeded in ensuring the word 'exclusive' could not be used with our *Sunday Times* story, 'Saddled with Suspicion'. The great cancer survivor, expected to win his third Tour de France, was then going for the world hour record.

Nobody expected the world hour record attempt to happen. And of course it never did.

It might have been worse. Pretty much every journalist who wrote about the Ferrari connection saw that the *Gazzetta* story was a pre-emptive strike by the Lance camp to lessen the impact of the *Sunday Times* investigation. For once I wasn't waterboarded or even shunned. It was as if with his cynical manipulation of the media, Lance had gone too far.

On the afternoon of the first stage the press centre in Boulogne had a healthy air of enquiry about it. When the stage finished, a pumped posse of reporters descended on the US Postal team hotel. Bill Stapleton smoothly fielded the enquiries. Hush everybody. A statement is being prepared and will be ready in five minutes. There was some grumbling. A statement. What about Lance? Give us Lance.

Sadly Lance was too exhausted to deal with questions.

Eventually the statement emerged. One issue only. Michele Ferrari.

Chris [Carmichael] and I met Michele Ferrari during a training camp in San Diego, California, in 1995. His primary role has always been limited. Since Chris cannot be in Europe on an ongoing basis, Michele does my physiological testing and provides Chris with that data on a regular basis.

Chris has grown to trust Michele's opinion regarding my testing and my form on the bike. And lately we have been specifically working on a run at the hour record. I do not know exactly when I will do that, only that I will in the near future. He has also consulted with Chris and me on dieting, altitude preparation, hypoxic training and the use of altitude tents, which are all natural methods of improvement.[30]

In the past, I have never denied my relationship with Michele Ferrari. On the other hand, I have never gone out of my way to publicise it. The reason for that is that he has had a questionable public reputation due to the irresponsible comments he made in 1994 regarding EPO. I want to make it clear that I do not associate myself with those remarks or, for that matter, with anyone who utilises unethical sporting procedures.

---

30 Years later I would meet Mike Anderson, Armstrong's one-time personal assistant. He remembers the hypoxic tent being kept in a shed at the Dripping Springs ranch. Once the Armstrong kids played with it, otherwise Mike never recalled it being taken out of the bag.

However, in my personal experience, I have never had occasion to question the ethics or standard of care of Michele. Specifically, he has never discussed EPO with me and I have never used it.

And for the time being, that was it. If the rest of the world thought Michele Ferrari had a thriving business as a doping doctor, the truth, according to Lance, was that Ferrari earned his money purely for diet tips and the rental of an oxygen tent.

Somebody, somewhere, was getting suckered.

9

'It's purifying to me that I've been honest.'

Lance Armstrong, 13 July 2001

Like a cat pawing at a nest of mice, Lance Armstrong saw us journalists as part of a game. There were those, the majority, who were happy to scurry along hailing him as the champion cat. And there were those who said, 'Hey, wait a minute.' This species were known as trolls. I lived and worked among the trolls and it's fair to say that, some of the time at least, Lance viewed me as the mayor of Troll City.

Trolls aren't especially dangerous. They're not venomous. Still, Lance felt it was best to keep the numbers under control. He knew that an infestation of trolls could hurt him and it irritated him that he couldn't always know what they were up to. So he paid attention. Pest control. When he came across an article online that he didn't like, he noted the name of the troll and mentally filed it with the others. He never forgot a name.

Every July we'd come out from under the woodwork in the

155

barn, appearing in front of him right before the start of the Tour. We had to be dealt with. Spray some pesticide, Johan. Beat them away with that sweeping brush, Bill. Lance was good at this, partly because he liked verbal sparring and felt confident with a microphone in his hand. But also, since his cancer, he had done a lot of public speaking and he knew how to hold an audience. He could work a room as well as any entertainer.

Before the oratory came the strategy. The trolls were a small minority and the plan was always to isolate them, make them feel out of step with everyone else. So Lance and his people noted who sat beside who at the press conferences, who travelled with them on the road; and when he figured out the associations, the message went out. Troll fellow-travellers, beware. Big Brother is watching you.

Once we were travelling on a long flat stage; my two old companions John Wilcockson and Rupert Guinness, the American reporter Andy Hood and me, when Guinness got a message from Jogi Muller, an ex-rider who did PR duties with the Postal team. 'Hi, Rupert, you guys like to break for coffee?' Nothing will stop a journalists' car quicker than an invitation from someone inside a team, especially the team of Lance. Also we thought the coffee might be free. We left skid marks on the road.

So there we were: a round of espressos in our paws and shooting the breeze with a guy who might well have spoken to Lance that morning. He had at least inhaled the same air. We talked inconsequentially for a while. Muller had the good grace to pretend that he enjoyed our company and we may have let him think that the feeling was mutual.

Later he would reveal to Rupert that the only reason for the coffee-stop business was low-level espionage. For the price of a few espressos he could report back on who was travelling with Walsh and what they were saying. Had the others been infected yet?

Through these years Rupert's access to the team depended on whether or not he was seen with me. 'You must choose your friends wisely,' Muller once told him, crooking his finger like a goofy Swiss Yoda. Rupert couldn't be friends with me and expect to get near the US Postal team. Why, it just wouldn't be proper. If this seems childish, it was the game Lance liked to play.

He needed to know the enemy, and the enemy's companions.

When the news of his relationship with Ferrari broke on that first Sunday of the 2001 Tour, Lance had refused to speak with the journalists who came to his hotel that evening. Too tired. Bless. Five days later selected journalists, mostly American and all considered sympathetic, were invited to his hotel for an audience.

It is normal for racers at the Tour de France to bestow favours on journalists from their own country: Jan Ullrich to the Germans, David Millar to the British, Lance to the Americans. But as Lance was Lance, twenty minutes of his company was the next day's big story.

The invitees weren't entirely timid or in Lance's pocket but they knew there was a line and the next invitation was dependent upon you not crossing that line. This didn't mean they couldn't ask about Ferrari. That would have been ridiculous and they wouldn't have accepted it. So Lance was asked about his controversial doctor.

'From what I've seen, I don't think he's guilty. And when you say "questionable reputation", this is cycling. Who's not in question? Who's not being investigated? But please, let's look at the facts. Let's get the evidence on the table.'

He rapped his hand hard on the coffee table.

'And then let's decide if somebody is a sinner or a saint. What you have in cycling is a lot of people who want to get caught up in innuendo, relations, rumours: "He's on this, he's on that, there's something new, he's not clean, it's fake. He's no hero, what a disappointment."'

He raps a second time on the table. 'Let's get to the facts. No, I never denied my involvement, my relationship [with Ferrari], and, number two, having talked about it, I feel better.'

Therein lay the power of the yellow jersey and, of course, the seductive power of Lance Armstrong. His style is slick, persuasive: cycling's problem is innuendo, rumours, the kind of nasty stuff that reputable journalists like you guys wouldn't engage in and, of course, the reputable hear what Lance is saying and think, 'Yeah, now that you put it like that.'

Facts are what matter; Lance likes facts. Evidence also. Let's get it all on the table. *I never denied my involvement with Ferrari.*

Hold on, Lance. Aren't you channelling Bill Clinton here?

No one knew about Ferrari.

So nobody asked about Ferrari.

So you never had to lie about Ferrari.

This isn't exactly a profile in moral courage that you are painting.

Six years into working with Ferrari, the relationship is uncovered. Now Lance looks around the table, looks into the eyes of men whom he knows will understand, and says, 'Having talked about it, I feel better.'

Phew. That is good news for everybody.

There is no grumbling or dissent from within the Lance Armstrong circle of trust. They don't say, 'But six years, Lance? You couldn't remember his name? You kept making memos to yourself to mention it sometime?'

Nobody will be so rude, not after Lance has invited them here. If one person crosses the line he will affect everybody's chances of getting invited into the circle again. In any case, this is good. He deals with Ferrari. So what. It sounds pretty plausible. Lance gives to the circle what he won't give to the common or garden journalist. Just come a little closer and let me say this.

'At the end of this bike race, if I'm lucky enough to win again, all the stuff that gets written – all the innuendo, all the speculation, all the critics, all the people who don't want anything good for cycling – it doesn't matter. It doesn't matter to my family, my friends or my team. It's purifying to me that I've been honest.'

That's it. That's the money line. Purified.

Everyone else in the *salle de presse* has to wait until the rest day, six days before the end of the Tour, to hear from Lance. That's how the game is played. By then Lance was assured of winning the race for the third consecutive time. Some carping comments from Jean-Marie Leblanc before the start of the Tour encouraged Lance to engage more with the public. He'd done that and, though he kept saying the Tour is not a popularity contest, the vibe was better this year. And if the vibe was good most of the mice were happy.

If it hadn't been for the Michele Ferrari stuff, a name that nobody in America knew, let alone cared about, this would have been the best of the three Tours de Lance so far. But trouble never goes away, not permanently. Trouble is always in the hallway doing press-ups. So here Lance is in the Palais des Congrès at Pau, south-west France, once again facing down a general gathering of the trolls.

The Trial of Lance Armstrong is in its third year, but nowhere near a verdict.

There are more than a hundred journalists in a relatively small room, twenty or more television cameras in a line at the back. Lance will be ready because this is like the race itself: you tell yourself the enemy is stronger than he is because that helps you prepare better.

An example.

Through the winter Lance monitored every interview given by his biggest rival Jan Ullrich and his Telekom team-mates. In every line Ullrich talked about focusing exclusively on the Tour de France. Because he studied his enemies, Lance knew this was a different approach from the German team to previous years. They will be stronger this time, he told him-self, and this thought helped him to train harder.

Now, he was sitting before the journalists who would ask about Michele Ferrari, but he knew what he would tell them. He could handle this. He'd coped with this sort of shit two years ago in Saint-Gaudens.

'Are you calling me a liar or a doper?' he'd said to that French guy knowing that the French guy wouldn't have the nuts to simply say, 'Both.' Sometimes you only had to act tough and these guys ran away.

I was in Australia when the race started. I arrived in France at the end of the first week's racing but I'm here now, feeling entitled to ask the world's cleanest cyclist why he works with the world's dirtiest doctor. The crowd of journalists milling around is far bigger than normal. *Anyone for the afternoon show? This way, this way!*

Before it begins, I speak with a Danish journalist, Lars Werge, who works for the daily newspaper *Ekstra Bladet*. He believes Armstrong is doping and indicates he will ask some doping questions, which is useful, because it can get lonely, the troll's life. Lars and I decide to sit far apart so Armstrong and his flunkies don't think we're some kind of double act.

Apart from his fireside chat with the American reporters, Lance hasn't publicly addressed his relationship with Ferrari yet, even though the story broke at the start of the Tour. My hope is that at least four or five journalists will want to make an issue of his relationship with the Italian doctor.

As we walk into the press conference, I feel sorry for Rupert because it so happens he is alongside me and the poor man has to decide what to do. If he sits next to me, he gets marked down as a troll mindslave and can forget about access to the Postal team. On the other hand he doesn't want to leave me because he's a decent bloke who doesn't like to be bullied. So he says nothing, just follows and takes the chair alongside me.

I'm glad but I know his discomfort is made worse by what he is wearing. That morning Rupert had plucked the most festive of Hawaiian shirts from his suitcase of sunshine. The troll police really can't miss him.

But everyone relax, this is a room teeming with sports-writers, and for most of them this is a good-news story.

Here goes.

Lance is asked about 'the look', that moment on the climb to Alpe d'Huez when he turned to scan his breakaway companions and seemed to allow his eyes to linger on the face of his principal rival, Jan Ullrich.

A German journalist snuggles up to Lance with, 'That look is being called one of the greatest moments of the sporting year?'

Maybe in Bavaria. *Ja?*

But Lance likes this question. 'I've heard about quote-unquote "the look" and of course everybody is guessing – what is the look? What was it? Was it bravado? Was it tactics? Was it a question? . . . [On the road] I had to examine the situation. It was not an arrogant thing. I did want to see his face, I wanted to see his mouth. I wanted to see the expression. But I also wanted to look back down the road and see who was there.'

There is an angle here. Lance and Jan, do-or-die rivals but also noble men who respect each other.

'The handshake between yourself and Jan yesterday: "the look" and "the handshake" are being seen as two symbolic moments of the mountain stages?'

Isn't this conversation more uplifting than prying about Lance and his Victor Frankenstein? Asked about 'the hand-shake', Lance looks smilingly at the questioner and says, 'I bet money you were going to ask a lot about that.'

He likes this question even more than the last because it is an opportunity to show graciousness, modesty, even a touch of class. It is only right to compliment the journalist on his discerning question.

'I really like Jan Ullrich. It's not a rivalry full of hatred. I think there's a serious amount of mutual respect there. To me, he's the only rider who really scares me. If he has a good day or a good year, he could be impossible to beat.'

And so the press conference saunters along in this way, as if there wasn't a troll in the building. But the sixteenth adoring question is too much: 'What makes you so superior to the rest of the field?'

I shoot a glance at Lars. Will Lance just say EPO and get it out there once and for all? 'EPO makes me the best. EPO and Michele!'

Lars' eyebrows are stretched skywards, and a few others are feeling the same way because it starts now, the doping debate. It is a French journalist who gets the ball rolling for, in a general sense, the French journalists, especially those working for *Libération* and *Le Monde*, have been the least gullible in the press tent. Lance is asked about doping. He gives the usual reply: this is an issue for sport, not just cycling. Global problem, he says: 'I think cycling is on its way out of the crisis because it has done more than any other sport.'

But of course there will always be people who don't want to believe. Trolls like me, suffering with cancer of the spirit.

And once the debate moves onto doping, a strange thing happens. Lance looks at me when he is answering, even though I've not asked the question, as if he's trying to convince me alone and not everyone in the room. Every time he talks about doping, he stares at me.

Someone wonders aloud if cynicism will follow him to the end of his career?

Lance answers straight to my face.

'I'm prepared to live with it. It's unfortunate. I can get up every morning and look at myself in the mirror and my family can look at me too. That's all that matters.'

Raising your hand to ask a question of a man who despises you is interesting because you're not sure how he will respond. I have heard him talk of cycling's problems and what the sport is doing to drag itself out of a mess and I ask if he feels a personal responsibility to promote a better image, and how does he reconcile that with his doctor/trainer being so associated with doping?

He has prepared for this moment.

'Well, David, I'm glad you showed up, finally. It's good to see you're finally here.'

Though soaked in sarcasm, he also wants me to know that he knows when I'm on the Tour, when I'm not. He cares.

'I'm confident in the relationship [with Ferrari]. I've never denied the relationship, even to you. I believe he's an honest man. I believe he's a fair man and I believe he's an innocent man. I've never seen anything to lead me to believe otherwise.'

He doesn't address the question of whether associating with a controversial doctor is bad for the sport but glides off into that sunset where Lance gets to interview Lance. It is a technique he has used many times in the past and it never fails to deliver the answer he wants.

'People will look at the facts, they will say, "Okay, here's Lance Armstrong. Here's a relationship, is that questionable?"'

'Perhaps.'

'Do they say, "Lance Armstrong tested positive?"'

'No.'

'Has Lance Armstrong been tested?'

'A lot.'

'Was Lance Armstrong's team put under investigation and their urine from the 2000 Tour tested for urine?'

'Yes it was.'

'Was it clean?'

'Absolutely.'

'Is there now an EPO test?'

'Absolutely.'

'Will he pass every test because he does not take EPO?'

'Yes he will.'

This Lance-interviews-Lance interlude is magical in its simplicity and effectiveness. He asks himself the difficult questions, but because he's the journalist and the sports star, he controls everything. And in fairness these are questions that 95 per cent of the journalists in the room wouldn't have asked anyway.

As for the trolls, they may as well crawl back underneath the rocks. But we don't.

Sitting well away to my left, Lars reminds Lance that he hasn't answered 'Mr Walsh's question' as to why a clean cyclist would want to work with a dirty doctor?

'Until there's a conviction, until someone is proven guilty, then I can't view them as guilty. Does that answer your question, David?'

It seems obvious to me that he is lying, but in this room it is a minority view. My question to every journalist I'd encountered on the race was: why would a rider who says he is clean and opposed to doping work with a doctor who has the dirtiest reputation in cycling and is about to go on trial for doping professional riders? Especially when the rider himself is dogged always by questions. So now I put this to Lance.

In the middle of my question, Armstrong interrupts: 'I have the proof, which you refuse to believe.'

'Let me finish the question,' I say with a firmness I barely recognise. I wait a moment for lightning from the heavens to strike me down. Nothing happens. I press on with my insubordination.

'Would it not be in the interests of cycling for you to suspend your relationship with Ferrari until he has answered the doping charges against him?'

He is taken aback by the reasonableness of the suggestion. 'You have a point.'

It's likely he's already considered with Bill Stapleton the possibility of publicly distancing himself from Ferrari. But 'the Adam of all your labours' cannot turn his back on Frankenstein. 'It's my choice. I view him as innocent. He's a clean man in my opinion. Let there be a trial. Let the man prove himself innocent ... how can I prosecute a man I've never seen do anything guilty?'

This press conference has lasted for an hour and ten minutes, another day at The Trial of Lance Armstrong, and he's defended himself ably. But he will have noticed that, as the conversation progressed, the number of journalists asking doping questions increased. More doping questions than at any previous rest-day press conference and they seem to think they had the right to ask. But he saw who they were, their faces were noted and soon their credentials, allowing access to the Lance Armstrong Circle of Trust, will be withdrawn.

He has done well here today and the tactic of staring at me throughout the doping debate will have left the subliminal impression that it was almost a private discussion between him and me.

Before he walks free from the court room, there is one last question.

'If you have to endure this questioning about your success, where does the happiness come from? Is it the actual winning, the performing in front of these people, or riding the bike itself?'

Ouch. Right over the line.

'All of the above,' he said. 'I mean, guys, I'm going to walk out of here in about thirty seconds and you're all out of my life. When I go back to the hotel, I get a massage and I relax. When this race is done I go back to my family and you're really out.'[31]

Lars paid a price for encouraging Armstrong to answer 'Mr Walsh's question'. Afterwards whenever he approached Johan Bruyneel with a question, the US Postal team director would say he had no time. Too busy. 'It was like he

---

31 This was a line spun often by Armstrong. His career would end, he would disappear, find himself a nice beach, have his family, a few cool beers, and we would still be back in the press room wondering how he'd done it. What actually happened is that he went away in 2005, couldn't live in retirement and came back in 2009. Had he been able to stay away, the likelihood is that the truth of his story would never have been fully revealed.

pulled down the curtain and I wasn't allowed in any more,' says Lars.

A few evenings later I was in the car with Rupert heading back to our digs when we made a short stop at a team hotel, as Rupert needed to check something with one of the Australian riders in the race. Unluckily for Rupert, this was also the hotel of US Postal. No sooner had he entered the lobby than he was confronted by Postal *directeur sportif*, Johan Bruyneel.

Bruyneel had seen Rupert with me. He collared poor Rupert to let him know that he couldn't associate with me and expect to have access to anyone on the Postal team. Bruyneel was livid. The finger jabbed close to Rupert's face. 'You're a fucking traitor, you're with Walsh. You come in here to talk to riders and you ride with Walsh. We know your game.'

Rupert defended himself. Bruyneel kept on and on until eventually Rupert told him that I was out in the car and why didn't Bruyneel just come on out and tell me directly what he was saying in the hotel.

Bruyneel turned and stalked off.

To people living outside LanceWorld, this must have seemed like the strangest encounter: two middle-aged men arguing furiously because one of them has been seen with another man. Bruyneel didn't take up Rupert's offer to come outside, something that on balance I was later pleased about; and although the whole thing might seen hilarious now, that wasn't how it felt on the night.

I'd known Rupert for more than twenty years; we'd run together countless mornings, eaten together in the evenings and we spent a good percentage of our lives sharing the back-seat of a car. In that time I only once saw him angry.

It was that night.

On the day Lance rides across the line on the Champs-Élysées to claim his third consecutive Tour de France, I have written another piece for the *Sunday Times* stating there's nothing to celebrate here as too many unanswered questions remain.

It was a piece I had written, on average, three times every July for three years, which was testimony both to my willingness to endlessly repeat myself and to my sports editor Alex Butler's patience. He could have decided he'd heard enough, as the majority of our readers felt they had, but he let me go on. The piece at the end of the 2001 Tour ran under the headline, PARADISE LOST ON TOUR, and it had one redeeming feature: I'd got Greg LeMond to go on the record about Armstrong.

LeMond had won the Tour de France three times and he knew that by criticising Lance on the day that he'd won his third, he left himself open to accusations of jealousy. But LeMond had heard things: first from his old mechanic Julien DeVriese, who was now Lance's mechanic, about the culture of secrecy around the team which, Julien said, was designed to hide the doping.

Then LeMond spoke with journalist James Startt, who told him that Lance's former teammate Frankie Andreu and his wife Betsy had heard Lance admit to doctors in Indiana University Hospital that he had used performance-enhancing drugs. That was in 1996 while being treated for testicular cancer. This put doubt in LeMond's mind, but the information was confidential and not something he would say publicly.

But Michele Ferrari was different.

Straw.

Camel's back.

LeMond believed that since doctors took over from old-school *soigneurs* (medically unqualified 'carers' who dispensed doping products in the old days), the situation in cycling had gone from bad to much worse. From everything he'd heard and read about Michele Ferrari, LeMond thought the guy was toxic. He read a line by the journalist Alex Wolff on the *Sports Illustrated* website that summed up his view of Ferrari: 'The only reason you go to Ferrari is to tell him to get the hell out of your sport.'

So, three days after the Pau press conference, I rang LeMond and caught him at a good time. He wanted to speak about Lance and Ferrari, but first he wanted people to understand this wasn't a jealous has-been knocking his successor.

'When Lance won the prologue to the 1999 Tour, I was close to tears. He had come back from cancer. In the middle of my career I had to come back from being accidentally shot [while hunting in 1987] and it felt like we had a lot in common.

'But when I heard he was working with Michele Ferrari, I was devastated. In the light of his relationship with Ferrari, I just don't want to comment on this year's Tour . . .' and then LeMond paused, considering if should say any more. He couldn't help himself: 'In a general sense, if Lance is clean, it is the greatest comeback in the history of sport. If he isn't, it would be the greatest fraud.'

That wasn't a quote Lance was ever going to miss.

A couple of days later, LeMond returned to his home city Minneapolis–Saint Paul following a business trip to London. Kathy, his wife, came in her Audi station wagon to pick him up.

'You wanna drive?' she asked.

'Yeah, I'll drive.'

Then his phone rang.

'Greg, this is Lance.'

'Hi Lance. What are you doing?'

'I'm in New York.'

'Ah, okay.'

'Greg, I thought we were friends. Why did you say what you said?'

'About Ferrari? Well, I have a problem with Ferrari. I'm disappointed you are seeing someone like Ferrari. I have a personal issue with Ferrari and doctors like him. I feel my career was cut short. I saw a teammate die. I saw the devastation of innocent riders losing their careers. I don't like what has become of our sport.'

'Oh, come on now. You're telling me you've never done EPO?'

'Why would you say I did EPO?'

'Come on, everyone's done EPO.'

'Why do you think I did it?'

'Well, your comeback in eighty-nine was so spectacular. Mine was a miracle, yours was a miracle. You couldn't have been as strong as you were in eighty-nine without EPO.'[32]

32 There is no evidence that EPO was being used by cyclists in 1989. Most agree, EPO made its cycling debut in the early nineties.

'Listen, Lance, before EPO was ever in cycling I won the Tour de France. First time I was in the Tour I was third [in 1984]; the second time I should have won but was held back by my team [second in 1985 behind teammate Bernard Hinault]. Third time I won it [1986]. It is not because of EPO that I won the Tour – my haematocrit was never more than forty-five – because I had a VO2 Max of ninety-five. Yours was eighty-two. Tell me one person who said I did EPO.'

'Everyone knows it.'

'Are you threatening me?'

'If you want to throw stones, I will throw stones.'

'So you are threatening me? Listen, Lance. I know a lot about physiology; no amount of training can transform an athlete with a VO2 Max of eighty-two into one with a VO2 Max of nine-five, and you have ridden faster than I did.'

'I could find at least ten people who will say you did EPO. Ten people who would come forward.'

'That's impossible. I know I never did that. Nobody can say I have. If I had taken EPO, my haematocrit value would have exceeded forty-five. It never did. I could produce all my blood parameters to prove my haematocrit level never rose above forty-five. And if I have this accusation levelled against me, I will know it came from you.'

'You shouldn't have said what you did. It wasn't right.'

'I try to avoid speaking to journalists. David Walsh called me. He knew about your relations with Ferrari. What should I have said? No comment? I'm not that sort of person. Then a journalist from *Sports Illustrated* called me. I've spoken to two journalists in total. Maybe I shouldn't have spoken to them, but I only told them the truth.'

'I thought there was respect between us.'

'So did I. Listen, Lance, I tried to warn you about Ferrari. This guy's trial is opening in September. What he did in the nineties changed riders. You should get away from him. How do you think I should have reacted?'

That conversation finished Lance with Greg. No more Christmas cards.

It was time to make LeMond toe the line. The first call came from Thom Weisel, the west-coast entrepreneur whose vision created the US Postal team and who has made a small fortune in providing financial services. He gently told Greg it wasn't good for him to say those things about Lance. After Weisel came Terry Lee, CEO of Bell Helmets, a cycle accessories company, and he too was conciliatory.

'If it was me in your position, Greg, I wouldn't do it.'

After Lee came a call from John Bucksbaum, chief executive of a real estate company, and another businessman who was in the Lance camp. He was calling, of course, as a friend. The full-court press went on. At the end of that week, Greg got a message to call John Burke, chief executive officer of Trek, the company that had a licensing agreement with LeMond to manufacture, market and distribute LeMond bicycles.

Burke told LeMond he was in a difficult position because his company also sponsored Lance and he needed Greg to publicly retract his statement about Ferrari and Lance. Only if that happened would Trek be able to continue its relationship with LeMond.

'It was like the troops were mobilised to shut Greg up,' said Kathy LeMond.

I spoke with Greg a lot during these difficulties with Trek and the pressure to which he was subjected by the group of high-powered businessmen in Lance's corner. He resisted for a time, but the endless conversations with his lawyer and the anxiety over what Trek were going to do with his business took their toll. He told his lawyer to do what was necessary to bring about some kind of closure because he wanted to extricate himself from all of this.

A little over two weeks after the fractious conversation with Lance had happened, Greg's apology appeared in *USA Today*:

> I sincerely regret that some of my remarks seemed to question the veracity of Lance's performances. I want to be clear that I believe Lance to be a great champion and I do not believe, in any way, that he has ever used any performance-enhancing substances. I believe his performances are the result of the same hard work, dedication and focus that were mine ten years before.

Sal Ruibal, a writer who was staunchly supportive of Lance through the early years, was rewarded for his work by being given the statement and Lance's gracious response to it.

'It is nice,' Armstrong said, 'to hear there was a clarification. I've always had a lot of respect for Greg as a rider and for what he's done for our sport. I respect and appreciate him even more for going out of his way to say that. I didn't have hard feelings before he made the statement and don't have them now.'

LeMond first saw that statement on the sport pages of *USA Today*. It sickened him. Not just because the statement did not represent how he felt about Armstrong's success but more because he had allowed himself to be browbeaten by men in powerful positions. It had happened once, LeMond told himself, but it would never happen again.

10

'Are we supposed to believe anything Betsy Andreu says?'

Lance Armstrong

Here's Betsy Andreu. Small, dark and wired. Implacable. From the moment you meet her you know that she is as tough and scrappy as a honey badger. If Lance Armstrong was any judge of character, he would have shut up the medicine shop the moment he met her. Nope. Here's Betsy Andreu. She was on the inside. Now she's on my side.

The downside of having broken the Ferrari story in 2001 was a falling off in the number of Christmas cards I received and the knowledge that my take on cancer's most famous survivor placed me out of the running for Humanitarian of the Year. Again.

One of the many advantages was that it put me on the radar of the other poor souls out there who cared about such things.

James Startt was an American photo-journalist for *Bicycling* who lived in Paris. He'd come to Europe to work and he'd got to know a number of the American riders. I'd met James on the Tour. Liked him. He knew Frankie Andreu. If you knew Frankie, you would know his wife Betsy. If you knew Betsy for any length of time, you got to know her views on the talented Mr Armstrong.

At some point either in person or on the phone Betsy, one of life's natural networkers, had asked James if she knew this guy David Walsh. As it happened James did know David Walsh and he was prepared to admit it.

'Tell him to call me.'

'Yes, Betsy.'

James duly passed on the message.

'She says she knows some things that you should know.'

I dialled the number straight away. In Dearborn, Michigan, US of A, somebody answered straight away. Betsy Andreu.

Sources are like blind dates. You meet a lot of duds before you talk to one that's worth the trouble. Sometimes, though, you just know when you have found the right person. The voice coming down the phone suggested intelligence and a fierce morality. Nothing I have learned about Betsy Andreu in the many years since has changed that first impression.

With Betsy, you didn't have to tip-toe around the subject of Lance Armstrong. Our first proper conversation was on a Friday evening. I'd flown into Heathrow from an assignment and had to drive cross-country to Cardiff for a rugby game which was happening the following afternoon. We started talking as I was leaving Heathrow. We were still talking as I pulled into my hotel in Cardiff. It says something for the support of my employers at the *Sunday Times* that the mobile phone bill was paid without demur, and if Vodafone had sponsored the journalist awards that year, I'd have got a prize.

Within minutes of me hitting the M4, Betsy was offering (to use a phrase of Lance's) liquid gold. She took me back to the gathering inside a consulting room at Indiana University Hospital in October 1996. Something about Frankie's combative and switched-on nature had earned him Lance's respect back in Europe. They were friends. When the news came of Armstrong's cancer in October 1996, it had hit Betsy and Frankie hard. They were six weeks away from a wedding and now their friend had cancer. Life was random and life was cruel.

They headed to Indianapolis for a few days intending to spend every spare minute keeping their friend company. Now the room with the bed in it had become too crowded and they had moved to a hospital common room, Lance clutching his IV as they went.

The Dallas Cowboys were on the television. The small group of friends and acquaintances watched with various levels of interest. In the room were Betsy Andreu, Frankie Andreu, Lance's coach Chris Carmichael and his wife Paige, Lance's then girlfriend, Lisa Shiels, and a woman called Stephanie McIlvain who worked as liaison with Oakley, who were Lance's sunglasses sponsor.

Two doctors now entered the room. They had questions for the patient. Necessary questions.

'We should leave now,' Betsy said, as the doctors began their checklist.

'It's okay,' said Armstrong. 'You can stay.'

And then Betsy heard the conversation that would change

her life and make her life and Lance Armstrong's life very difficult.

'Have you used performance-enhancing drugs?' asked one doctor.

Matter-of-factly, Armstrong listed them: 'EPO, testosterone, growth hormone, cortisone and steroids.'

Betsy was stunned. The message to Frankie Andreu, her fiancé, was flashed with her eyes: 'You and me, we gotta speak outside. Now.'

Frankie knew enough to sense that this wasn't good. He'd better follow. 'If you're fucking doing that shit, I'm not marrying you,' she said.

Frankie was a tough man of the roads. He learned bike racing in harum-scarum rides around the Dearborn Towers near home, at hard races in little-sung placers like Downers Grove. And he kept getting better. That summer he had been fourth in the road race at the Atlanta Olympics. This time, however, he was in trouble.

When Armstrong asked Frankie a while later how Betsy had reacted to his disclosure, two words sufficed: 'Not good.'

Over the years, Betsy stuck to her account of what had happened in that room. In the days after, she had called friends Dawn Polay, Piero Boccarossa and Lory Testasecca and spoke to them about what had been said. She was still shocked and upset. Could she marry Frankie after what she had heard? Should she? The advice that came back was to talk it out long and hard. They did.

Frankie promised to be clean. Betsy Kramar became Betsy Andreu when the pair got married just over two months later on New Year's Eve 1996.

It was a lonely road, though. Never for a second did Betsy understand why she should lie and cover for Lance Armstrong. When her view became known, when people learned that she was slurring an American icon, she had only the support of her friends, her mom and a few others to fall back on. From the world in which her husband lived and worked, only Greg LeMond, his wife Kathy, Jonathan Vaughters, an old teammate of Frankie's, and James Startt were supportive; and, for a long time, so too was Stephanie McIlvain. But Betsy didn't care. Honesty needs no approval.

When she first told me the hospital-room story, so early in our relationship, it stunned me. It was such a small human thing for Lance Armstrong to do. He assumed so much of people. Later, people would say: surely he would never have admitted taking performance-enhancing drugs in front of six friends?

Betsy and Frankie talked about this. 'Frankie, why would he be so indiscreet?'

'Honey,' Frankie said, 'the previous day he'd had lesions removed from his brain. He wasn't sure he was going to live. Right then performance-enhancing drugs weren't the biggest thing on his mind.'

And this room in Indiana, where the disease eating his body changed the context of everything, this room far away from pesky testers and shifty Europeans, this room with its poorly drawn borders of confidentiality, this was where it happened.

A small human thing, but Betsy's account was utterly believable. Lance was comfortable being surrounded by people who all had a stake in him one way or another. He misread the terrain. He didn't ever think it would matter. He never understood that Betsy's concern would be for the man she was due to marry, for his honour and health.

The clincher was Betsy hauling Frankie outside for the most frightening random test of his career. '*You and me gotta talk.*' Lance Armstrong, even the Lance of 1996, couldn't imagine that he would be such a bit player in the drama of that conversation.

Betsy told me that story and, like everybody she has told it to before or since, I believed her. It wasn't proof. It wasn't the smoking gun. For journalists in doping cases there is no such thing. I remember in Atlanta in 1996 meeting a prominent American journalist who told me about a lengthy investigation he had carried out into the drug practices of a hugely admired American athlete. Finally, after a drip feed of damaging stories, the athlete had let loose his lawyers and a meeting was called between the journalist, his employers, the athlete and his lawyers.

The paper, unnerved, either by celebrity or by the sight of so many assassins in fine suits, just caved in. It was agreed the reputation of this fine man was being impugned and the paper assured the lawyers that it would all stop. Everybody got up and shook hands. Very civil and cordial. The last shake was between my friend the journalist and his quarry, the athlete. Eye contact and an aggressively firm shake. The athlete left with a backward glance and the smile for which he was famous.

My friend looked down at his palm. Pressed into the skin was a small dianabol pill.

'Fuck.'

He showed it to his bosses with whom he was already very displeased. Wow, they said. Look at that. You were right. But, listen: that proves nothing. You can't even write it because of what it would imply.

Betsy's story was a little blue pill in my palm. And luckily it had come to me without the hindrance of lawyers or injunctions. It wasn't proof because for years it would be a he said-she said debate. For me, though, it was confirmation. Reassurance. Keep going. Keep looking. Keep talking to people. Keep asking the questions. Keep writing. It was an irony Lance wouldn't enjoy, but I found Betsy's information to be performance enhancing.

For her part, she always asked at least as many questions as she would answer. 'What do you know? How do you know? Have you put that to him? What did he say?' A sports editor like her and I'd have burned out years ago. She scanned the newspapers around the world and knew which writers were taking which positions. Those without a spine she wanted me to get phone numbers for so she could call them and ask what had happened to their self-respect.

Betsy is a one-off. Her humanity and her morality made her instantly believable. The daughter of a Serbian jeweller and a Slovakian librarian, Betsy grew up as a devout catholic in Dearborn, Michigan, graduated from University of Michigan and met Frankie in April 1994 in a pizza joint. He was a stringy professional cyclist with a blue-collar work ethic and a flashing smile. When they met, Betsy was just getting ready to open an Italian-themed coffee shop.

Italy! Frankie lived a world away in Como, Italy. He hung with a loose and lively cycling community with a strong constituency of ambitious Americans. Frankie was a flatmate of Lance Armstrong's and the two seemed close; neighbours included guys like Kevin Livingston, Jeff Pierce and Bob Roll, all of whom had found their way to the area.

Frankie had been cut up by the death of their teammate Fabio Casartelli on the 1995 Tour. Fabio died descending Col de Portet d'Aspet. Betsy had seen the pictures. Blood on the road. Frankie and Lance hurting during a minute's silence in the aftermath. Black armbands. Frankie with a pair of wrap-around shades hiding his pain. Lance just weeping. They were brothers of the road, living life and learning.

Cycling, which for the amateur seems like the most pure of endeavours, was making itself known to the Americans in the hard, professional sense. They watched in awe and bemusement as riders like Mario Cipollini came to early-season races and devoured the climbs. WTF, man? Rumours were everywhere. People talking about r-EPO, comparing their haematocrit levels, the sound of ice rattling in a thermos, a necessary prop for a drug that needed to be chilled.

There were spooky stories of riders who were so hopped up on this stuff that their levels were up above 60 per cent. They had to wear pulse meters at night so that when their pulse rate dipped below a certain point an alarm would sound and they would get up and exercise furiously before their blood turned to treacle. This was the shit that killed eighteen or so Belgian and Dutch cyclists in the nineties? And it works?

But Betsy Andreu didn't care what races Frankie won or how much he earned, if the means to the end was cheating and endangering his health. EPO was meant for sick people, right? Some wives and partners were like Betsy, but others

saw doping as part of the deal and even assisted in their partners' wrongdoing.

The doors were opening to a world that Frankie didn't
much like. He was a good professional, a cool and able strate-
gist on the road, and he had a natural abrasiveness which
earned respect among his peers. He hadn't gone into professional cycling to start messing with drugs, but all these
rumours and the talk were a dust cloud which was about to
float over his life. He didn't know how he would square any
of it with his future wife's black-and-white sense of right and
wrong.

What I remember most vividly about so many conversations with Betsy Andreu is that they seemed to pass in a flash,
yet I would come away with an almost cinematic memory of
whatever she had been describing. The stories never wanted
for detail or consistency. Bill Clinton used to tell people that
he could feel their pain. If he'd met Betsy he could have felt
her pain, her frustration, her anger, her humour, her loyalty.
She put it all out there. When she'd describe a row with
Frankie, no shrinking violet himself but the man on the
frontline of the old dilemma about whether to go along or
get along, I would agree with Betsy's point of view but feel
sorry for Frankie. He was facing into a force of nature.

Frankie knew he'd got lucky, though. As I was to find out,
it was good to have this particular force of nature as an ally.
Asking questions about Lance Armstrong, sporting hero and
pioneer in the fight against cancer, could make you feel like
something of a cancer yourself. And if you didn't feel that,
there were people willing to help.

One of the early letters to the *Sunday Times* came from a

reader, Keith Miller, who hadn't been impressed by my scepticism. 'I believe Armstrong's victory was amazing, a triumph in sport and life. I believe he sets a good example for all of us. I believe in sport, in life, and in humanity ... Sometimes we refuse to believe for whatever reason. Sometimes people get a cancer of the spirit. And maybe that says a lot about them.'

'Betsy, let me tell you what this guy said in a letter ...'

And here on the phone from Michigan, she was listening, somebody who would be a companion on the road ahead. 'I told Frankie, I ain't lying for Lance.'

If people around me were bored of me teasing out the details of the story in their presence, there was somebody a phone call away who never got bored with the topic. Betsy was in this for the long haul and she would suffer as much abuse as anybody, and she would take it without flinching.

After they had got married, Frankie and Betsy lived together in Europe for a while. Frankie had raced with Lance in his pre-cancer days at Motorola, and when Lance recovered and signed for US Postal, Frankie followed. Armstrong continued to be a part of their lives.

The conversation in the hospital room in Indianapolis was not forgotten. Betsy had married Frankie with love and a few caveats. She decided, though, that perhaps the drugs trail began and ended with Lance. Frankie was different. He didn't have the assassin's cold remove, the same driven ruthlessness. Lance could live his life. Betsy and Frankie would live theirs. That was okay.

There were tensions. Life is that way when you live in the shadow of a volcano. Frankie and Lance were pulling in different directions.

Back in 1998, when Willy Voet was caught driving his little shop of horrors, Frankie thought out loud on the team bus after the prologue in Dublin. He had some sympathy for Willy but he hoped that this was the beginning of the end of the doping culture in the Tour. He hated it and hated the pressure and hated that Betsy worried over it. And above all it wasn't fair, he said. When he'd come into the Tour you could ride the three weeks on spaghetti and water. Now?

Frankie had joined French team Cofidis before Lance's illness in the expectation that his old friend would be at his side. Instead he rode the 1998 Tour for the French team while Lance was elsewhere, rebooting himself.

Betsy travelled to the Tour that year with Kevin Livingston's wife Becky. As the scandal unfolded with police raids, and teams ducking for cover and withdrawals and sit-down protests, many around the world of pro cycling felt that things had gotten out of hand. Frank was a little ambivalent. He hoped this would be the watershed, the end of the pressure he felt to dope. But, hey, the police didn't have to be so heavy-handed. No way. Betsy's reaction was distinctive as usual. If the riders were that upset they must have plenty to hide. End of story.

Funny, Betsy's problem was never really with Kristin Armstrong. When Kristin was pregnant in the spring of 1999 Betsy and her fell into a conversation on the subject of hiring nannies. They were in the car on the way to the Milan–San Remo classic. Betsy felt that if you had a child and could be there for it then a nanny was unnecessary. Kristin agreed. Sometime later Betsy was trawling a cycling forum and came upon a discussion of Kristin's pregnancy. Somebody speculated with a sneer that the Armstrongs would be hiring a nanny. Betsy, ever the lioness, logged on and posted a reply that she knew Kristin and there would be no nanny, so put an end to the bullshit, please.

Next time she was talking to Kristin she happened to mention the online exchange, the nerve of somebody making a post like that. She told Kristin she had backed her up and put an end to it. To her surprise Kristin burst into tears. Inconsolable for a while, she later apologised. She was feeling very hormonal, she said. Betsy understood.

A day later, though, Kristin must have mentioned the whole business in innocence to Lance. Armstrong confronted Frankie, jabbing him in the chest: 'Tell your fucking wife to get out of my wife's face, you tell her to stop fucking upsetting Kik.'

Soon there was a full-scale shouting match between two of the tougher *hombres* in cycling, the boys butting heads like stags in the glen. Lance was unhappy anyway because Betsy had become close to Kevin Livingston's wife Becky and they hung out together. Which meant that Kristin Armstrong was a little isolated and this annoyed Lance, who took it out on Frankie in the most crass of ways.[33]

Things cooled a little between Frankie and Lance by the summer of 1999. What happened didn't destroy their friendship but it was never quite the same again. Betsy sent Lance

---

33 Interestingly, Armstrong showed Emma O'Reilly the offending email from Betsy on a significant day in a significant place: Sestriere on 18 May 1999. That same night Michele Ferrari came to dine with several team members in the Last Tango restaurant. Armstrong and Ferrari sat together and talked all evening. If only Betsy had known.

an email pointing out to him that he didn't treat people the way he would like to be treated, that he had a habit of walking all over anybody who got in his way.

And then there were good times. Breaks in the weather. Nights out drinking and plotting in Chez Wayne, their local in Nice; evenings when Betsy and Frankie would have the Armstrongs over and Lance would talk sweet to Betsy about the wonder which was her risotto. He'd go to the supermarket with her, she challenging his atheism, he arguing against her belief in God. They used to get along.

The best of times and not quite the worst of times. Lance had got better. Frankie and Lance had gone back to work. They had been flatmates in Como before the gang moved to Nice. That couldn't be wiped. US Postal was a serious team, the best Frankie had worked for. Lance was becoming the star he had planned to be when he came to Europe. Good times again.

In July Lance duly won his first Tour de France with his team pushing him all the way. With Frankie busy, Betsy went back home to Dearborn and watched most of the race from there between visits to friends and family. She told me about that day to Sestriere, the first mountain stage. She had been at home looking on in alarm as she saw her husband drive the race up the early Alpine climbs on the way to Lance's first win in the mountains. She knew Frankie Andreu like nobody else did. This wasn't a recognisable version of her Frankie. She called up a friend in Paris, Becky Rast, who was married to James Startt, to see if Becky was seeing what she was seeing.

'Isn't it great?'

'He isn't a climber. What the hell is he doing pulling at the front on a first-category mountain? Frankie is about as much of a climber as the Pope is an atheist.'

Towards the end of the race, she flew to France with her two-month-old son Frankie. They joined the Tour at Carcassonne in the deep south, but it wasn't the time or the place to confront her husband.

The boys went all the way to Paris with Lance in the lead. She watched her husband at the moment of his greatest triumph on the shoulder of the champion. The famous and giddy ride down the Rue de Rivoli, onto the Place de la Concorde and then up the Champs-Élysées. She let Frankie have his time.

That night she went to join the boys at the victory party in the Musée d'Orsay. The world wanted a part of this now. She thought of the Motorola years and the subdued Sunday nights they'd spent in Paris in other years. The mood here was jubilant and a little triumphalist. They had conquered Europe. By now, though, there was only one subplot which interested Betsy: drugs.

At the party she was expected to congratulate Lance Armstrong, to take her place in the line and kiss his ass like everyone else.

'Did you shake hands and congratulate Lance?' said Frankie, when she caught up with him.

'No.'

'You gotta shake his hand. It'll look bad.'

'I don't care. I want to talk to you about EPO.'

When Betsy told me this story, I smiled. By now we were talking every day, sometimes twice a day. People warmed to her because of her passion for the truth. Even though it was clear to everyone she was a non-believer in The Legend of Lance, she had regular conversations with a member of Lance's extended family, she spoke with someone very close to Bill Stapleton and she knew far, far more than the libel laws would allow me to print.

She would track down stories and reports and pass them on. Two, three, four emails, with links to Lance stories. 'See what this idiot wrote,' she'd say. I couldn't help, though, imagining tough Frankie Andreu having ridden through three weeks of hell getting to the victory party only to face his biggest challenge.

'By the way, Betsy, did you shake Lance's hand in the end?' I asked her much later.

'I thank God for giving me the strength not to shake the hand of that asshole.'

A short time after that first Lance Tour, Betsy found a thermos with EPO in Frankie's fridge at their flat in Nice. It brought things home in a harsher light than just seeing him lead the way to Sestriere. This stuff was in their home. After all the conversations that followed the hospital visit in 1996, all the reassurances and promises, it felt like a betrayal. Betsy confronted her husband.

'What's this?'

'Nothing,' he said, but instantly he caved

He explained that before the Tour, with expectations high, Frankie had felt the pressure like never before. He couldn't let the boys down. The culture was that if you weren't doping you weren't committed. Frankie didn't want to dope but his commitment was the greater influence. He drove to Switzerland and rattling with nerves bought some EPO over the counter in a chemist's. He administered it to himself in the flat in Nice, jabbing himself in the shoulder with the needle and getting on with the day quickly so he could forget what he had done. He didn't bring his little thermos to the Tour but he felt the benefits of its contents.

He was contrite and he was sorry but there was nothing he could do. In Betsy's world things might be black and white. In Frankie's world it was different.

Betsy recalled a discussion she'd had with Kristin earlier that season, the day at Milan–San Remo. Betsy asked Lance's wife what she thought about the EPO thing. 'A necessary evil,' Kristin had shrugged.

Betsy Andreu never saw an evil which she found to be necessary. For Frankie bringing home the corn meant that sometimes he had to go along to get along. They argued.

'You don't understand. This is the only way I can ever finish the Tour now. After this I promise you. I'll never do it again.'

She hated the argument because this time of year, winding down and recovering after the Tour, was one of her favourites. She had a bottom line, though. If the team was making Frankie dope, he had only one option.

'Get off the US Postal Service team. Just get off it.'

'This is a problem for every team though, hon.'

'You've got to promise me you won't do it again. I don't want you to do this, even if you don't ride as well.'

'I am not going to do it again.'

So Betsy won out, as she always knew she would. After the 1999 Tour de France win, it fell to Frankie to go to Armstrong to ask him to pay his eight teammates the $25,000 each he owed them for helping him win the Tour. It told Betsy much that Armstrong had to be reminded. By then Armstrong was moving into a different stratosphere as an earner and as a celebrity. Those who shielded him from the elements, paced him on the climbs, led him on the descents, needed every dollar they could earn.

Lance could never understand why Frankie wouldn't go with Ferrari. He called him a cheapskate, too mean to pay and, for sure, Frankie didn't like the idea of handing over a significant slice of his salary to a doctor in Italy, but it wasn't just the money. He knew Ferrari meant big-time doping and that wasn't what he wanted to do. And, in any case, Betsy would have killed him.

By the end of 2000 Betsy had got her wish. Frankie rode an ordinary tour. He was dead when it finished and was cut loose from Postal. Lance, who had the power to stop him going, just shrugged.

When I caught up with Betsy she had already been through the mill a few times. She would tell me the story of how some time after Frankie was cut adrift from US Postal, having refused to submit to the ministrations of Ferrari, he took a call one night from his *directeur sportif* Johan Bruyneel.

If Lance was, as the French liked to say, cryptically, on 'another planet', Bruyneel was his representative on earth. Not a voice to make Frankie skip to the phone in excitement.

When the call came, Frankie was in the process of putting his professional life back together. The culture of US Postal had changed quickly since 1998 and if you didn't commit to doping you were considered not to be committed. Period. Frankie had received offers from two other teams to work as *directeur.* He had the brain and the toughness to be good at that, and the passion for the sport to want to do it.

'What teams?' asked Bruyneel.

Betsy signalled across the room for Frankie to shut his mouth. Don't tell Bruyneel anything. Frankie blurted out the names anyway. Fuck Bruyneel. Frankie wasn't afraid.

Within days the job offers had evaporated.[34] Word was out that Frankie Andreu, with nine Tours as a *super domestique* on his CV, just wasn't a team player. Bruyneel resurfaced. He offered to put Frankie back on the payroll. American director for US Postal. Betsy and Frankie saw the play right then, they didn't like it but they had a family now and couldn't afford not to go with it. Bruyneel put Frankie back on the books. Kept him in America, away from people asking the wrong questions. And bought his silence for a while longer.

Incidents like that meant that, in the early days of our contact, Betsy didn't want to go public straight away. Whatever trappings his drug-fuelled success had brought to Lance Armstrong's life, Frankie Andreu's reward for being a lieutenant was a life determined by tight domestic budgets. Small things like Armstrong's refusal to pay him a mere $6000 when Frankie's contract with US Postal was ended had a serious effect on the family budget. In the larger scheme of things within US Postal, $6000 wasn't a lot. To Frankie and Betsy it made a difference.

The difficulty was always Frankie's job. He had quit riding

---

34 It wasn't the last time this would happen. Most notably in 2006, after Frankie's deposition in the SCA case was leaked, he was suddenly removed as *directeur sportif* of the Toyota United team. No satisfactory explanation ever emerged.

in 2001 but had remained in the sport. Pro cycling was the only job he'd ever known and Betsy knew that Armstrong could hurt her husband's career. Frankie wanted her to step back and let others lead the race to find out the truth about Armstrong.

'Who, Frankie? Who will do it?' she would ask before delivering her usual bottom line: 'I'm not lying for him; don't dare ask me to do that.'

It frustrated the hell out of Betsy that she had to be so guarded about what she said about Armstrong. As much as she wanted the truth out there, she knew the consequences for Frankie and their family if she was the one accusing Lance. Yet she was also able to take a longer-term view and she believed that one day she would be able to say exactly what was on her mind.

Parallel to the conversations Betsy and I had through 2003, I spoke on and off with Pierre Ballester. Though he didn't cover the Tour any more and had left *L'Équipe*, we remained friends. I learned from the Ferrari story in 2001 that a good newspaper – and the *Sunday Times* was a very good one – could only ever tell part of the Armstrong story.

From the moment on the 1999 Tour that gut instinct said, 'This guy ain't clean,' my sports editor Alex Butler had said, 'That's how you see it, that's how you write it.' In the English-speaking world, it was a story we had on our own; an 'exclusive' our rivals were happy to pass on. But the newspaper pieces could only stretch so far. It was time to write a book.

Pierre Ballester and I first discussed the possibility in August 2001, and knowing why he'd fallen out with *L'Équipe*,

I thought he would be a perfect co-author. He believed in the story and, with his contacts in France and his knowledge of the sport, he would bring a lot to the project. We agreed to put out feelers to my contacts in London publishing houses; he would try in Paris.

Most London publishing executives were enthused; all of their legal people were dead against. With a different set of libel laws, Pierre got a better response in France and in no time we were speaking with La Martinière. The deal was soon done and towards the beginning of 2002 we were dividing up the various angles. At the time it felt like the most exciting thing I'd ever done. Betsy was pleased with the news: 'A book,' she said. 'You know I'll help you whatever way I can.'

I flew to America in December 2003. It was a four-pronged trip. I spoke to riders Marty Jemison in Park City, Utah and Jonathan Vaughters in Colorado (while there, I also squeezed in a chat with Andy Hampsten). I went to Minnesota to meet Greg LeMond and to Dearborn to meet a woman I'd never met but who felt almost like a sister.

The trip was mainly an information-gathering exercise. In stories like this there is always a big difference between what you know and what you can actually print. For now I was happy to just know more. So the interviews with Jemison, Vaughters and Andreu took place in two parts. One general section, which I was allowed tape, were unsurprisingly bland. And then a juicier section, where I would only take notes. This was the good stuff. This was what they wanted me to know but couldn't be seen to tell me. I'm not sure about the legal status of such an arrangement but we all trusted each other to stick to the rules.

In Michigan I stayed at a plush hotel near where the Andreus lived in Dearborn. It would be the only time they let me stay at a hotel: I got the room in the basement of their home after that. A friendship grew out of what had been a business relationship: I went to Betsy's church, had coffee at her favourite diner; we walked through the pretty university town of Ann Arbor, she took me to a college football game involving her beloved University of Michigan. I went with big Frankie to watch little Frankie play ice hockey.

And Betsy and I talked, and talked. She lectured me on the need to pursue the truth. We laughed, too, and had fun seeing each other as Lance saw us. So I called her 'the crazed bitch' and she called me 'the troll'. (Not even in my top ten list of the worst things I have ever been called.)

I loved watching the dynamic of the relationship between Frankie and Betsy. One evening early on, Betsy cooked these amazing steaks with a lovely dressed salad. Frankie sat down, surveyed the table and frowned.

'Where's the ketchup?'

'You want ketchup? With this? Frankie? That's disgusting?'

'Yeah. I want ketchup.'

The ketchup was fetched and Frankie wrapped his hand around the bottle and shook it until a sea of red sauce covered half his plate. Betsy shook her head for the benefit of the visitor but flashed a little Mona Lisa smile to her husband.

On the cycling internet forums and in places where people have tried to tease out the multiple ramifications of the Lance Armstrong story, Betsy and Frankie's relationship has been a source of intrigue. There is wonder they survived as a couple, and many firmly believe the strain on their marriage was close to breaking point.

But that was simply not true. Of course there was a lot of stress, but the remarkable thing about that was the more stressed Betsy felt about the Lance situation the closer she felt to Frankie, and it worked the same the other way. At the time when Frankie was losing jobs and being passed over for positions that were made for him, they were at a low point, and Betsy suggested to Frankie that he should tell people they were getting divorced.

'Just say we're splitting up and you'll get a job.'

'Don't say that,' he said. 'That's not funny.'

'I'm not being funny. Just tell them we're getting divorced. You get a job and you tell them we've changed our minds.'

'Betsy, I'm not going to do that. I would never do that. Don't ask me to do that.'

She thought this was sweet because Frankie didn't often get mad, but she could see he was upset at her suggestion. And, anyway, she would never get divorced because of Armstrong.

Because Betsy and Frankie needed to go on raising their family with earnings from the cycling industry, we knew that Betsy couldn't go public with the hospital story. The retribution would be swift. So we decided to see if somebody with no stake in cycling or in Lance would confirm. The obvious person to track down was Lance's former girlfriend, Lisa Shiels, who had also been in the room that evening some seven years previously.

Back in 1996 Lisa had been a chemical engineering co-ed from the University of Texas. Lance had the reputation in the cycling world of being a legendary ladies' man and teammates

197

referred to him for a while as FedEx ('When you absolutely, positively have to have it overnight'). Doubtless as he mellowed he became more US Postal. Lisa had stuck with Lance through his diagnosis and treatments and it was said that he had intended to get engaged to her ... then he came across Kristin and fell in love. Since that time Lisa had, presumably, returned to a normal quiet life. Betsy undertook to make a few phone calls in an attempt to track her down. Then I would step in and see what Lisa was prepared to say about that day in the hospital.

A few years later, Betsy would wonder and spend a little time investigating if someone had been hacking into her computer. A lot of strange things happened and when the experts looked into it they agreed something was going on, but it would cost a lot of money to find out who was behind it. Betsy had a lot of things but not a lot of money. In any case, Lance always had a retinue of loyal flunkies who would call or email him if there was the slightest word of dissent in the winds. He got wind of Betsy's search for Lisa pretty quickly. Betsy had asked Becky, wife of Kevin Livingston, if she had a number.

On 15 December 2003, at 4.22 a.m., the Andreus' computer blinked out the news of a newly arrived email. It was directed to Frankie. From Lance, with love. He referenced a previous exchange where he had chastised Frankie for the behaviour of his wife.

Frankie, thanks for the help here. The more I think about this though the harder I find it to understand why your wife did what she did. Let me get this straight: you work for the team (or some form of USPS), oln [TV network] (where we work together on a daily basis), and all she cared about was getting left alone by this little idiot . . . to go around and say to Becky, 'Please don't tell Kevin,' is as snaky and conniving as it gets. I know Betsy is not a fan, and that's fine, but by helping to bring me down is not going to help y'all's situation. There is a direct link to all of our success here. I suggest you remind her of that. Again, not to be a dick but this really stings, and I cannot for the life of me, get my arms around it.

thanks, la

It was clear I was the 'little idiot' being referred to. That would change to the 'little troll', and I was grateful for that. Trolls have a little more about them. And I had come to terms with the fact that Lance and I were no longer in love. Of more concern was the situation Betsy and Frankie were in.

Frankie replied to Lance later that day. Wisely, he chose not to mention that a couple of hours later he would be sitting down to dinner with his house guest, the little idiot.

15 December 2003, 4.50 p.m.

I told you I would talk with Walsh. I tried to get some information for you and he finally called back. Betsy answered the phone and he started to ask her some questions but she told him she had nothing to say and called me to the phone. Generally he asked some questions about [Michele] Ferrari. I don't think he will call back again so I don't know if I can follow up at all on anything. I don't know if this helps at all but I tried.

And that was it. Somewhere out there Lance Armstrong was waiting and watching. The pulse just ran a little faster.

11

'When Johan Bruyneel and Lance advocate and support the use of performance-enhancing drugs and then make out they are cleaner than the driven snow, discrediting those that don't toe the line; well, you can't get away with that for ever.'

Emma O'Reilly, *L.A. Confidentiel*, 2004

One of the good things about working on a story that nobody much approves of is that you don't have any competition. You work away on the story, you check your facts, write your transcripts, dot your i's and cross your t's and all the time you sleep soundly at night. You know that there is no eager young super sleuth out there ready to scoop you in cold blood.

Take Emma O'Reilly. Another paper could easily have taken Emma but, in May 2003, just a few months after finding Betsy Andreu, Emma fell out of the sky and into my life.

I'd heard of her. An Irish name had cropped up in several

accounts of the early years of US Postal. O'Reilly? Emma? Irish? Who knew?

Paul Kimmage's contacts in the Dublin cycling community were better and fresher than mine. I had tried to get a contact number or a lead for this Emma O'Reilly and had failed. Paul hit a wall as well. Could be nothing. I'd come back to her again perhaps. Then one day an English colleague approached me at an event we were both covering. He knew the cycling game. Knew it well. He agreed there were questions about Armstrong and he didn't think I was wrong to ask them and, by the way, he said, 'I think Emma O'Reilly might talk.'

I kept a stiff upper lip. In my heart I wanted to embrace him.

'Any way of getting in touch with her?'

'Her former husband is a guy called Simon Lillistone. Get in touch with him and he'll get you a number for Emma.'

It surprised me that my colleague was prepared to try to put me in touch with Emma. It wasn't like we wrote for the same newspaper and the only explanation was that he was fearful of the consequences from the US Postal team of writing a piece that might be critical of Armstrong. From what he said, he knew Emma was going to spill some beans. I had a laptop which ran on spilled beans.

I rang Simon. He cautiously agreed to email Emma, and seemed like a guy who did everything cautiously. I explained and asked him to see if she would speak with me. Four or five days later I got a call from Emma O'Reilly.

'No, I don't mind telling you what I saw when I worked with the team,' she said. 'It wasn't right.'

John Walsh, almost two, sitting on Paul Kimmage's bike, wearing Paul's ACBB gear, and looking serene in the front garden of 10 rue Kléber in Paris, 1984.

A scene from the 1984 Tour de France with two of my heroes at the time, Sean Kelly (centre) and Stephen Roche. Eighteen years later I would be invited onto Ireland's number one television programme, *The Late, Late Show*, to debate with Roche evidence that appeared to show he was given EPO by Dr Francesco Conconi.

Two weeks short of his 22nd birthday, Lance Armstrong became the third youngest world road race champion when winning in Oslo in August 1993.

After spending 1997 recovering from testicular cancer, Lance Armstrong returned to racing with US Postal in 1998 and is seen here in his home city, Austin, with the State Capitol Building in the background, before setting off on a training ride.

Postal team member Jonathan Vaughters plays doctor as he and Armstrong goof around at the medical before the 1999 Tour de France. According to Emma O'Reilly, this was the occasion that Lance asked her to use her make-up to cover needle marks on his arm.

After feigning fatigue earlier, Armstrong was strong on the final climb to Alpe d'Huez in the 2001 Tour de France. In control, he had the energy to turn and check on his rivals, especially the German Jan Ullrich. This became known as 'the look'.

At a press conference in the Tour of Georgia when Armstrong announced he would retire after the 2005 Tour de France. Alongside him, the ever-present (at least from '99) Johan Bruyneel at his right shoulder.

Armstrong returned to professional cycling in January 2009 when he competed in the Cancer Council classic in Australia and he would be part of the peloton for a further two years.

Though Armstrong had the yellow jersey seven times on the Champs-Élysées and Floyd Landis once, Greg LeMond now stands as the only official winner of the Tour de France to have come from the United States. Here LeMond stands above his Z teammates after winning in 1990.

23 July 2006 seemed like the happiest day of Floyd Landis's sporting life as he enjoyed the triumphal ride down the Champs-Élysées after winning the Tour de France. The following week everything turned sour as Landis was told of the positive drug test that would take away his victory and destroy his reputation.

At the height of their powers, US Postal was the dominant team in the peloton and here, at Spain's Bicicleta Vasca in May 2001 are four of their strongest: (L-R) Robert Heras, Lance Armstrong, Tyler Hamilton and Jose Luis Rubiera.

Press Association

Press Association

Getty Images

A smiling Dr Michele Ferrari first teamed up with Armstrong in 1995 and he would have a significant input until the rider's final retirement in 2010. According to USADA's report, Armstrong paid Dr Ferrari over $1 million in fees.

Armstrong's agent/manager since 1995, Bill Stapleton is a former vice-president of the United States Olympic Committee and was part of the committee that helped bring the United States Anti-Doping Agency into being.

Frankie and Betsy Andreu suffered both professionally and personally because of their willingness to tell the truth in the story of Lance Armstrong, but the more stress that came their way the closer they felt as a couple.

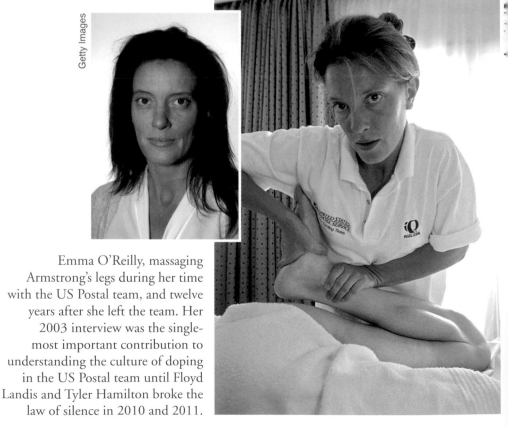

Emma O'Reilly, massaging Armstrong's legs during her time with the US Postal team, and twelve years after she left the team. Her 2003 interview was the single-most important contribution to understanding the culture of doping in the US Postal team until Floyd Landis and Tyler Hamilton broke the law of silence in 2010 and 2011.

Rex Features

Rex Features

L.A. Confidentiel became a bestseller in France but didn't go down so well in the world of Lance Armstrong and would be the cause of multiple lawsuits.

Pierre Ballester, co-author of *L.A. Confidentiel*, has most recently written a book about his sister Anne who has lived with the Yanomami people in the Amazon for the last eighteen years.

Getty Images

Quietly spoken Stephen Swart was the first witness to alert the world to Lance Armstrong's doping when giving an interview to *New Zealand Herald* journalist Phil Taylor in 1997.

Press Association

Sandro Donati, the Italian anti-doping campaigner who has done so much to expose corruption in his own country.

Press Association

Travis Tygart, chief executive officer of USADA, whose investigation into Lance Armstrong would reveal the truth behind the story of the 'seven-time Tour winner'.

The Edenbridge Bonfire Society in Kent, south-east England, burnt a 10-metre effigy of Lance Armstrong on 3 November as part of the community's traditional Guy Fawkes' night celebrations.

After the decision of the UCI to accept USADA's report stripping Armstrong of his seven Tour de France titles, the former champion then changed his profile on Twitter, deleting the words '7-time Tour de France winner'. A couple of weeks later Armstrong was more defiant, posting a photograph of himself in the company of his seven yellow jerseys at home in Austin.

I don't know if this was the happiest moment of my life but it would give the others a run for their money.

Emma O'Reilly came from Tallaght, a massive suburb to the south of Dublin often referred to as Tallaghtfornia for its sense of urban grey sprawl. Tallaght is an overgrown town that generally lacks the quality of being a town, but Tallaght produces feisty and proud people, all the same. They have a tribal quality. Emma O'Reilly is feisty and a little tribal. You wouldn't want to cross her.

There was cycling in her family – not a lot, but enough. Her brother Norbert rode locally with the Irish Road Club, and when Emma began going to his races she liked the easy atmosphere, she enjoyed the company of the weekend warriors. She was a runner herself, competing for the Tallaght club Cú Chulainn, but cycling seemed like better fun. From then on she ran only to keep fit.

Emma had that sense of adventure that has scattered Irish people all over the world. She began training as an electrician, a mildly unusual job choice for a woman in the Ireland of the early 1990s, and then decided that if she could become a massage therapist as well and get her name around the cycling community in Ireland there might be a chance to get to see a little bit of the world.

It worked. She finished training as an electrician in 1991 but, for the final couple of years of her apprenticeship, she had taken night courses in massage therapy and sports injury as well. She dedicated herself to this, got herself noticed and was soon working with the Irish national team. The work and travel dream materialised. The electrician work put bread on the table; the massage work brought travel. She worked a few

World Championships, brought her table to Britain and France again and again. Good times, but her feet itched. There was even more to the world.

At a race one day she got talking to a guy who was a mechanic with the LA Sherriff team on the west coast of America. She'd been thinking about the US for some time and when the mechanic saw her working he recommended her to his team as a *soigneur*.

So far so good. She got her visa paperwork sorted and took it to the US Embassy in Dublin. I'm Emma O'Reilly and I'm off to live in Santa Barbara where I will be working as a *soigneur* for a cycling team. They looked at Emma and her qualifications. Electrician and massage therapist? Of course. Of course. Get a fake job as a '*soigneur*', whatever the heck that is, and then disappear into the world of contractors and building sites? Not on our watch, Missy. They declined to stamp her visa.

As somebody would later tell her in times of crisis: what goes around comes around. The following year she won a green card through the US immigration lottery system. She touched down in Boulder, Colorado, in the spring of 1994, not long before her 24th birthday.

She began working with the San Francisco-based team Shaklee, but they said they couldn't offer her work for the full summer. So she went back to Boulder and began working in electrical sales. The next year Shaklee came looking for her again, which was not a surprise because Emma was a good massage therapist. This time she ran away with the circus and stayed.

The cycling world is small and reputations are made

quickly on the basis of character and efficiency. Emma was good and had a way with people. She didn't defer, she had a sense of humour and a spark. She was a team player. A rider called Mike Engelman knew her work and when he moved from Coors to US Postal (or Montgomery Securities, as the team was known at the time before becoming US Postal in 1997), he put in the good word.

Still, it wasn't a done deal. She had no idea at first what she was getting into. She got a call telling her that the team would fly her to San Francisco for an interview. 'Could they not just call me?' she thought, but she was impressed. Montgomery Securities sounded to her like the sort of operation that sold home alarms. She didn't want to seem grateful for being flown out to San Francisco, but it did give the sense that this team meant business.

By accident she found out at the eleventh hour that she was dealing with a firm of financiers. Change of dress code. Bye, bye jeans. Buy, buy business suit.

She hit San Francisco and took the shuttle to the Financial District where she found the Pyramid Building, as instructed. Even for a finance company, the building was pretty impressive. So this was how the other half lived. A security guard accompanied her in the silent lift to the 23rd floor and ushered her towards the office of Thom Weisel.

It went well. For a few minutes she fretted that they intended putting her to work with a new women's team they hoped to start. The prospect was none too exciting. She made her feelings known: 'I don't want to be involved in the women's programme, thanks. I know it's terrible to say this but I can't handle women riders. It's better to have a guy deal with them.'

The women's programme never materialised. Thom Weisel's dream was of a serious team that would compete in Europe. Everything was geared toward that dream. Emma left San Francisco with the feeling that all had gone well.

That was December. She came home to Tallaght for Christmas. Flew back to Boulder in January and the next day she found herself in Ramona, near the Mexican border, about three quarters of an hour inland drive from San Diego. Training camp. The adventure had truly started.

This was the ticket to the big time.

Emma and I spoke a few times on the phone. She was prepared to talk but was cautious, too. There would be consequences. Finally it was agreed I would travel to meet her in Liverpool where she was living with her boyfriend, Mike Carlisle. I would try to sell her the idea of a major interview to be published within the covers of a book that would ask a range of questions about the state of cycling and the reign of Lance Armstrong.

She would be one voice among many.

I had no idea as to the story she would tell, but I knew she had spent five years with the US Postal team, and worked as personal masseuse to Lance for two of those years. She knew a lot more than I knew.

That first meeting in Liverpool was a pure getting-to-know-you occasion. We went for supper to Villa Jazz in Oxton out on the Wirral peninsula. Her boyfriend Mike came along, and for much of the evening we spoke about his beloved Manchester United. The other stuff could wait. Impatient as I was, I didn't bring a recorder or notebook.

Emma had to get a sense of who I was and of my reliability and sincerity. I had to get an idea of her credibility.

I was interested in sussing out her motivation for wanting to speak publicly about her time with US Postal. She hinted several times that doing this might cause her problems, but on the other hand she didn't see why she shouldn't speak about what she had seen. That evening I didn't want us to get into any of the stuff that went on in the team. It could wait.

My sense was that Emma believed cycling had lost its soul, that doping was rife, that this wasn't the sport she had fallen in love with as a teenager in Tallaght, hitting the road with the gang from the Irish Road Club. Yet she still felt an affinity with and loyalty to various people within the cycling world.

As she mentioned in that first call, she knew of riders who had died because of doping. She had been an employee of a major team and I would learn that, in the end, she had been treated unfairly. A pragmatist, she didn't resent that overly, but she felt that it excused her from the law of *omerta* that held the whole thing together. If she didn't want to carry US Postal's secret practices around in her head she wouldn't. First, though, she would have to find somebody she could trust to handle what she had to say.

In our early discussions, I think that what attracted Emma to the idea of being interviewed for the book (which would become *L.A. Confidentiel*) was the idea of being one of a number of voices speaking out. That seemed preferable and more manageable than the fall-out from a one-off interview. That first night in Oxton we got on well, and at the end of the evening we agreed to stay in touch by phone and to meet up a few weeks later to formally do the interview.

It would be early July before we sat down and faced each other again. We met in Emma's home at Oxton, sitting on the sofa in the living room, my digital recorder between us. Coverage of that day's Tour stage had already started when we met, and we watched a short burst of Eurosport before we started talking. It was a flat stage and not very interesting.

We watched for a while before Emma said decisively, 'We don't want to watch this, do we?' and banished the picture with the zapper. If it had been a half-decent mountain stage that would have been different.

Emma's story would take six hours to tell and the transcript would run to about 40,000 words. As she spoke, I realised Emma O'Reilly's voice in this story wouldn't just be one of many. Among the many, hers would stand out. This was a world that had possessed her. Now it was letting her go.

The nascent team with which Emma linked up in Ramona in January 1996 might have had the backing of money but it didn't have the smell of money. Ramona was a one-horse place and in the evenings they all ate together in the local sizzler. There was another female *soigneur* too: Alison Baker, the sister of Darren, a rider in the team.[35] The team director's nephew was working as a mechanic. The atmosphere was good and the plan was to do a few smaller European races over the following two years and then to hit the old continent

35 When the house of cards came tumbling down in October 2012, two former US Postal riders issued a statement calling on statement calling on UCI president Pat McQuaid and honorary president Hein Verbruggen to resign. One was Scott Mercier, the other Darren Baker.

full time. Emma couldn't quite see it all working out so smooth, not there in tatty little Ramona, but it was an adventure gift wrapped in steady pay cheques.

Then Andy Hampsten joined. Hampsten was a veteran on the descent but he was a name, which suggested intent, and he could still climb better than anyone in the team. There was potential in guys like Tyler Hamilton and Eddy Gragus, but no one was getting carried away.

That first year was the Galibier of learning curves: long and steep. Emma worked the domestic programme Stateside in the early months but found herself in Europe from April. The team stuck to competing in the smaller races. Any time they traded pedal strokes with the big boys they got crushed. As the year progressed, riders began to come up with reasons why they were so far behind other teams.

It was a source of tension in the team. By the Tour de Suisse, riders were lobbying the team doctor Prentice Steffen for something with a bit more poke than Anadin and the vitamin pills he was dishing out, but he wouldn't shift. Doping was a constant topic of team conversation. Emma, still in love with the sport, stayed out of the chat. She didn't want disillusionment to spoil the adventure.

As her responsibilities grew she gained a reputation for being efficient, for being a top-class masseuse and for taking no shit. The crew had a distinct Polish flavour at the time and a guy called Waldek Stepniowski was the head *soigneur*. First, Waldek had to learn a thing or two.

One day he said, 'Emma, I need to know what your time of month is?'

'You what?' she asked.

'Just so I understand your mood swings.'

'Hey. I have an excuse. What's yours?'

Another day she caught Waldek looking her up and down appreciatively as he talked to a buddy.

'Don't you ever fucking eye me up and down like that again,' she said. Soon she had made proper space for herself in the testosterone-splashed world of the team.

Late in the year they won a stage of the Tour of China and the money was divvied among the team. Emma got about $3000 which went on top of her $20,000 a year salary. It was a pittance for a life on the road, a life of 24/7 availability, but she figured that she had no expenses when she was on the road and that this was what she'd come to America for.

From that first meeting with Thom Weisel at his offices in the Pyramid Building, she knew that whatever results were achieved in '96 they would be bettered in '97; and that prospect excited her. Good wages or bad, she wanted in.

Of course other things were happening in late 1996. Lance Armstrong, the young American rider with Motorola, had cancer. And rival team Motorola were departing the scene. By the time Emma got back to Ramona for pre-season work the following January, her team, now known as US Postal, had acquired some Motorola trucks and a biggish name, Viatechslav Ekimov. Too big a name for most of the team to get their mouths around actually. He was known ever after as Eki.

Andy Hampsten had retired and the team also had a new *directeur sportif*, a friendly Dane by the name of Johnny Weltz, and a new doctor, a Spaniard, Pedro Celaya. And another promising American rider, George Hincapie.

Emma worked the American spring races, but the word

coming back from Europe was that Johnny Weltz and Waldek weren't hitting it off. Neither were Waldek and Pedro Celaya enjoying their new togetherness. Emma smiled. In time the call came. An SOS. *Soigneur* needed. Emma arrived in Europe in time for April's Tour of Flanders.

That season they weren't competitive or particularly organised but they got through, and continued to learn the ropes. Still much of the talk was about drugs. Riders would comment that they had ridden *pan y agua* or on 'bread and water'. Some riders never rode that way apparently. In the US Postal set-up, they were looking at some astonishing performances from rivals and often they would shake their heads and ask each other just where that had come from. 'What planet is he on?'

The culture was changing, but it was still acceptable within US Postal to dismiss a rival who evidently doped as a cheat or a moron.

Emma felt that if there were drugs around US Postal that summer it was minor-league stuff compared to what seemed to be going on elsewhere. The only time she thought awhile on the question was when a colleague from the Rabobank team said to her, late in the season: 'Well, we all know that you have a good doctor now.'

Emma took the compliment at face value. They had nine riders and all had stayed healthy, so Pedro Celaya must have been a good doctor. But maybe something else was being implied.

Johnny Weltz had brought a Spanish *soigneur* in with him as part of his deal. A guy called José. He wasn't greatly appreciated for his massage, but his facility with a needle was revered. What was in the syringes which José so deftly applied and disposed of wasn't Emma's business. Some of the European 'culture' was seeping in, however.

Late in the year, Emma travelled to the World Championships in San Sebastián with the Irish team. She got a call in the hotel from a Postal colleague. 'They've signed him. This will be great. Things will change.'

'Him' was Lance Armstrong. Things did change.

Emma is a natural teller of stories. I knew from that first dinner we had had that she had things to tell me. I knew it would be worthwhile but I never guessed at her sense of detail. Also she had a diary in which she had kept notes. A smart, articulate woman with a diary. No downside. Better still, she had a sense of humour and had retained affection for Lance Armstrong. He wasn't perfect but he had treated her right and respectfully. She hoped that might continue.

Lance Armstong arrived in Emma's life in 1998 in, where else, Ramona. He arrived with Christian Vande Velde. Emma shook hands with Vande Velde: 'Hi, I'm Emma.'

She had the impression Armstrong was speaking to somebody on the phone as he came in, so she ignored him. Vande Velde laughed and when she looked again Armstrong was standing with an outstretched hand.

'Here, he's trying to say hello,' said Vande Velde.

They shook hands and from there out they got on just fine.

Emma was a good worker and bright enough to see the deficiencies in the organisation. Armstrong had been with Motorola before his illness and he had helped 'Europeanise' their attitude and preparation. Now that nobody else would give him a shot after his recovery he had settled for this, a small contract with a middle-sized team – but big bonuses would accrue if he performed well.

He too could see what the team lacked in comparison to bigger, more successful outfits. That bonded them. He liked to work with Emma because she was the best of an average lot.

In 1998, though, despite two years of virtually holding her hands over her ears whenever there was talk of drugs among riders or crew, she got dragged into the circle anyway. George Hincapie overheard her say that she had to go to Belgium for a trip. He asked if she would mind picking up something for him from a friend. No problem. The friend was a person known to her but no longer associated with the team.

Emma arranged a meeting at the Hotel Nazareth in Ghent. The package was handed over. She was surprised by how small it was but said she would try to get it to Hincapie if she saw him down in Girona in Spain, where several of the team were living. If not, she would catch up with him in the States and hand the package over there. There was a pause. Her contact said: 'Emma, don't do that. Give it to George. It's testosterone and you don't want to transport it yourself.'

'Really. And why would George want testosterone?' she asked, unable to help her own curiosity.

'He needs to have strength for a sprint at the end of long stages.'

'Oh.'

By the end of 1998 this minor piece of work as a drugs

mule would look distinctly innocent. The Tour de France began in Emma's home town Dublin, so she headed back to Ireland a few days early for some family time. She arranged to meet the team as they came off the ferry.

Unbeknown to her, as she'd been spending the day with her family, Willy Voet, the Festina *soigneur*, had been arrested carrying a cornucopia of performance-enhancing and leisure drugs in his car. So when she got to the ferry, which was an hour late, the Irish police were present. She thought for half a second they were giving the team an escort to their hotel and thanked them.

'No,' they said, 'we're customs officers. We have some searches to do.'

This was home turf for Emma O'Reilly and on this particular turf nobody is very impressed by uniforms. She gave the customs officers some advice.

'Lads, let me tell you, for your own sakes, don't even try it. There'll be a riot. They've been travelling all day, they're very grumpy. Come to the hotel in the morning if you have to.'

And remarkably, as the biggest scandal in Tour history was breaking all around them, the customs men left it at that. It stayed like that for the duration of the Tour. US Postal were somehow protected by their innocence, their American-ness and their big brand backers; they seemed somehow to be set aside as war loomed between the police and the teams. And when it got a bit scary one afternoon, with the police in the field where the team vehicles were parked, US Postal flushed a lot of stuff down the drain.

It is the summer of 2003 as we are sitting and talking in Emma's house: almost exactly four years since I watched

Lance ride the 1999 prologue and came away scratching my head. It's been four years of circling a fortress, finding little cracks but never anything big enough to let me in. I've been on trips all over the place speaking to scientists, cyclists, police, doctors, testers.

Now here I am chatting with a woman from Dublin and, incredibly, she is from the inside. She's talking about Lance Armstrong, the world's favourite sporting icon and medical miracle. And she has the goods. Just like that. I keep glancing at the tape recorder making sure the little red light is still illuminated. I try to keep my mouth from hanging open. It gets better, stranger. I can't believe I've been sent down this trail. Emma tells me stories and anecdotes and this is an interview I never want to end. Maybe to pause for a second, bring the world in by the ear and say, 'Listen to this woman, just listen.'

Lance didn't compete in the 1998 Tour, but afterwards he was back in Europe to ride the Tour of Holland. Emma drove him to the airport after that and, as he was getting out of the team car, he handed her a bag and said, 'Look, Emma, I didn't get rid of these, will you get rid of them for me?'

The bag was full of empty, used syringes.

She accepted the bag but didn't know what to do. She was heading to Ghent in Belgium and when she got over the border and relaxed a little she found herself getting pulled over for being marginally over the speed limit. She cursed and cursed before winding down the window for the policeman. She noticed she was shaking with fear.

'I'm sorry about that, officer.'

'No. Do you know Mark Gorski?'

'Yes. He's my boss.'

The policeman was a former rider. She gave him a contact number for his old friend. Emma and her syringes drove off into the night leaving the policeman behind on the road waving cheerily.

The casual nature of it all astonishes me. Sure, there's a cloak-and-dagger element to what Emma is relating, but there is a bravura too. An arrogance. Just dump these for me.

She tells me she deliberately refused to get involved in finding out who was taking what, as most European *soigneurs* would. Her style was to open the truck where the medications were kept and tell the team, 'There you go, lads: help yourselves.'

Armstrong's view of the other *soigneurs* never really changed while Emma was there, so he tended to work with her exclusively and she would massage him and listen to what he had to say, his complaints and his views on other riders. In terms of staff, Lance was the kingmaker. People came and went at his whim. Johan Bruyneel arrived as *directeur sportif* for 1999 and became Lance's enforcer. He promoted Emma to the post of head *soigneur*, but the honeymoon period between them was brief.

She paints a comprehensive picture of a team more ramshackle on the inside than it ever appeared from the outside. The characters, the incompetents, the savants, the bluffers. Again and again she makes me laugh. Her relationship with the Bruyneels, Johan and his former wife Christelle, was a book all in itself.

'I know this is terrible but he [Bruyneel] wore cheap clothes, even though he was quite wealthy; he was a team director, but he never dressed really appropriately. When everyone else wore khakis, he would wear those stupid things with the zips on them and stuff like that. Things you could turn into three-quarter-length shorts!

'Oh god, the poor fella got beaten up by the ugly tree coming down.'

While the world thought he was Lance's lieutenant and enforcer, Emma viewed him differently. Lance's lap dog.

What fragments I'd gathered over the years about life inside the US Postal team, Emma was able to glue together easily. She had been in the Last Tango restaurant in Sestriere the night that Michele Ferrari came to dine with the team. She wasn't surprised to see Ferrari with Lance. It confirmed a lot of things.

'I knew his role in cycling was dirty, that no rider he worked with was known to be clean.'

She described the deterioration of her relationship with Johan Bruyneel, and the surprise she felt when having been asked to drive to Spain from France in May 1999. That day at the team's base in Piles, Bruyneel even managed to squeeze some pleasantries out of himself as he slipped a pill box into her hand to be brought back to Lance.

She told Simon, her boyfriend at the time, what was happening as part of their journey. It created a sort of giddy nervousness in the car. During an earlier squabble, Bruyneel had commandeered the last team car available, leaving Emma and Simon to hire a rental. As they waited to be waved through at the border, Emma wondered if Bruyneel hadn't planned the entire thing this way because a rental car was less likely to be stopped than a pro-cycling team car.

She brought the pill box to Armstrong and left it at that. Soon after, her relationship with Bruyneel began to become intolerable.

The 1999 Tour was a triumph, of course, and she had written in her diary before the start, 'We're going in to win the Tour.'

And then there was that strange incident the day before the prologue, when Lance noticed the syringe marks on his arm *en route* to the pre-race medical. He wanted Emma to spread some of her make-up over the needle bruises, but she said her make-up would be no good for that job. She went to a pharmacy and got some proper concealer. With some horror she looked at the job she'd done, thought it looked terrible, but he seemed happy.

One evening well into the race, she was giving Lance his evening massage when there was a big kerfuffle about a positive cortisone test. Two team officials were there, then a third, and they agreed that a backdated prescription was the best way to deal with the problem. That was accepted and she got the impression everyone just wanted a 'clean' Tour.

They said Lance had saddle sore, but he never mentioned that to her and she didn't believe it. She did see the team doctor Luis del Moral, who had taken over from Celaya at the start of the season, getting all hot and bothered about the prescription, as if he'd been asked to rewrite the law of gravity. But that took care of it. Lance Armstrong. Pure as driven snow.

'Now, Emma,' Armstrong said at the end of that night, 'you know enough to bring me down.'

The Tour de France of 1999 would be Emma's last. The

relationship between her and Bruyneel deteriorated quickly after that. She believed that Bruyneel felt threatened by the respect that Armstrong had for the *soigneur*. Emma knew she was empowered by that respect. Something had to give. The lap dog knew how to bite. Bruyneel marginalised and bullied her to the point where she knew for a considerable time that this part of her life was ending. After stealing her diary, Bruyneel went to her colleagues and lied about her writing nasty things about them.

Emma resigned her job in early 2000.

It was another staff member who had told her about the intrusion into her diary. The same guy told her not to worry.

'In one conversation with him he twirled round the front wheel of the bike he was working on. "See, Emma-*tje*," he said, using the affectionate version of my name in Dutch, because we were friends. "Look at the valve there. When I spin the wheel it goes round but the valve always comes round too. Remember it, Emma-*tje*: what goes around comes around."'

It was coming around now. Surely.

12

'One must not cheat anybody, not even the world of its victory.'

Franz Kafka

One evening, when things were going badly, Jan Swart turned to her husband Stephen and asked him a simple question.

'Stephen, why did you do this?'

This. This had brought fire and brimstone down upon them. For this they had lost friends and business. For this they had been excoriated in low-rent media. For this her husband was portrayed as a bitter loser. That hurt her so much.

This. Why had he done it?

And Stephen said: 'Jan, when I'm on my rocking chair at eighty-four years of age and I don't have a lot of time left to live, I will look back on this and I will regard it as one of the finest things I've ever done in my life.'

That was all she needed to know. A good man is hard to find. They would battle on.

When Lance Armstrong unravels his life and pulls apart all the strands, he'll wonder (just perhaps) at the serendipitous nature of events that would eventually undo him. Stephen Swart was an early piece in the jigsaw: a former rider and, as they say, a stand-up guy.

He came into my orbit in a roundabout way. Consider the odds. An Irish journalist, through a series of life events, comes in middle age to make a new start in England. He and his wife, their five kids and their new daughter Molly wind up in Cambridge. Molly might not go to school but she'd meet the scholars.

In Cambridge they would meet a distinguished New Zealander, an investigative journalist who, having done a fellowship in Oxford in 1996, was now completing a fellowship at Cambridge. For his fellowship at Wolfson College, Phil Taylor was studying sports doping. He trawled the internet for UK journalists who wrote about doping and, as this was the very month when I happened to be in France interviewing Lance Armstrong, my name was soon in his net.

He's a journalist, so he got the number easily enough.

'David, you wouldn't happen to live anywhere near Cambridge?' he said.

'About four miles,' I said.

He came for lunch, stayed for the afternoon and the time flew. I told him he had to go see Sandro Donati in Rome, which he did. He, too, loved Sandro. We talked about the Armstrong case and he told of an interview he had in 1997 with a compatriot of his, Stephen Swart, who had ridden with the Motorola team and been in the same team as Lance Armstrong for two years.

Phil wanted to do a story about Stephen's particular experience in the Motorola team and how it was decided that only by using EPO could they hope to compete. Twenty-three-year-old Lance Armstrong was one of the strongest advocates for doping in the team. Phil wanted to write a story about Stephen's personal experiences, but it was too soon for Stephen: he was in his first retirement season and he wasn't ready for the backlash. Soon afterwards, Phil gave me a transcript of Stephen's recollection of doping in the Motorola team.

I wanted to meet Stephen Swart.

Now Auckland, New Zealand, is one of those places in the world where you can't really claim to be just passing through. So when preparing to cover the Rugby World Cup in Australia in 2003 I mentioned to Alex, my long-suffering friend and boss, that it might be the mark of a great editor to send a winged minion across to New Zealand to do a piece on Jonah Lomu, the great All Black wing who was suffering from kidney disease at the time.

Not long afterwards, Alex had the idea of sending a winged minion to Auckland to do a piece on Jonah Lomu. Selflessly I undertook the four-hour flight from Sydney and – why not? I was going to be passing through anyway – made time to see Stephen Swart. I met him at a hotel in the city and he drove us to the port where the yachts rocked gently on their anchors and the Tour de France seemed to be part of another universe.

'Is it here that the *Rainbow Warrior* was sunk?'

'Ah, those French …' Stephen remembers with a grin. 'Over there. That one. She won the America's Cup.'

We found a restaurant, kept the harbour and yachts in our sights, and talked about things in general. If he didn't mind, I wanted to do the interview at his home the next day. He was cool with that. Very little in Stephen's life was a hassle. I told him about Betsy and Frankie Andreu, Greg LeMond, Jonathan Vaughters, Prentice Steffen, Emma O'Reilly and many others who had all helped to show that Lance Armstrong was part of a doping culture at both Motorola and US Postal.

It mattered to him that he wouldn't be the only one putting his head on the chopping block.

Stephen grew up in Morrinsville on the North Island and in his junior racing days he and his older brother Jack were big names in the New Zealand cycling community. Jack would be New Zealand cyclist of the year six times, but Stephen would be the one to have the pro career and get to ride the Tour.

In middle age the two of them are still cycling. There's a clipping I saw from just a couple of years ago where Jack won a stage on a race in New Zealand on the same day that Stephen was voted 'Most Aggressive' rider. They make them different down there.

Just eight years before our meeting in 2003, Stephen had been earning his bread in Europe riding a bike. He'd loved Europe, even if it hadn't showered him with reward. He'd become a hard and respected pro and the Tour de France was for him the most exhilarating time of the year, a career highlight.

When he stopped cycling, he and Jan and the kids had come back home. Having been a rider all his life, Stephen worked for a while in a company associated with cycling, then he started his own company as a property developer. He finds a place that needs some attention, buys it, does the work and puts it back on the market. Not easy, but it's a living and life is good.

There's a gap there, which he is conscious of, though. I've heard Paul Kimmage and other guys talk about the same thing. The void of not knowing. Stephen gave the best years of his life to cycling and when the sport spat him out he felt as if he had been short-changed, duped.

Doping had done that. He couldn't throw himself into the life of the needle, not in the way you needed to. He tried it and felt uncomfortable with it and with himself. He'd never know how far he might have gone if he had been racing in a clean peloton.

The transition back to ordinary life had been difficult. The Swarts didn't have a lot of money and then suddenly the dream was dead, and the rest of life looked like it might be something they just settled for. It had been easy to unpack the suitcases, but it was harder to deal with their contents.

'I said to myself, "Did I really learn the profession?" In other words, did I know enough on the medical plan? Maybe I wasn't a good enough pharmacist? But why was it necessary to learn that? You do not get into sports thinking that you have to learn this type of thing. You don't go to school saying to yourself: "Well, I want to be a racing cyclist, and to be one, I'll have to know medicine and get a pharmacist's diploma." I felt that I had more than average abilities, that if you remove everything and just look at the guys naked on their bikes, I would have had an advantage. I knew I had this advantage, but that, against professional cyclists, it meant nothing.'

Stephen Swart became a pro back in 1987. There were no firework displays. It wasn't breaking news. A nation didn't see him off at the quays. He signed with the English team ANC-Halfords. Meanwhile, fate had taken up kickboxing. Six months later, Stephen wasn't getting his monthly wage of £500. The team was broke.

Back then he was a wide-eyed and innocent Kiwi. Before the team dissolved, the riders had been rounded up by their old-school *soigneur*, Angus Fraser, and each injected with an undetermined substance. They all wondered but nobody asked.

'We had complete confidence in this guy, because we thought he knew what he was doing. Like if you go to the doctor when you're sick, you have confidence in him. You think it can't be very bad since it doesn't test positive. And I wasn't a big enough cyclist to have the right to ask questions. I remember two cyclists from the team who carried their own briefcases, and it wasn't papers that they carted around with them.'

Having gone over the edge with Halfords, he headed for the glamour of Belgium. He joined the SEFB outfit in 1988, noting that the team was sponsored by a bank. At that time, some people believed that cycling was clean and others believed that banks were a safe bet. Stephen believed both.

He arrived in Liège to find that SEFB was a modest organisation and one of cycling's wallflowers. The team struggled to get invited to decent races. Their *directeur sportif* was a character: Ferdinand Bracke, record holder for the hour in 1967, when he rode 48.093km in 60 minutes. Bracke was winner of the Tour of Spain in 1971, third in the Tour de France in 1968 and an old cyclist straight from central casting.

Among Stephen's teammates was a guy at the other end of the colour scale, a rider called Johan Bruyneel.

Back then Bruyneel was a young professional and not yet a member of the boss class. He was riding for the first time in the peloton, having forged himself a good reputation on the Belgian amateur circuit. His teammates had high hopes for him.

SEFB's small budget and half-filled-out dance card meant that there was no doctor attached to the team, and in the matter of doping everybody was left to choose for himself. The *soigneurs*, of course, were more opinionated than taxi drivers.

'One evening, I went to a *soigneur*'s room,' Swart remembers. 'All the products were there and the cyclists came to use them as they wanted. Another evening during the Tour de Suisse, we were sitting in a room and the *soigneur* came in with medications. Everyone helped themselves. The guys filled up these enormous syringes like you use for horses and shot up. I can tell you it wasn't the first time. It was the culture.'

Swart doesn't know what he took. Because he was young, and he didn't speak Flemish or French, he was left to himself. Afraid of medications and ignorant of their use, he generally avoided them. This was before the time of EPO, when people still cheated in minor chords. On his day, a clean rider could still catch a cheat.

Swart had a natural exuberance in the saddle and when he was going well he loved his job. He finished 13th in the general classification of the Tour de Suisse. In the big mountain stages he was equal to the best. After the finish, he went back to Belgium by car with Bracke. They talked a lot.

'Bracke was crazy; he couldn't even drive normally. He was anxious over nothing. Something in him wasn't working right. During this trip he told me about all the big projects he had for me.'

The best laid plans, etc.

The season ended prematurely for Swart, whose mother became seriously ill and died two weeks after his return to New Zealand. He took a job in a bicycle shop in Auckland, and slowly got back his desire to train. Around the end of the year, he decided to reboot his career in the United States, a place Swart appreciated because the races weren't as hard there and the sport had a more hip, more middle-class, slightly alternative feel. The doping culture, which was everywhere in Europe, was practically non-existent.

He began riding with a club in California and before long he had won enough races to come to the attention of Jim Ochowicz, *directeur sportif* with the Motorola team. Ochowicz offered him a place on the team and an opportunity to return to the European circuit.

Swart couldn't resist the temptation. He'd become bored with the States. He was riding with Coors, a decent team, but the landscape was limited: an enthusiastic culture, but the same races every year, and it wasn't competitive enough. He wasn't getting any younger and whatever he was winning was being eaten by utility bills. Time to shoot for the moon.

When he got back to Europe he found that things had changed, changed utterly.

'In 1994, everything was completely changed. The increase in speed was incredible. Especially in the mountains. In 1988, I had been as good as some of the best. On the climbs, I could stay in the top ten. On the 1988 Tour de Suisse, I was at the summit with the Dutchman Gert-Jan Theunisse and Steven Rooks, the best climbers of the Tour de France three weeks later. And now, though I knew I had made progress, I couldn't keep up.

'They didn't use the same gears as before. No one put on the little brackets any more. All that had disappeared in five years. Incredible, the level had gone through the ceiling. I understood pretty fast that I was going to have to face something. I had heard EPO talked about, the word had made its way to the United States. We knew that it doped the blood, increasing the oxygen capacity, but I never thought that it could have changed things so much.

'At Motorola, some of the old guys were a little demoralised. For example, in a race at the beginning of the season like Tirreno–Adriatico [an Italian stage race held at the beginning of March], we spent a week racing full force, only to survive. Just to finish the race. It was completely crazy.'

Competition was counterfeit. This was a pharmaceutical trade with a sports theme. The teams that used EPO were stronger than those that didn't. Full stop. And the authorities didn't seem to mind. You joined the arms race or you got out. Those who used the most, those who doped to the edge, dominated the races.

One of Stephen Swart's teammates now in Europe was an

impatient young American called Lance Armstrong. He'd become world champion the previous season. The class of the team. Their paths had crossed on the American circuit not twelve months previously. Stephen told the story of how Lance came to win the Thrift Drug Triple Crown of Cycling. Back in 1993, an elbow of the US season was a three-race series in the eastern states. Three races: the Thrift Drug classic in Pittsburgh, the K-Mart West Virginia classic and the Philadelphia CoreStates Championship.

Three races and the prize on offer for the overall winner of the Thrift Drug Crown of Cycling was $1 million.

Lance was the hotshot of the field. After Pittsburgh, where Lance showed his dominance as a one-day racer, the series continued on through West Virginia. Lance proceeded to boss the five-day stage race. Before the end, Stephen Swart's Coors Light team were approached with an offer.

The contact, as far as he could remember, came from Frankie Andreu of Motorola through Scott McKinley of Coors. The offer was simple. Don't attack and there'll be a $50,000 kickback. A discussion took place on the road as they cycled and, afterwards, they held a meeting in Lance Armstrong's and Phil Anderson's hotel room. Lance was the kid; Anderson the old Aussie gunslinger who'd slugged it out with Bernard Hinault at the 1981 Tour.

Stephen didn't feel he had it in him to challenge Armstrong anyway. If anybody else did they didn't say so. Not McKinley. Not Mike Engelman, their big-name guy. Nobody. And $50,000 for mislaying their aggression would make for a nice little bonus.

So they just played along accordingly. In the race Lance was leading, and Coors' Mike Engelman and a guy called Steve Hegg were the only riders with the remote chance of a challenge. Lance Armstrong led them home for the second leg of the Triple Crown. And in Philadelphia he wrapped it up. The Coors Light boys were unclear as to whether the *entente cordial* was supposed to continue in the city of brotherly love, but Armstrong made it irrelevant by being untouchable.

A few weeks later the contents of an envelope containing $50,000 in cash was divided among the Coors Light boys. Nobody was any the wiser.[36]

Swart was there and Armstrong was there on one of the watershed days for doping, the day in 1994 when the Michele Ferrari-doped Italian team Gewiss-Ballan came home one-two-three in the Flèche Wallonne.

From the start of the season they'd been exceptionally strong but now they were flaunting it. Now Ferrari was advertising his programme in a way that made everybody else take notice. And if anyone was still so blind as not to see, Ferrari casually equated EPO to orange juice the next day. He didn't say the Gewiss cyclists used EPO, but he went as close as he could. EPO briefly emerged from the shadows, introduced itself to the world at large, and retreated again with the words, 'You know where to find me.'

36 The story would be fairly unremarkable were it not for the ironies sown. The buying and selling of stages, one-day races and criteriums is an age-old practice in cycling, but after his retirement Stephen Swart's next turn in the limelight would be when he told this story as part of his testimony in the SCA case in 2006. SCA were withholding money due to be paid to Lance Armstrong. SCA were an insurance company who accepted premiums to guarantee big prizes like that due to Armstrong for winning successive Tours de France. (Or the million dollars for the Thrift Drug Triple Crown of Cycling.)

At the time, EPO had been banned for three years by the UCI but, while there was no test capable of detecting its presence in the urine, this performance enhancer was all the rage. It was open season.

One rider who sat up and took good note of what was going on was Lance Armstrong, who was wearing his rainbow jersey as world champion that day. Armstrong was in good shape and he was hungry. He drove himself furiously, trying to catch the three breakaways, but just couldn't reach his prey. He was one of the big losers that day. And it being Lance, he felt cheated, not defeated.

A year later, in March of 1995, after the Milan–San Remo race, Stephen went to Como where a number of the Motorola team were living, including Lance, Frankie Andreu, Kevin Livingston and George Hincapie. Team doctor Max Testa lived nearby as well.

The day after the race, the Motorola boys hit the roads for a recovery ride, just a simple stretch and pedal down the road. No pressure or intensity, just for a couple of hours turning the pedals while shooting the breeze.

One of the topics of the day was EPO and how, after the pastings they had taken the previous season, the team was still riding at such a disadvantage to the European teams. As professionals they felt they would have to look seriously at how to rectify the problem. Or else they'd all be home competing before ten people on lonely roads in West Virginia.

It was a freewheeling conversation in all senses. They'd break into different pairings as they rode and talk about it. They were mostly young Americans who had grown up in a different cycling culture to Europeans. Guys who never thought doping would be part of the deal. As a New Zealander, Swart could see that. Lance Armstrong agreed that this wasn't what he'd got into the sport for, but at the end of the day you had to step up.

He told the team that if they were going to go to the Tour they were going to have to produce. Armstrong didn't spell out explicitly what he intended to do or when he was going to start doing it. There were no rocket scientists on the ride that day but they all worked out what he meant.

Feeling he should commit to Armstrong's philosophy (i.e., if you aren't doped you aren't committed), Swart went about getting himself EPO. Like Frankie Andreu and others in the team who didn't have access to paid Italian consultants, he went to a chemist in Switzerland and bought some EPO over the counter.

The Tour de Suisse, approximately three weeks before the start of the Tour de France, was his testing ground. He used EPO throughout the Tour of Switzerland and couldn't stop worrying about what he'd got into. Whatever extra energy came with the increase in red cells was drained by the stress of his leap into the darkness.

'I can't remember how long the box of EPO lasted, but I basically took it every second day. Then in the race I was just going backwards. Then at the Tour de France the EPO ran out after the prologue and at that point I just decided it wasn't for me.'

That was it essentially. He recalled the team doing internal tests to measure their haematocrits as the race hit the mountains. The machine could process ten samples at once so everybody got tested. The numbers were called out like a lotto. Stephen was around 46, 47, which in the brave new world was sort of lamentable. Pretty much everybody else including Lance was 50 or above. He tells this as if unsure whether he was witnessing the death of sport or he just didn't have what it took to be a proper doper. He got through the Tour, made it to Paris but without truly competing with those benefiting from EPO.

There is sadness, that's for sure. On a mantelpiece sits a photograph from the Champs-Élysées at the end of the 1995 Tour de France. It shows the five Motorola riders that finished that year, not just lucky to have made it but, remembering the tragedy of their teammate Fabio Casartelli who crashed on a descent that year and died, lucky to be alive. Sitting on the handlebars of Lance's bike in that picture is Stephen and Jan's daughter, the then four-year-old Olivia.

The photo is the only evidence in the room that Stephen was once a racer. He doesn't see there's much to boast about. He was part of a world where your sport told you to cheat or get screwed. He didn't want to cheat; he didn't want to get screwed and he ended up in a kind of halfway house, unclean and still screwed.

Listening now as he recalls the Motorola years, the team haematocrit tests and Lance scoring one of the big numbers, my mind goes back to another sofa, the one in the lobby of Hotel La Fauvelaie in eastern France two and a half years before. There I asked Lance Armstrong about these same two Motorola years.

'When did you become aware of the doping subculture?'

'I don't know the answer because Motorola was white as snow and I was there all the way through ninety-six.'

'How conscious were you that EPO had become a factor in race results?'

'We didn't think about it. It wasn't an issue for us. It wasn't an option. Jim Ochowicz ran the programme that he set out to run, a clean programme.'

Armstrong gave one version, Swart offered another. Black and white. I thought about Swart's motivation. He had retired six years previously, returning from Europe with his family to begin a new life in New Zealand. It'd been a good while since. He started a new career as a builder and small-time developer, and he'd raised his family in one of the better cities. Why would he go back to his career to lie about it, especially to tell stuff that hurts him and his family? Why bring this on them?

He did so because professional cycling shouldn't have been like that, and it mustn't be like this for the next generation.

I've listened to these two accounts of the Motorola years and know it is Swart who doesn't lie.

Deepening the conviction that he's telling the truth is the matter-of-fact way Stephen Swart describes his own use of EPO. He was never going to be the poster boy for the drug. Despite having bought and then used EPO through the Tour de Suisse and at the beginning of the 1995 Tour de France, he hadn't blossomed as promised. The duck didn't become a swan. In fact, he had raced better the previous year when he wasn't using EPO.

He'd struggled on, though. Three weeks. His entire season came down to a merciless fight to survive Le Tour and fight through another season. One more summer with the circus. At the end of the '95 Tour he was still pedalling, and he actually enjoyed that mad final day and the colour and fun of arriving on the Champs-Élysées. He hadn't won, of course, but being there at the end was victory in itself. It told his employers that he was still strong and healthy and good to go for another year.

The evening the race finished, Motorola organised a small party for the cyclists, their immediate families, and the team's technical staff. It was a congenial atmosphere, but there was always the sense that elsewhere in Paris there were more substantial celebrations going on.

Swart and Steve Bauer were both warmly congratulated for their selfless contribution to the team effort. It brought a smile to Stephen's face. This recognition was a good sign. If he and Jan still had doubts about the renewal of his contract, they were being swept away now by the gratitude that the team showed him that evening.

After the Tour, the cyclists rested up for a week, then prepared for the end-of-season races. First, in August, for the Leeds classic in England, and the Grand Prix of Zurich, then for the Vuelta a España that started in September. The day before Zurich, Jim Ochowicz asked Stephen to come to his room. Out of the blue Ochowicz told him that his contract would not be renewed in 1996.

'It was completely unexpected. We should have discussed it during the Tour de France, but we hadn't, so I presumed everything was okay. Jim asked me to come to his room and told me that there was nothing for me. It's like saying to me, "There's a plane that's leaving in two hours, and since you're not racing tomorrow, we reserved you a seat on it." I tried to come to terms with it, and could have started looking for another team, but I thought: "No, that's enough. I don't want to keep going in this direction." I didn't want to go on with Motorola. I could have maybe started again with another team, but I wasn't interested.'

Swart went around to the rooms to say goodbye to his teammates. They already knew. He particularly wanted to shake hands with Sean Yates and Frankie Andreu, who he thought were decent guys.

'I tried to keep my head high and remain proud. I said, "Good luck, see you around sometime."'

Stephen knew the politics of the team well enough to suspect that Ochowicz had discussed his situation with Armstrong but he wanted to say goodbye to him anyway.

'I knocked on his door. It was open and I went in. I saw that he was in the bathroom. I called out that I had come to say goodbye to him.' He just stuck his hand outside the door.

'"See you around."

'"Yeah, see you around."

'He didn't say, "Hang on a minute." He didn't try to take leave of me properly. I understood then that he had been a part of the decision and he didn't have the guts to look me in the face.'

The manner of the goodbye added another twist of sadness. Swart believed that Armstrong had greatness in him and has said that if doping didn't exist the Texan would still have been a champion. Still, it saddened him to see such smallness in a man who might have been great.

'When he had his cancer, I thought he would have the opportunity to say in front of the world: "I made a mistake." If that had been the case and he had gotten back to a good level, I would see him in a different light. He had the chance to do something positive for the sport; instead of that, he helped keep things the same as they were before his illness. Since the scandal of 1998, what has changed?

'Nothing. The doping culture has just become more sophisticated. I think he is fooling these people, the cancer survivors. He has become a spokesman for them, but his past is troubled. Of course, he was a cancer victim, but you can't help but ask yourself if he contributed to its development. Personally, I have more respect for a cyclist like the Swiss Alex Zülle who at least raised his hand and confessed, "I did it. I'm sorry." Lance had the chance to be honest. By being cured of cancer, he could have, in a small way, helped the sport, and he chose not to do it.'

For Stephen that summer of '95 was a glimpse of the future. He was old enough and mature enough by then to know that Europe could no longer promise anything like the pure joy he had known growing up, watching his brother Jack compete on the two-lane blacktop around New Zealand. These weren't the footsteps he had dreamed of following.

He'd had his pro career, he'd done the Tour, done the lot. If he didn't take EPO he was going to be left behind. Instead he left cycling behind. He came home to New Zealand. His story took four or five hours of a pleasant antipodean evening to tell. He was a strong character and a guy who had found his happiness beyond the peloton.

Stephen's wasn't evidence that would bury Lance Armstrong, and neither was it intended to be. Telling about his career was something he needed to do for himself.

I left Auckland though with a better feeling for the pattern of things in Lance's life in the mid-nineties, before cancer; a sense of when he had first been beguiled by Michele Ferrari. It was a place far away and a time long ago, but Lance had been riding so hard and fast he crossed the borders without noticing. Guys like Stephen Swart just stepped off the ride and got away when they had the chance. His story made a deep impression. I left Auckland with something else too.

A sense of responsibility to people like the Swarts.

13

'For most of my life I had operated under a simple schematic of winning and losing, but cancer was teaching me a tolerance for ambiguities.'

Lance Armstrong

I can still remember that one of the satisfactions of sitting talking to Emma O'Reilly on that July day in 2003 was a small, spiteful pleasure. The sort of thing I would never confess to Sandro Donati. Somewhere off in France Lance Armstrong was busting his gut chasing after another Tour. He might have noted, perhaps with sorrow, my absence from press conferences. He may have thought that I'd given up, been pulled from the case, finally been admitted to a home for the bewildered.

As I sat with Emma I hoped he'd noticed that I was missing and I hoped he'd wondered for a second: 'What's the little troll up to now?' Because now, right now, as he sweated through the French countryside bossing the peloton, I was sitting with one of the people who had been spat out from the US Postal machine. I was looking at this smart, bright young woman and wondering what was wrong with Lance Armstrong that he couldn't have seen the sense of retaining her loyalty. Did he not know she was from Tallaght?

By the time I spoke to Emma, the business of writing the book which would be called *L.A. Confidentiel* was a significant part of my life. After Ferrari in 2001, I realised that if all this really mattered to me I couldn't continue on the basis of going to the Tour every year and sending the *Sunday Times* my annual three dissenting pieces. It wasn't enough.

Pierre and I conceived the book and then like proper journalists took a long time to do anything serious about it. It had become evident early on that English publishing houses weren't going to risk their lives in a scrum for the publishing rights, so it would be a French book, and we were determined that it would be a good book. Years on and I'm glad to say that there is very little which appeared in the USADA report of 2012 which didn't appear eight years previously in *L.A. Confidentiel.* Admittedly, the report had more detail but the stories were the same.[37]

---

37 There were conflicting reactions to *L.A. Confidentiel* at the time and even now commentators disagree on what it achieved. Below are two recent takes on the book.

'Here's what was so surprising about Wednesday's Lance Armstrong evidence dump from the United States Anti-Doping Agency: not all that much. Sure, USADA filled in many shocking details about Armstrong's doping practices, but the basic outline of this story has been known since 2004, when David Walsh and Pierre Ballester published *L.A. Confidentiel,* a groundbreaking investigative work that was mostly ignored at the time.'

Outside magazine, 2012

'It's just so easy to say, "Yeah the journalists should have dug deeper." Well, my god Walsh and Ballester dug as deep as you could dig and, you know, they didn't get anywhere. They really did not get anywhere. I've gone back, in fact, and looked at some of the things that I wrote at the time and I don't find any of it embarrassing. Now of course, I did find it uninformed.'

Samuel Abt, *New York Times, Herald Tribune,* 2012

Setting to work, we divided up the tasks and somehow I ended up with the glamour and Pierre ended up with the grit. If you're from County Kilkenny and dealing with a charismatic Frenchman, this is as good a deal as life has to offer.

While I stacked up the air miles, Pierre did the dog work. Pierre has a talent for the forensics of doping, an understanding of the scientific implications of numbers and figures and graphs. I went around sticking my tape recorder under people's noses and asking questions. Pierre went to laboratories and offices and doctors, and pored over figures and then went back again looking for explanations. At the end of it, he could have passed himself off as an oncologist.

I put some batteries in the recorder and headed off. I'd been to San Francisco in 2001 to interview the former US Postal team doctor Prentice Steffen.[38] That piece would be a starting point.

Steffen was the team doctor for US Postal in 1996, the year before Armstrong joined the team. Steffen had been with the team since 1993, when it was known as Subaru–Montgomery, and continued as team doctor in the first year of US Postal's involvement. He saw the team as distinctly American and felt it should represent the mores of American cycling.

With US Postal's backing and money, however, came the

---

38 The repercussions of that interview would be long lasting. In 2005 Steffen told *L'Équipe* that some time afterwards in 2001 he had received a phone call from Lance Armstrong. Lance said: 'I have a lot of money, good lawyers, and, if you continue to talk, I'll destroy you.'

In 2008 at the Tour of Utah, Steffen ended up getting a punch in the face from Marty Jemison, whose name featured in the interview.

ambition to compete against Europe's best. In 1996 they entered the Tour of Switzerland. A big step up.

Then Steffen recounted a conversation which causes trouble to this day.

'We were wiped out,' said Steffen. 'Two of my riders approached me saying they wanted to "talk about the medical programme". It was said that, as a team, we weren't able to get to where we wanted to go with what I was doing for them. I said, "Well, right now I am doing everything I can." They might have come back with "more could be done" and I said, "Yeah, I understand, but I am not going to be involved in that."'

Steffen was sure that he was being asked to help the two riders, Tyler Hamilton and Marty Jemison, to dope. Jemison, the more experienced of the pair (he had ridden in Europe on European teams before), did all the talking. Hamilton listened.[39]

After that informal discussion, relations cooled between the doctor and his riders. Four months later, a message was left on Steffen's voicemail telling him that the team no longer needed him.

Steffen sent a letter to his boss, Mark Gorski.

Dear Mark,

I've had a week now to consider the message you left for me concerning your decision to use Johnny's doctor

[39] Hamilton claims not to remember the conversation. Prentice Steffen sticks to his version still. Jemison says he was asking about B12 injections and legal means. It is possible that Jemison and Steffen were merely at cross purposes in a time of stress.

[Johnny Weltz, the team's new *directeur sportif*] instead of me next season. I'm afraid you've seriously misjudged me and that you will need to reconsider your position.

I feel that, by my efforts with the team since the '93 season, I've earned the opportunity to provide medical support for the team as we enter a new and exciting phase of our development. Certainly my training, qualifications, experience, knowledge and dedication cannot be questioned. So why your decision?

As is my habit I discussed the situation with two of my close friends. The explanation soon became clear. What could a Spanish doctor completely unknown to the organisation offer that I can't or won't? Doping is the obvious answer.

November 1996, and Steffen received a letter of reply. It came from the firm of Keesal, Young & Logan, attorneys for the US Postal team. The letter said Steffen's suspicions about his departure were incorrect but he would be held responsible for his comments if he made them public.

Steffen departed. Pedro Celaya came in as team doctor. At the 1997 Tour de France all nine US Postal riders made it to the finish. Prentice Steffen was pretty sure he knew why.

That interview was a useful building block.

In late autumn 2003 I saw the former Postal rider Stephen Swart in New Zealand. Then I went to Park City, Utah, and sat and talked with Marty Jemison. In Colorado I met Jonathan Vaughters (who now runs the Garmin team; Prentice Steffen is the team doctor). I went to see the LeMonds in Minneapolis and on up to the Andreus in Michigan.

I just about made it home to Mary and the kids for

Christmas 2003 in Cambridge. The New Year came with a mountain of writing to be done.

When the book came out in the summer of 2004 it was the claims in the interviews which made the impact. Newspapers always go for the drama: Wife of ex-teammate slams Armstrong. Former masseuse rubs Lance wrong way.

Obviously Emma was the star turn of the book. She had been longest and furthest into the belly of the beast and her descriptions of the internal culture she witnessed were compelling. The Indiana hospital story went over big as well but, overall, the impact was hard to see in the blizzard of legal actions which Lance Armstrong launched to greet the book.

His response was more of a story than anything in the book.

A lot of the real nourishment in *L.A. Confidentiel* was provided through Pierre's work. This was largely ignored on the grounds that it was insufficiently sexy. Pierre did the science. Science has no ambiguities.

Pierre raised questions which we have never really got answers to. Lance signed for the Cofidis team from Motorola just weeks before being diagnosed with stage iv cancer. According to the Englishman Paul Sherwen, who was public relations manager for Motorola at that time, 'For a very long time, Lance Armstrong felt a shooting pain that did not worry him overmuch. We even made him a special cushion.'

A key rider in a Tour de France team was experiencing pain severe enough for the PR flunkie to know about it, but it doesn't seem to have come to the attention of the medical staff who would have fussed about him every evening.

If they did know, why no disclosure to Cofidis? And what

were Cofidis doing spending so heavily on a new signing with no medical test required?

And then there was the question of the human chorionic gonadotropin.

Human chorionic gonadotropin, or hCG, is commonly referred to as the 'pregnancy hormone' because elevated levels of hCG are present when a woman conceives. Produced by the placenta, these higher levels of hCG are detectable eleven days after conception, and are what urine-based pregnancy tests use to calculate a positive result. So far, so good.

In addition to pregnancy, there are other health-related factors that may cause hCG levels to be elevated. After a cycle of steroid use, many users take hCG to boost their natural testosterone levels again. A slowing down of the work-rate in the testes is a side effect of steroid abuse.

In men and non-pregnant women, high levels of hCG are sometimes associated with cancerous and non-cancerous tumour growth. Tumour growth that causes increased hCG usually occurs in the reproductive glands, like the testicles or ovaries, but can also be caused by other tumours in the abdomen.

Which leads us back to 1996. In its synthetic form, hCG has for a long time been a banned product for male athletes. Lance Armstrong was tested thirteen times during the summer of 1996. If he was suffering from stabbing pains and using a special cushion on his saddle and was to be diagnosed with stage iv cancer in the autumn, it is more than reasonable to assume that he was showing distinct levels of hCG in those tests.

Armstrong himself has said:'I knew that hCG was looked

for in anti-doping controls. I would like to know what my level was at the time of the control [he's talking about the anti-doping control given at the Swiss Grand Prix, in August, six weeks before his cancer was detected]. If it's true that the UCI keeps all the results, it should be possible to know where my cancer was at that time.'

Oddly enough, Lance never pushed the issue any further. Or communicated it, so far as we know, to the UCI. And the UCI have carefully avoided giving any explanation.

At the time the French national anti-doping laboratory was under the control of Jean-Pierre Lafarge. Questioned by *Le Monde*, Lafarge said, 'Control of hCG was systematic. The cases are rare, probably lower than one case out of 10,000. In Lance Armstrong's case, it is surprising that no trace of the illness was detected during the controls.'

Pierre knew that the anti-doping controls taken on the Swiss Grand Prix in August 1996 were analysed at the Institute of Biochemistry of the German sports university based in Cologne.

Its director, Wilhelm Schänzer, has confirmed that his 'laboratory had the capacity to find traces of hCG'. It seems quite clear that the beta-hCG content in Lance Armstrong's blood in August 1996 was screened. At the time, the Cologne laboratory detected a slight abnormality in the analysis of testosterone, but did not find it suspicious enough and sent a negative result to the UCI.

The only official reaction to this contradiction came from Anne-Laure Masson, who was then the medical co-ordinator of the UCI.

'I'm perplexed because if the level of hCG was also high,

Lance Armstrong should have tested positive, in principle. For now, it's inexplicable.'

We know that at the time his cancer was detected Armstrong's beta-hCG level was through the roof. Beta-hCG is a tumour marker for the specific type of cancer Armstrong had. Normal level in males is 1-2 nanograms per millilitre of blood and pretty much always under 5ng/ml. Armstrong has given several different numbers for what his level was when he was diagnosed.

The figures vary according to which source you give credence to: 52,000ng/ml or 92,380ng/ml or 109,000ng/ml. The first figure came from Armstrong himself in an interview with Pierre in *L'Équipe* in November 1996. The other two figures are extracted from his autobiography *It's Not About the Bike*.

This is extraordinary. Even if we accept the lowest figure, Armstrong's beta-hCG levels had to have been enhanced for quite some time. Stranger still that in the years since then Armstrong has apparently satisfied himself with these vague answers.

Was there negligence? Were riders passing tests regardless of findings? If Armstrong's urine was carrying hCG, shouldn't he have been immediately informed and it be ascertained whether he was doping or had some kind of cancer, unrelated to doping?

One of Armstrong's attending physicians, Dr J. Dudley Youman, has attempted to place a date on the birth of the cancer. 'In my opinion, this cancer was in his organism for several months.'

Other medics told Pierre that there was a mathematical

relationship between the level of the hCG marker when properly noted and the extent of the illness.

Testicular cancer advances rapidly, but for Lance Armstrong to have had his cancer for less than a month before being diagnosed 'is just not possible'.

Pierre delved into this world page after page, report after report, doctor after doctor. It is impossible to do his journalism justice here, but it was never done justice anywhere, and those questions which he raised were just left hanging in the air.

It was Pierre's quiet excavations which uncovered what for me is still one of the mysteries of Lance: a letter from Alain Bondue of the Cofidis team to Bill Stapleton with a copy to François Migraine, head of Cofidis. The letter is dated 22 April 1997:

> I must inform you that during his period of training in January [at Marcq-en-Barœul], Lance was in Italy to see Dr Ferrari, and that Cofidis made the reservation and paid for his airfare, although the trip was considered a personal trip that had not been decided by Cofidis.

This still strikes me as extraordinary. The Cofidis press conference to launch the team for the year took place on 8 January. The team then went to Marcq-en-Barœul to train. Armstrong was just three weeks over his last chemotherapy session. He was not expected to work with the team, who were indeed flabbergasted to see him turn up for the press launch.

Ferrari, as we know, received no mention in Lance's autobiography, yet even before he was given the all clear from cancer (February 1997), Lance was going out of his way to spend time in Ferrara. At the time Dr Craig Nichols, his physician in Indiana, was firmly on the record as saying that it was at that point unclear as to whether Lance would be able to resume a career as a professional cyclist.

What was in his head? What decisions had he made?

Someday I hope he tells us about all these things.

14

'*Litigation: A machine which you go into as a pig and come out of as a sausage.*'

Ambrose Bierce

I walked out of my boss's office knowing what I had to do. Alan English, the deputy sports editor, was seated at a desk to the left.

'Alan, I'm leaving the *Sunday Times*. I don't have an option.'

I had been at the paper for more than eight years and had been chief sports writer for the previous three. Something the footballer Teddy Sheringham once said about Manchester United reflected how I felt about the *Sunday Times*. 'When you leave United,' Sheringham said, 'you accept that where you're going won't be as good.'

I felt nothing but intense sadness. Eight years and then at the very moment when *L.A. Confidentiel, les Secrets de Lance Armstrong*, is about to appear on book shelves all over France, I am leaving a job and a newspaper that I love.

Alan could see how I felt. 'I'll walk with you to the car.'

We went in silence.

'Think about it,' he said, as I got in the car.

'I have. I don't have a choice.'

It was a Thursday evening, a little after seven o'clock and London's rush hour had passed. Knowing what was going on, I was in no rush to get home.

The more I thought about it, the worse it seemed. Emma O'Reilly, Betsy Andreu and Stephen Swart were putting their necks on the line for me and now, when I needed the newspaper's support, I didn't feel I had it. Anger passed, replaced by sadness and a sense of hopelessness. I dialled Alex's number.

'I don't think we need to fall out over this but I'm resigning from the paper.'

'I'm sorry you're doing that,' he said. I could tell he felt let down by me.

'I'll send you an email when I get home confirming it.'

'Okay.'

I rang Betsy.

'I've resigned from the *Sunday Times*,' I said.

'Oh my God, are you kidding?'

'No. It's true.'

'What are you gonna do?'

'I'm not sure. Hopefully, there will be options.'

'I cannot believe this. This is crazy. No wonder we broke away from the British, with the stoopid libel laws you got.'

At home I wrote a short email to Alex, confirming the resignation. Telling Mary wasn't the easiest bit, but she could see the sadness and tried not to think about the consequences. 'If that's what you think you had to do, then you didn't have a choice.'

It should have been one of the better weeks of my working life.

L.A. Confidentiel was the product of two years' work; of finding sources, earning their trust, reassuring them, and then convincing them to allow their stories into the light. With our book in draft form, I had sent emails to Lance Armstrong and Johan Bruyneel asking questions that gave them the opportunity to address many of the allegations contained in our book. I sent eleven questions to Bruyneel; eight to Lance.

> Question to Bruyneel:
> According to several sources, some US Postal riders are known to use doping products. What can you say about this?
> Did you ever transport doping products? Did you ever ask any US Postal staff member to do so?

The questions for Lance weren't any less explicit:

> I have heard you once admitted using performance-enhancing drugs to your cancer doctors?
> Witnesses claim they saw needle marks high up on your arm. What do you say about this?

These questions were sent in late May 2004, about three weeks before printing presses would begin churning out copies of *L.A. Confidentiel*. We had enough time to include responses from Armstrong and Bruyneel in the book but not enough to allow them to launch some form of legal offensive that could have delayed publication. The emails deliberately did not mention whether I was writing a newspaper article or a book, merely that I had been researching the team and needed some answers. An alarm was triggered inside Lance's world, caused no doubt by the aggressiveness of the questions.

His response was delivered through the London law firm Schillings in a letter addressed to me and faxed to the *Sunday Times* on Tuesday 8 June. They guessed we were planning to run a piece in the newspaper about Armstrong and now it was over to Schillings, representing the team's owner Tailwind Sports llc, Lance Armstrong and Johan Bruyneel. Schillings' first letter was short, just to say they anticipated sending a fuller response the following day. 'In the meantime, please note our interest in this matter.'

On that same day, a meeting was taking place in the sports department of the newspaper attended by sports editor Alex Butler, Alan English, the *Sunday Times* lawyer Alastair Brett and myself. They wanted to know the most convincing evidence in the book. I went through it:

> **Emma O'Reilly**: former head *soigneur* at US Postal and Armstrong's masseuse in 1998 and '99, who had given me an explosively frank account of her five years in the team. She dumped Lance's used syringes, went on a 'drug run' to Spain, applied some women's concealer to hide the needle marks on his arm, witnessed the cover-up of his positive test at the Tour de France, and picked up testosterone for another Postal rider. I had done a taped interview with Emma.

Stephen Swart: former teammate of Armstrong at Motorola in 1994 and '95. He says the team decided to use EPO in 1995 and that Armstrong was a strong advocate for the team resorting to banned products. Swart admits he used the drug for '95 Tour de France and did so because it was a team decision.

Betsy Andreu: she told me she heard Armstrong tell his doctors at Indiana hospital in October 1996 that he used performance-enhancing drugs before his cancer. Another witness in that room, Stephanie McIlvain, confirmed that she too had heard this. Because Betsy's husband worked in cycling and Stephanie worked for Armstrong's sponsor, Oakley, they didn't want to openly say they heard it but they would testify under oath to having heard it if there was a need.

Greg LeMond: LeMond and his wife Kathy had told me about an incriminating conversation between Greg and Lance after the 2001 Tour de France when, according to Greg, Lance said he could get ten witnesses to say he, LeMond, had used EPO and that 'everyone used EPO'.

Since I had first raised questions about Armstrong, the challenge had been to get people who knew things on the record. Alex was cautiously excited by the possibilities, Alan was very excited, while Alastair was nervous but appreciative of the fact that much new evidence against Armstrong had been uncovered. I was asked to go away and put together a long extract that could be broken into ten or twelve different stories, as the plan was to run four pages of Armstrong/US Postal material in the *Sunday Times*.

The material ran to 11,000 words and, for me, this was the moment to say, 'This is our case against Lance Armstrong; how do you feel about him in the light of this evidence?' I was proud of the book but frustrated that it would be printed only in French. All of my sources for the book were from the English-speaking world and I saw the four-page report in the *Sunday Times* as the right platform for their stories.

On the Thursday, three days before publication, I turned up with my 11,000-word extract from *L.A. Confidentiel,* feeling the nervous excitement journalists feel when there's a potentially explosive story sitting inside their laptops. Before me, a courier had arrived at the security office of the *Sunday Times* on Pennington Street in Wapping. His letter, marked 'Private and Confidential', was addressed to me and from my friends at Schillings. This was their 'response' to the expectation that we were planning to run a piece about their clients, Armstrong and Bruyneel, on Sunday.

Their clients had passed on the questions I had emailed to them. According to Schillings, the allegations implicit in the emails were false, highly defamatory and extremely damaging. They concluded from the emails that I believed Armstrong and US Postal had achieved their success through cheating, in particular by the use of performance-enhancing drugs. They wanted me to understand that it would be highly improper to publish false and very serious allegations concerning their clients.

And if the allegations were published, 'our clients' would have no alternative than to resort to law.

In other words, print and be sued.

One of the consequences of being consumed by a story like

this is that it detaches you from mainstream society and takes you into a smaller world where only your sources and your desire to expose the wrongdoers matter. I saw Schillings as the legal wing of an operation well versed in intimidation. For the previous five years I'd experienced, firsthand, the many ways the Armstrong machine tried to discourage accusers and doubters. This threatening letter was just the latest example.

Alastair, the company lawyer, didn't see it quite like this.

We discussed the story and what could be done to firm it up. Alastair wanted me to get emails from Betsy and Stephanie McIlvain confirming they would stand over the hospital-room confession in the likelihood of a lawsuit. 'Okay,' I said, 'I'll call them.'

Stephanie McIlvain's situation was extremely difficult. She and Lance went way back, and though their friendship ebbed and flowed, her job with Oakley depended upon her having a good relationship with him, which she managed to do most of the time. Her husband, Pat, was a vice-president of global marketing for Oakley, and, between them, the McIlvains had much to lose if ever they fell out with Lance.

After Stephanie met Betsy in the Indiana hospital room in 1996, they became friends. Through Betsy, I got to know Stephanie. During the early months of 2004, I began calling her and we spoke many times. She was a keen runner and we would talk about how far she'd run and her pace and, of course, we spoke about Lance. In the beginning, before the 'Inc' would be tagged onto the end of his name, she and Lance were close and she recalled how he had consulted with her about his choice of agent. There were some big players pitching for the business but she suggested he go with the Austin-based lawyer Bill Stapleton, and she was pleased he did.

We spoke too about the hospital-room admission and she told me she had heard it but, given her position and her husband's position with Oakley, she couldn't publicly say that. She and Betsy spoke all the time and both were in that position of not wanting to lie about it and not being able to tell the truth. For the purpose of telling about the hospital-room admission in *L.A. Confidentiel*, we agreed a compromise that would make it clear Lance did admit to using banned drugs without the two women having to say he did.

So, in the book, the hospital-room scene was described, the visitors listed, and I then question Betsy about it:

'Were you there when Lance admitted to his doctors that he used banned performance-enhancing drugs?'

'I've nothing to say on that. It's a question more for Lance than me.'

'But did you hear him say he used performance-enhancing drugs?'

'I've told you. I've nothing to say on that subject.'

'If you never heard him say this, just say so.'

'I've got no comment.'

This routine was repeated with Stephanie:

'Were you in the room that day?'

'Yes, I was there.'

'Did you hear him tell his doctors he used performance-enhancing drugs?'

'I am sorry, I have nothing to say on this subject. It is a question for Lance. I have nothing to say.'

'But listen, just say yes or no. Did he say he used performance-enhancing drugs?'

'Sorry, no comment. If you have any questions that need to be answered, you must put them to Lance.'

Betsy, Stephanie and I believed that no one could miss the significance of these conversations. They admit they were in the room and all they've got to say is, 'I never heard him say that,' but they refuse, leaving readers to believe they did hear it but were afraid to admit it. Both women reassured me they would not lie under oath about the admission. Betsy also said that her husband Frankie, who was also present, would not lie under oath about it.

Alastair was still nervous about running anything on the hospital room without written assurances from Betsy and Stephanie, and so I left Alex's office where we were discussing it and set up a conference call with my two sources. I explained to them what I needed. Betsy was willing to write the email but Stephanie was unsure, fearing the consequences of Lance finding out about her complicity in the story.

'Stephanie, you've got to do the right thing,' Betsy said.

It was a fraught phone call. Stephanie was afraid and upset. Betsy was certain and unwavering. Eventually they agreed to send emails confirming they would stand over what they heard in the hospital room. I was so impressed by both women's willingness to tell the truth about this incident because they had so much to lose. Without Lance's goodwill, Stephanie wouldn't have had a job, while Betsy's forthright views on Lance had hurt her husband's career.

I returned to Alex's office, convinced I'd done enough to make sure we could get the hospital-room incident into our story; but with more time to reflect and no doubt to think more about Schillings' letter, Alastair had grown more cautious.

'They will write emails,' I said.

'I think we need affidavits from them,' he said.

'That's ridiculous. Now we're just looking for ways to keep this story out of the paper. These women are being incredibly brave and we're trying to make it impossible for them.'

'We're just trying to protect ourselves,' Alastair said. 'We've had that letter from Schillings and we pretty much know they are going to sue, so we've got to do everything we can.'

Knowing how difficult it had been to get Stephanie to agree to the email, I couldn't just go back to her now and say we need an affidavit. Instead I turned the flame-thrower on Alastair.

'Alastair, three weeks ago I was in Paris when we had a meeting to sign off on all the legal issues arising out of all this stuff and we worked with a lawyer there, Thibault de Montbrial, who, from the first moment of the meeting, convinced Pierre Ballester and me that he was on our side. He wanted our story in the public domain and wanted every detail in there. Then he showed us how we could do it. He was inspiring to work with. This is fucking depressing.'

Alastair was upset by my withering put-down and had every right to be. It was grossly unfair because it did not take into account the significant differences between French and

259

English libel law. The French allow journalists who are honestly seeking the truth to do their jobs, but this is not the case in England. Here we had five witnesses – O'Reilly, Swart, Andreu, McIlvain and LeMond – who were all offering direct evidence that linked Armstrong to doping, but somehow it wasn't enough.

Whatever I brought to this discussion, it wasn't objectivity. My loyalty was to the people who had gone out on a limb for me, risked much so that Pierre and I could get more of the story out there. In all of the debate that Thursday afternoon and into the early evening, I didn't get the significance of the Schillings' letters and how difficult it would be for us to defend a case against a multiple Tour de France winner and cancer icon.

My understanding of the threat wasn't helped by some simplistic thinking. The previous day the Dutch newspaper *De Telegraaf* repeated comments made by Armstrong about me: 'Walsh is the worst journalist I know,' he had said in an earlier interview. 'There are journalists who are willing to lie, to threaten people and to steal in order to catch me out. All this for a sensational story. Ethics, standards, values, accuracy – these are of no interest to people like Walsh.'

'So,' I raged at Alastair, Alex and Alan, 'he can say that about me and we can't run the interviews we have done with people who worked with him and rode with him and give a completely different picture of him to the one fed to the public? Where's the fairness in that? Is there any chance that the *Sunday Times* might support its journalist?'

Over the years I have discovered that anger hasn't helped me to convince those on the other side of an argument. I didn't consider that Dutch libel laws are very different to England's, and Armstrong's comments about me in *De Telegraaf* were probably not libellous and, anyway, I wasn't going to sue. Alastair knew Armstrong would sue us regardless of what we printed about him. There was nothing veiled about Schillings' threat.

I went out and called Betsy and discussed the possibility of getting an affidavit from her, but what was the point? Stephanie wasn't going to be able to do this. Betsy, of course, was more than willing: 'I ain't lying for Lance. I told Frankie that.' The more Alastair thought about it, the more he felt the 11,000-word piece was unusable without affidavits from both of them. If I had been able to stand back and assess things dispassionately, it would have been obvious to me that the dice were just loaded against us in England.[40]

Deep in the back of my mind, I knew Alastair was right.

Emma O'Reilly's recall of all that happened at the US Postal team during her five years was detailed and wholly convincing. You listened to her story and knew she was telling the truth. But Armstrong would say she was lying and he could probably have produced five witnesses from within the team who would claim everything Emma said was a lie. What then?[41]

---

40 Years later, Alex Butler would say that as we were going to be sued no matter what we wrote, we should have run the original piece and be shot for a sheep as a lamb.

41 In the nine years that have passed since she and I did that first long interview, Emma O'Reilly has despaired about Britain's libel laws. All she ever wanted to do was tell the truth and she discovered it was possible to do this in the US and in France but not in England. Judge Leveson and his inquiry into the media could have done worse than to invite Emma in to tell them her experience of British libel law.

When I went back in to Alex's office, Alastair said he had to recommend not running the Armstrong story because of the certainty we would be sued and the likelihood we would lose. Alex couldn't overrule the lawyer, especially when it was clear to everyone but me that the lawyer was right. They hadn't any doubts about my evidence and they, too, were certain Armstrong was doping, but their responsibility to the newspaper meant they couldn't dive headlong into a legal battle they felt we would lose.

I understand that now, but didn't understand it then. Demoralised, I made the decision to resign.

The morning after you've resigned from a job you didn't want to leave isn't going to be the brightest of your life.

Alan English thought it wrong that I should leave the newspaper this way and wanted to find some way to undo it. He reckoned the position I'd taken meant it would be difficult for me to come back, even if the newspaper wanted me, if nothing about Armstrong appeared in that week's paper. He spoke to Alex and asked if he could look at the 11,000-word piece I'd originally submitted to see if he could take it and distil a piece that Alastair would pass.

Alex told him to go ahead and then sent me an email saying that the newspaper was seeing if there was a way out of this and to hold off in relation to the resignation. Though still feeling incredibly low, I was happy to do that. I didn't want to work for any other newspaper.

Paul Kimmage had joined the *Sunday Times* two years before and that weekend he was in Florida on a golf story. When told I had resigned, he felt he too would resign because he knew how much I'd put into the Armstrong story and he was almost as keen as I was to see it in the newspaper. It wouldn't come to this, as Alan wrote a story that contained many of the allegations in the book and made a strong case for the need to ask questions of Armstrong. Alan's piece had the balance that my piece lacked, although it didn't have a few of the most serious charges against Armstrong.

Mindful of how Britain's libel laws work, Alan quoted Lord Justice Brooke's recently expressed view that the media are the general public's eyes and ears. 'In a free society,' he said, 'fearless reporting has often exposed information which it has been in the public interest to expose.' It definitely was in the public's interest to know there were good reasons for suspecting Lance Armstrong was not who he said he was.

In his piece, Alan also argued that with lawyers charging a £400 hourly rate, newspapers could be held to ransom by those with the financial wherewithal to do so. The *Sunday Times* knew Armstrong had the means to commit to this battle and that the further it progressed, the more our libel laws would serve his interests.

In the piece Alan refuted the suggestion, made by Schillings in their letter, that I had a vendetta against their client. He insisted my opposition was to the cancer of drugs in sport and that was true. I had written about doping in athletics, doping at the Olympics, Ben Johnson, Linford Christie, Michelle Smith and Stephen Roche, and he reminded readers that young cyclists were dying because of doping.

In a two-month period at the turn of the year, the '98 Tour de France winner Marco Pantani had died, so too his contemporary the great Spanish climber José Maria Jiménez, and also the 21-year-old Belgian Johan Sermon. Here, Alan was attempting to reflect my concern for cycling's deep-rooted culture of doping, and he was pleased the piece was passed with few changes by Alastair, Alex and the editor John Witherow.

They knew Armstrong had his finger on the trigger but they weren't ducking for cover.

At around five o'clock on the Saturday evening, an hour or so before deadline, Alan emailed me the piece. I told him I didn't think much of it, feeling that it hadn't gone far enough and had left out too much of the most damning evidence. It was a thoughtless and classless response to a friend and colleague who had done so much for me. Alan was furious but, still seeing myself as the victim, I never even saw that.

Alan's piece would cost the *Sunday Times* £600,000: £300,000 as a contribution to Armstrong's legal fees and £300,000 to cover its own legal expenses.[42]

Two years were spent fighting the case, reams of evidence were gathered, many witnesses pledged to come and testify on our behalf, but after a ruling decreed that the meaning of the article was that Armstrong doped, and that to win the case the *Sunday Times* would have to prove that he doped, the game was up. How do you prove a rider has doped? We were supposed to wait for him to test positive. British libel law wanted to make cheerleaders of us all.

Tim Herman, Armstrong's long-time lawyer from Texas, came to London to finalise the settlement with the *Sunday*

42 In the light of the USADA report in October 2012, the *Sunday Times* decided to seek re-imbursement of that payment to Armstrong and legal costs of its own during that 2004-2006 case. The file remains open.

Times' then managing editor Richard Caseby. It was civilised and Richard recalls Tim saying they were never going to allow the case to go to court. Something about Lance one day going into politics and a court case about doping not being that helpful.[43]

In France, Armstrong sued the publishers of the book La Martinière, the authors, and *L'Express* magazine who published extracts. After lodging the complaint in France, Armstrong had three months to press ahead with the case. Shortly before the three-month deadline passed, the case was dropped. His climbdown was hardly noticed.

In America, Armstrong showed how masterful he had become at dealing with doping allegations. By now there was a pattern: every six or nine months brought a new wave of allegations, but he spun this to his advantage. 'This is not the first time I've lived through this,' he said. 'Every time, we've chosen to sit back and let it pass. But we've sort of reached a point where we really can't tolerate it any more and we're sick and tired of these allegations and we're going to do everything we can to fight them. They're absolutely untrue.

'Enough is enough. We don't use doping products and we will sue those who suggest we do.'

---

43 Armstrong's legal team were the masters of brinkmanship. At one point they were proceeding against the *Sunday Times* and me over an article about *L.A. Confidentiel*, dealing with an unfair dismissal claim by former personal assistant Mike Anderson, and a counter-claim by Armstrong. Along with a public defamation suit by Italian cyclist Filippo Simeoni, to be heard in Paris; a libel action, also in Paris, against me, Pierre, Emma O'Reilly and Stephen Swart; a libel action against La Martinière, publisher of *L.A. Confidentiel*; and one against *L'Express*, which published extracts from the book. Lance was also facing an Italian police inquiry into sporting fraud. He ultimately managed to avoid going under oath in any of the cases.

Judith McHale, president of Discovery Communications, the company that had committed millions of dollars to Armstrong and the team, was reassured. 'Lance is a role model known for determination, integrity and a spirit that never gives up. There is no better ambassador for quality and trusted information.'

In England, the fall-out was very different. Emma O'Reilly felt the strain more than anyone else. She was exposed. She'd come from Tallaght, brought the resilience of the area with her, but you couldn't be prepared for this: running her own business, living in England with a good man who was dealing with multiple sclerosis, and, when the door bell rings, it is a policeman who wants to serve you with a subpoena. And not just one.

In the run-up to publication of *L.A. Confidentiel*, Marc Grinsztajn, a slight, engaging and clever man who worked for our publishers, had said to me a couple of times to look out for Emma in the aftermath. Of all of us she would be the one most vulnerable. I nodded but didn't see it.

Her interview with me had come to just under 40,000 words of transcription. I'd gone back to her and asked her to check through all of it again, which she did assiduously. I'd edited them down, asked her once more. I'd produced about 25,000 words of Emma-related copy and gone back a third time to ask her to confirm she was happy with it. All this and a stream of calls confirming things which weren't clear to me, or looking for a steer here, or new information there.

When we had first met I had spoken to her about her input in terms of the book being a chorus of voices who would be speaking out at once. As it turned out, she was becoming the star attraction and everybody else was on backing vocals. Pierre and I were almost made of Teflon by this stage: none of the comments or abuse hurled at us ever stuck. But Emma was doing so much of the work and taking so much of the risk.

In the end Pierre and I spoke and agreed we would each contribute 2500 Euros in order to give Emma a modest sum for about five weeks of evening- and weekend-work on the book. It wasn't a payment. It was a small thank you.

I volunteered this information to Joe Lindsey during an interview for *Outside* magazine in the US and, unsurprisingly, this was used to single out Emma again and make her a target. In retrospect she had been vulnerable right from the start. When Lance held his press conference in Maryland in June 2004 to launch the Discovery sponsorship it was Emma he personally attacked.

Armstrong was by nature a straight-talker but, when necessary, he could do slyness too. 'It's not going to be my way to speak badly of her,' he said of Emma, at the Discovery Communications press conference, and then did just that, 'but there were issues, within the team management, within the riders, and she was let go.' He didn't specify what the issues were, just let it hang out and the darker your imagination, the more he had succeeded.

By that point I'd spoken to many people Emma had worked with and each spoke highly of her professionalism and her personality. Three riders – Frankie Andreu, Jonathan Vaughters and Marty Jemison – all said they liked her, both as a therapist and as a person.[44] So for Armstrong to suggest impropriety and not explain what he meant was nasty. Emma thought it low, but she wasn't surprised. 'Lance is Lance,' she often says, as if this explains everything.

With Emma I never understood how guilty she would feel about betraying people in the Postal team she liked: Tyler Hamilton, Jonathan, Frankie, the head mechanic Julian DeVriese with whom she was friendly. Julian was old school: Belgian, once mechanic to Eddy Merckx and later Greg LeMond. He looked after Armstrong in Emma's time. Old enough to be her father, they still liked each other.

He wouldn't understand why she would spit in the soup.

Then, pretty soon after publication of *L.A. Confidentiel*, the lawyers came over the hill and charged into her life. The subpoenas began to arrive, so frequently for a while that the local police officer serving them would ring Emma's home and tell Mike to put the kettle on because he had another. Keith Schilling, a lawyer representing Armstrong, asked to see her. Emma called our dashing French lawyer, Thibault de Montbrial, who gave the go-ahead for her to speak to him. Mike said he wanted to be with her when Schilling came.

She told Schilling that everything in the *Sunday Times* and in *L.A. Confidentiel* was the truth. He wanted to know if the interview had been taped. She said it had. But, at this time, she

---

44 In September 2012 Tyler Hamilton spoke publicly about Emma O'Reilly. 'Emma was the best *soigneur* I ever had. A great, great person. You can see it in her eyes: she's the salt of the earth and everyone in the team knew that. When she came out with the doping stuff about Lance, I couldn't be seen to support her but I knew what she was saying was true. And I liked it in a strange way. "The ass-hole," I thought, "is getting some heat." I kind of felt he deserved it.'

was in something way over her head. She will never forget what Schilling said during their conversation. 'I'm surprised the paparazzi aren't already outside.' It stayed with her because she and Mike didn't feel he said it out of concern for her wellbeing.

The effect on Mike was what hurt Emma the most. They knew the stress would worsen his multiple sclerosis. He became agitated by what Armstrong was allowed to do to his girlfriend, causing a noticeable deterioration in his condition. Emma's final decision to let her testimony go into *L.A. Confidentiel* had come when she'd been upset by the death of Marco Pantani in early 2004. But now she felt responsible for Mike. And she wasn't pleased with me, feeling I should have known how things would play out.

Sometimes on the phone or in an email I got one barrel, other times I got both. Things were bad between us through the summer of 2004. She asked me to contact her former husband Simon Lillistone, who had been in the car with her on that journey to Spain to pick up drugs for Armstrong. 'He can verify that story.' I called Lillistone, who at first tried to say he didn't know but then admitted he did. On a follow-up phone call he was upset and said he didn't want his name used, that it would damage his career. He now works for British Cycling, had a high-profile role at the London Olympics and his career has blossomed.[45]

Emma never changed her story and never ran away from it. Tough woman from Tallaght.

---

45 During his relationship with Emma, Simon got to know different people in and around the US Postal team, and perhaps his reluctance to publicly support Emma's account of the drug trip to Spain was based in part on a desire to preserve those friendships. Up until recently he was exchanging tweets with Johan Bruyneel.

She would tell me later that the experience really made her feel exposed and guilty for a long time. She was sad to have put people through so much and sad that it seemed to be acceptable for Lance Armstrong to attempt to take everything from her: finances, reputation, self-esteem.

In the end the UK's libel laws gagged Emma. She got no protection in the country that she lives and works in. She did an interview with the American weekly magazine *Sports Illustrated* and they told her that what she said would be fine in the US, but if Armstrong sued her in Britain it could be a problem.

'So I shut up. Plenty of others were running scared so why should I risk ruining the lives of those closest to me by speaking the truth?'

Enough said.

Armstrong frightened every media outlet in the UK, but that didn't explain why so few journalists were interested in Emma's story at the time. Her allegations against the US Postal team were detailed and indicated a pervasive doping culture within the team. I remember Sam Abt, a veteran editor on the *International Herald Tribune* at the time, who would also cover the Tour de France for that newspaper and the *New York Times*, writing a cutesy little piece on Emma during her US Postal days.

I knew Sam well, and asked how he found her. He said he'd really enjoyed meeting her and the piece reflected his enthusiasm for her. In my naivety I wondered if Sam would go back to Emma and see what motivated her to speak out and try to satisfy himself as to the truthfulness of her story. But by then Sam was friendly with Lance, and if there was one of those little Lance gatherings to which a journalist needed an invitation, he would have been near the top of the list.

Emma was trouble: trouble to get to in England and much more trouble when you got back and had to write the piece.

I spoke with Sam after the book was published and went through a lot of the allegations in the book, saying there was a lot of evidence, especially from Emma and Stephen Swart, but there wasn't a smoking gun. Of course, that was the one line from me that Sam emphasised in his piece. I felt like the late Severiano Ballesteros, who had been let down by his caddie: 'Please,' said Seve, 'don't blame yourself, I'm the idiot who hired you.' Well, I was the idiot who gave that quote to Sam. What did I expect?

It had been an interesting June 2004 at the *Sunday Times*: the legal threat, endless discussion over the extract, a chief sports writer so consumed by one plot he lost sight of all the others, then a page-long article that I thought wasn't strong enough and London judges of libel thought had blasphemed St Lance. Can we ask some questions about this guy setting out to win his sixth consecutive Tour de France? No, you can't.

But we did anyway and paid for it.

A service to our readers, we thought, but they too were unimpressed. To convey the general reaction, two of the letters were published:

How many times does Lance Armstrong have to defend himself against drug allegations, and why does David Walsh feel the need to keep digging? Is it because the Tour

David Walsh

de France is about to begin, and by bringing out a book questioning the favourite, he may get good sales? Martin Clayton, Holmfirth.

I was shocked to find the *Sunday Times* used to promote a book co-written by David Walsh, one of your journalists, condemning Lance Armstrong. As someone who has gone through the same chemotherapy as Armstrong, the thought of taking drugs that could cause more damage is abhorrent. Why not print something positive about him and his work involving testicular cancer?' Colin Millsop, Les Lecques, France.

15

Liège isn't a city you'd lose your heart to. It's not so good that they've named it twice. Nobody croons about 'my kind of town, Liège'.

But me?

I'll always have Liège. I'll always feel something for the biggest rivet in the Belgian rust belt.

The Place Saint Lambert in Liège is a very large square which loosely links the old part of the town with the new. The square is bordered by some interesting buildings but, as a precaution against charm, the Belgians have filled the entire square with concrete.

Twice I can remember being a speck in this grey vastness. The first time was for the start of the much-loved one-day classic cycling race known as Liège–Bastogne–Liège. It was a Sunday in April 1984, and I still have a photograph taken that morning shortly before the start of the race.

It was shot by a photographer who we knew back then only as Nutan, and it showed the great Belgian cycling champion Eric Vanderaerden worming his way through the masses of fans to the start line. As he did so, a man in his early thirties held a baby in his left arm, and with his right hand he stretched the child's left hand forward until the infant's fingers touched the cyclist's back.

Devotion to a sport had never been so poignantly expressed or beautifully captured. Back then I could identify totally with the innocence in that act of adoration.

Twenty years later, I was back in Place Saint Lambert. The same grey square but my world was a different place and cycling had changed utterly: Paul Kimmage had retired and written *Rough Ride*, the book which would begin cycling's long period of painful introspection. And now Pierre Ballester and I had produced *L.A. Confidentiel*. We'd nailed our theses to the door of the cathedral. We awaited the whirlwind.

Well, I awaited. Others had wearied. My co-author and friend Pierre had walked away from covering Tours. He couldn't write about doping, and fiction wasn't his thing. Benoît Hopquin of *Le Monde*, the journalist who revealed Armstrong's positive test for a corticosteroid during the first Tour victory in 1999, was gone too. He was now writing about the environment and feeling like he was doing something.

Even Jean-Michel Rouet, who was the thoughtful lead writer for *L'Équipe* on that 1999 Tour, the man who had, with subtlety and eloquence, expressed his early doubts and had, for his trouble, received a personal chastisement from the Tour . . . even Jean-Michel has dismounted and walked down to the football stadium.

It is now Friday evening, the day before the start of the 2004 Tour de France, and the innocence with which I'd come to this square in 1984 is just a memory. This will be Lance Armstrong's sixth Tour de France victory, and though present to cover this race, I have come also to defend the book Pierre and I have co-authored.

It will need defending. In the past few weeks I have been in Portugal, a place that I love, covering the European soccer championships. I leave for Portugal the same day that I've un-resigned from the *Sunday Times* and though I spend two weeks at the football, the time is spent dealing with endless phone calls from journalists wishing to speak about *L.A. Confidentiel*.

Other things have been happening, though. Last month in Maryland, Armstrong announced a brand-new sponsorship deal with Discovery Channel. Dull enough, but coverage was boosted by the exposure given to his legal team. The previous day he had leaked the joyous news of the filing of the libel suit in London against myself, the *Sunday Times*, my colleague Alan English, Emma O'Reilly and Stephen Swart.

Meanwhile, a court in Paris had rejected Lance's attempt to force our publisher to insert his denial of doping accusations into all copies of the book. With a little welcome French style, the judge, Catherine Bezio, called Armstrong's request an abuse of the legal system and ordered him to pay Pierre, me and the publishers a symbolic $1.20 fine.[46] That was a bit

---

46 I never received that $1.20. Lance, you still owe me.

of fun, but the forecast for the legal climate ahead was more serious.

The book would sell more than 100,000 copies and reach number two on the French bestseller list, but to Armstrong and those around him it was *The Satanic Verses*.

In the *salle de presse* just now, US Postal team director Johan Bruyneel saw me arrive and said at the top of his voice: 'Hey, Mr Walsh, good job, good job, eh!' Poor Bruyneel, he lacked so much class that his was almost a medical condition. I could imagine him skipping off to tell Lance the clever thing he had said to the troll.

No surprise that Bruyneel would be here today. Armstrong is just about to give a press conference to launch his Tour. Bruyneel was usually to be found around his boss's coattails being a good goon. He lived vicariously. As Armstrong was to comment a few years later, *J.B. Confidentiel* wouldn't have been much of a seller.

For late arrivals, it was standing room only, but I found a seat in the second row, not far from the stage where Armstrong would sit. I felt that I should have given the journalists either side of me T-shirts with the legend 'I'm Not With the Troll' on the front.

Early in the Liège press conference, Lance was asked about *L.A. Confidentiel*. He dealt with it well. In all the time I watched Lance in press conferences and around journalists, I was invariably impressed by how he handled himself and how he seemed to be aware that many of the men in the room longed to be just like him. He knew they would be the ones laughing hardest at his wisecracks and nodding most vigorously at his aphorisms. Today Lance hit a home run.

A journalist sent in a cowering shivering wretch of a question to set him up nicely.

'Lance, have the controversial allegations upset your preparations in any way?'

The question should have carried a placard with it saying, We Mean No Harm, We Mean No Harm.

'I'll say one thing about the book,' replied Lance. 'Especially since the esteemed author is here. In my view, I think extraordinary accusations must be followed up with extraordinary proof.

'And Mr Walsh and Mr Ballester worked for years and they have not come up with extraordinary proof.'

The soundbite was good and it pleased many of those in the room. I could understand that. Many of the guys in the seats around me simply preferred to write about an exciting Tour rather than to roll up the sleeves and delve into the murkiness of drugs. They didn't want to know. And that was okay: I didn't want to stop them doing their jobs. I just resented that so many of them wanted to stop me doing mine. They had no appetite for this stuff. This 'extraordinary proof' line from Lance was good enough to lead with and then wrap up the whole drug thing.

Marc Belinfante, a Dutch journalist, attempted twice to ask serious questions.[47]

---

47 Belinfante could see I was the black sheep of the cycling family. Pitying me, he asked if I'd like to do an interview for his television station. In October 2012 he sent a link to the piece, recalling a time and a Tour de France that wasn't much fun as it happened.

The last question he asked was if I thought Armstrong would win the 2004 Tour. 'This is a strange answer,' I said, 'but I mean it: I don't care. I don't care who wins the race. What I care about is clean sport. We must come back to the Tour believing in it more than we do now. This is a bad time for cycling but I hope the times will get better and they will get better if we're honest.'

'How did Lance feel about what Stephen Swart had said?'

'No comment.'

'Or Emma O'Reilly's allegations?'

'Next question.'

All over. The media had read the book. Lance had given them several dozen words of response. The mood of the afternoon was reflected in a rare expression of gratitude from Armstrong to his friends in the cycling media.

'I have received many, many calls from journalists in this room who've read the book, people who've read the book and said to me, "Okay, what's the big deal? There is nothing there." And I appreciate the support.

'Y'all know who you are and I just want to say publicly to you, "Thank you for reaching out to me at a time when I think there was a lot of expectation but there wasn't a lot of delivery."'

Wow. Lance Armstrong. Cancer survivor. Troll survivor. Thanking the guys. It was masterful stuff. Ronald Reagan meets John Wayne.

I knew it was supposed to make me and a few others like me feel isolated. To some extent it worked.

For Pierre and me that whole month of June 2004 had seemed seminal and surreal. Microfilm of *L.A. Confidentiel* had been whisked to a secret printing house in the French provinces, and from there the printed word was escorted to a secret warehouse from where it would be distributed throughout France. The secrecy was because of the publisher's fear that an injunction sought by Armstrong could lead to the book not reaching the public. For two journalists used to smudgy notebooks and chaotic desks, the whole business of microfilm and secrecy was pure James Bond.

Now things weren't quite as much fun.

I recalled suddenly a small incident which took place on a rest day during the 2002 Tour de France. With literally nothing much better to do, a Danish journalist, Olav Andersen, and I had travelled to the village of Miribel-les-Échelles in south-east France, where the US Postal team were staying at a favourite hotel, Les Trois Biches.

Close to the village, we saw the actor Robin Williams out on his bike with some friends. Williams and Armstrong were friends even though at that stage I think Armstrong had appeared in more decent films. It wasn't unusual, though, to see Mrs Doubtfire at the Tour supporting the team.

At the hotel a waiter told us that the team were out training. Andersen decided to have a coffee in the hotel bar while I sat on a wall on the village green. Part of me didn't want to be actually in the team hotel when the boys came back. Another part of me wanted to sit out on that wall knowing full well that Armstrong would see me on his return. I'd look at him. He'd look at me. Maybe I'd wave. He'd know that I was there.

I'd been sitting and contemplating for about forty minutes when the small train of US Postal riders zoomed back into Miribel-les-Échelles. Armstrong was at the front and he immediately noticed my presence. He gave me a slightly more surprised version of the much ballyhooed second glance he had given to Jan Ullrich in 2001. The Look. Well, The Look Lite. I didn't feel his steely blues piercing my soul.

Poor Andersen sipping his espresso didn't know this was happening at all. As soon as Armstrong returned to the hotel, he spoke with the owner and the atmosphere in the bar changed.

Immediately the owner was moving through it, looking closely at the few wastrels who were having a coffee or a drink.

He came to Andersen and could see the outline of an accreditation badge dangling beneath a T-shirt. He stood eye-balling the Danish journalist for a while. He wanted to ask Andersen to leave but he didn't dare. It was a public bar and hard for the patron to eject a customer, even if it was on sus-picion of being a journalist – but it was a close-run thing. If that accreditation badge had been on the outside of the T-shirt Andersen would have been on the outside of the hotel pretty quickly.

It was certainly a demonstration of the fact that, in the month of July at least, Lance Armstrong could usually get what Lance Armstrong wanted.

Two years later now and that fact was about to be demon-strated to me again not long after the Liège press conference. That year I was due to travel on the race with three journal-ists – Wilcockson, an American, Andy Hood, and my old Australian pal, Rupert Guinness – in the *VeloNews* car as so often before.

John Wilcockson and I had travelled together on the 1984 Tour and had shared car space on any number of Tours after that. Since 1999 and the ascent of Lance, of course, we'd had the slightly combative relationship detailed earlier. Guinness and I were still friends and still hauling our ageing bodies over French fields on early-morning runs during the Tour.

Now, an hour after the press conference, John collared me with a bit of news. The expedition was going ahead without me. It was pretty bad luck but they couldn't take me in their car this year because, well, Armstrong would find out. And then Lance would no longer co-operate with *VeloNews*. The sun, quite possibly, would cease to shine.

John looked at me as if to say, 'Chin up, old chap.'

I was stunned. I asked him with whom I could now travel?

John shrugged his shoulders compassionately and said that he was sorry but there was nothing they could do. They needed Armstrong like fish need oxygen.

John certainly did. In 2009 he would write a book, *LANCE: The Making of the World's Greatest Champion*. By 2009 John was the last man on earth selling Lance Armstrong hagiographies.

'That leaves me on the side of the road,' I said.

He shrugged his shoulders again.

'Fuck you,' I thought. 'I've been ditched in better joints by better doyennes.'

Still, it stung.

Guinness would later apologise for what he felt had been a very bad judgement call. Years later Wilcockson would write that he had been acting on orders from on high: the executive suite on Floor 100 in the *VeloNews* building no doubt. Whatever the truth, it was a long weekend in Liège: taxis everywhere until reporters from the French newspaper *Le Monde* offered me a place in their car. I needed to travel in an accredited vehicle to follow the Tour and so couldn't just hire one. There was no English-speaking journalist I could have asked with any confidence.

At this time the difficulty in discovering the truth about Lance wasn't just timid journalism or the challenge of substantiating wholly credible allegations. It was the entire framework in which we were operating. In June, Armstrong's London lawyers had sent a letter to virtually every print house in Britain urging the proprietors to keep their hands clean of *L.A. Confidentiel* and the fall-out. What was printed in the British media after the book surfaced were a few small reports giving quotes from the press conference in Liège and little round-ups of who was suing who. No debate took place.

And, of course, the British legal system actually worked against journalism and whistleblowers in the Armstrong case. In a time when we hear much discussion of the vileness of the tabloid relationship with celebrities and the desirability of fostering a culture of investigative journalism, it is the libel laws that are sorely wanting.

English libel law seemed to state that asking questions implied that you had come to a conclusion. If we listed the questions which we felt Lance Armstrong needed to answer, then those questions in themselves implied that we didn't consider Lance Armstrong to be unimpeachable, just as he was. The law protected Lance's defence of first resort: he didn't test positive. Beyond that any expression of doubt could libel him.

It was like trying to follow the logic of *Alice in Wonderland*.

He looked like a duck, walked like a duck, sounded like a duck, but until the laboratory actually came out and said that he was a duck, we weren't supposed to even ask a question about His Duckness.

In France, when Lance got us into court with his attempt to make us insert a rebuttal into every copy of the book, he made himself almost a figure of fun. The judge wanted to know why he had declined, for almost a month, to reply to the questions raised in the book. They had been put to him again and again. Our lawyer argued that investigative journalism could not be practised if those under suspicion refused to answer questions but were then allowed to insert broad denials into everything written about them.

In her decision Judge Bezio noted that the questions and allegations in the book 'do not necessarily constitute defamation'. In France no libel is committed if allegations are made in good faith, without malice, or if they turn out to be true.

The *Sunday Times* tried its best and in the end had to work within the legal system of the land. Part of the reason why *L.A. Confidentiel* had come about in the first place was because, quite early on in the Lance years, I had become convinced that the drip, drip of small, tightly legalled stories in a newspaper wasn't going to be enough to make the argument.

In one way I might as well have sent the pieces to the shredder instead of to France. *L.A. Confidentiel* sold well in France – over 100,000 copies – but its impact elsewhere was small. Lance handled the book effectively in that Liège press conference and his lawyers did the rest.

Our experience with the French legal system was a breath of fresh air compared to England. Thibault de Montbrial went through the legal aspects of *L.A. Confidentiel* in two hours. When he decided who the good guys were, he gave all of his amazing energy and intellect to them.

His position was that he wanted this book published. All of it. If there was anything he wasn't happy with, he enthusiastically told us what to do to make him happy. His position from the start was that we were going to find a way to get this done. I have been in so many rooms with lawyers who want nothing more than to save their backside by keeping something out of a newspaper altogether that I felt I had died and gone to heaven. Two hours to go through the book and then in the weeks afterwards we happily went about the tasks he had set us. It was a liberating way to work.

In the end at least I felt the satisfaction of having got the book out: I knew we had succeeded in putting a lot of good journalism between two covers. The system, though, seemed tilted to me. At no stage did I, Pierre or any other journalist I met want to do a hatchet job on Lance Armstrong. We wanted to believe in the great race more than anybody. To us the cynics were the guys and women who just wanted to pretend, who wanted to be a part of pushing what might be a bogus event on their readers. The system did a hatchet job on us.

And Lance Armstrong can be smart and very decisive. He saw the system, he understood it and he played it beautifully. America was his principal market and his sponsors' principal market. So he would have small intimate round-table press conferences with American journalists, who would be flattered to be texted a summons to come on over and sit down with Lance at the hotel in twenty minutes or so. The French, German, Spanish, Dutch, Italian media? Really, how many people in heartland America were going to translate and analyse that stuff? Euroweenies out to get Lance.

That left me, an English-speaking writer on a very credible paper. For all the talk and bluff in his years of prominence, the *Sunday Times* and I were the only legal battle Lance really took on and suggested he was prepared to take all the way. And he did enough to claim a win but never wanted things to proceed to the spectacle of a trial and witnesses being called to testify under oath.

Legally he got the bragging rights, and with that came something more important: the gagging rights.

In 2004, I left Liège behind without so much as a glance in the rear mirror. In no part of me could I find a trace of the wide-eyed innocence I'd had in this same place twenty years before. The thrill was gone, stolen by gimlet-eyed doctors and oily administrators and brainless riders who betrayed the thing they loved the most and screwed the friends who refused to join their brotherhood.

Lance was starting his campaign for a sixth Tour de France in succession. I could see nothing that would stop him winning numbers seven, eight or nine.

The road ahead seemed to stretch for ever. And I was tired.

I had no real right to feel jaded.

There are worse things in life than being dumped in the middle of Liège by John Wilcockson! Pierre and I had done the work and seen a bit of the world. The satisfactions and rewards were internal. Other people were having it harder.

The LeMonds had each other and they had been in the firing line since 2001. Greg went through tough times because he dared to say that working with Michele Ferrari was a bad thing and if Lance's story wasn't true it was the greatest fraud in the history of sport. What's there to disagree with? We spoke a lot during the two years after 2001 and my feeling was that without his wife Kathy's strength, it might have been impossible.

Stephen and Jan Swart in New Zealand would get some nasty backdraft. They worried how their three children would react to their dad admitting he had doped during his career, especially as so many in the media wanted to portray Stephen as the bad guy. The remarkable thing was the kids understood better than people paid to be loudmouths hosting radio phone-ins. Not once did they question their dad's decision, and when Stephen and Jan went on television in New Zealand to explain why Stephen had broken cycling's law of silence, the kids ribbed them about being famous.

One time Jan came across a nephew of Stephen's, who had come to visit, on a cycling website. She trawled through the comments, one more ignorant than the last. She got so angry, then so sad, then angry again because these snipers would fire only from behind the cover of aliases and she wanted to go on there and give them a mouthful. She thought better of it. What was the point?

She kept all that stuff from Stephen because it would have only upset him. And there were so many times when she questioned why he'd done it. And what did he say? 'One of the finest things I've done in my life.' Storms are weathered best by those with the right clothing.

The others? In Michigan I felt Betsy would be protected by two things. Her part of the book was structured so that she appeared to be a reluctant witness fending off our intrusive questions. Secondly, Betsy Andreu could handle herself and protect those around her. She would look any detractor in the eye and say, 'I was never going to lie for him, never.'

Frankie, though, was right here in Belgium and Lance was pissed. He sensed the Andreus had given me more than I was letting on. In short, he didn't believe that Betsy hadn't talked. To compound matters I had suggested on Irish radio that although she wasn't named as a source she was one of a number of witnesses who would come forward in a court case and back up allegations made in the book. With Frankie still dependent upon cycling for his livelihood, Lance thought there was no way Betsy would do that.

Frankie was summoned to Lance's room in Liège. Lance told Frankie that Bill Stapleton wanted to talk to him about the possibility of having Frankie persuade Betsy to put out a statement saying she had not been a source for the book and to generally discredit me. Frankie was uncomfortable. He knew Betsy would be reluctant to do that, but he also knew he wouldn't have much of a life in cycling if Lance was pulling against him.

Following Bill's call, he and Frankie agreed to meet near the start at Charleroi the next day, shortly after the Tour had pulled out of town. Stapleton came with his colleague Bart Knaggs, and they probably knew getting Frankie to put the frighteners on his wife wasn't going to be straightforward.

The previous night Frankie had called Betsy and told her about what was happening. He was feeling the pressure. If Stapleton and Armstrong could use their influence in cycling to get Betsy to sign a statement discrediting one of the authors of *L.A. Confidentiel,* it was game, set and match to them. To Betsy's surprise, Frankie had a plan. He intended to tape Stapleton and Knaggs the next morning. Betsy always knew that she had married a genius.

'If it's not taped, they'll deny the conversation ever took place.'

She told him to be careful and wished him luck.

The next morning Frankie slipped an ordinary digital recorder into the breast pocket of his shirt and waited for Stapleton and Knaggs to come across the car park.

Stapleton got to the point quite quickly: 'You know your wife is a source for Walsh?'

Frankie: No, no, no. My wife is not a source for Walsh. When David Walsh called the first time, I called up Lance and told him – cuz Lance said. Lance told me specific to talk [to him]. I talked with him two times and the other time when David Walsh called I wasn't home, and that was when he asked about the hospital room [inaudible]. And then she [Betsy] said, 'No comment. I got nothing to say.'

Bill: That's it?

Frankie: About talking to him?

[inaudible comments]

Bill: Yeah.

Frankie: Well, yeah.

Bill: Yet he claims she's a source for that conversation. Would she be willing to clarify that though?

Frankie: I read in the book that LeMond's the one who gave him that story.

Bill: No. Walsh was talking to LeMond and I think LeMond told him he heard it from Betsy and he [LeMond] claims Betsy is the source.

Frankie: Greg LeMond and Betsy don't even know each other. One hundred per cent don't know each other . . . and Betsy did not tell Greg LeMond about the hospital.

Bill: Well, is Betsy willing to issue a statement that – or go on the record that – she didn't give [inaudible] no comment to Walsh and was never interviewed by him?

Frankie: She'll say that when he called she said: 'No comment.'

Bill: About everything that she talked to him about?

Frankie: No, because there were other conversations. When I was there I talked to him and the one time I was there, there might have been some nicky picky nothing stuff, but she didn't really talk that much, you know. I don't know exactly, but dealing with the hospital-room thing, that is what she said.

At this point there is some discussion punctuated by inaudible sections about my radio appearance in Ireland, where I had said that, if needed, my anonymous sources would back up their version on oath. I then mentioned Betsy as one of these.[48]

Frankie: Well, I'd like to get a transcript of that [the radio show].

48 It was brainless of me to mention Betsy by name as a source for *L.A. Confidentiel* and it brought trouble Frankie's way, but neither Andreu complained. Remarkable people.

Bart and Bill: Okay.

Frankie: David Walsh is lying. He does not have a taped thing of Betsy saying that she would do that.

Bill: All right.

For some time Frankie sticks to the version of events that involves Betsy saying 'no comment'. Stapleton and Knaggs are not to be diverted from their plan, however. Again and again they press.

Bill: It would be very helpful if she would . . . was just willing to make a statement, cuz, see [Walsh] has talked to other people about her and said that she's very courageous, and she's willing to take a stand against Lance, [that] she knows these things about Lance. That she's told him [Walsh].

And again.

Bill: [Walsh is] trying to take the people that gave him very little . . .

Bart: . . . and build them up . . .

Bill: . . . and make them bigger, like LeMond. LeMond's not going to testify against Lance and all those people.

And once again.

Bill: The question . . . the question is, if she'd be willing to take a strong position that she [inaudible] didn't give him anything about the hospital room [inaudible].

That's very important, cuz it says that he's lying [inaudible], he lied about sources … and if she's willing to make a statement that she'd never testify against Lance: again, that makes him a liar …

The fascinating aspect of this conversation and the Armstrong camp's attempt to destroy my credibility is that at no stage does Bill Stapleton attempt to convince Frankie Andreu that the hospital story is untrue, and at no stage does Bill Stapleton try to convince Frankie Andreu that he – Stapleton – had been in the room at the time. Stapleton and Lance would both later claim this to have been the case.

In the end – the conversation took about twenty minutes – Bill Stapleton sums up the overall strategy for Frankie:

Bill: Because the best result for all of us is to [inaudible] pick away at him [inaudible] enough between his witnesses that he has taken things, pieced this hodge-parcel together, and show the *Sunday Times* and show his publisher that it really is falling apart, and [at] that point extract an apology, drop the fucking lawsuit and it all just goes away [inaudible]. Because the other option is full-out war in a French court [inaudible] and everybody's gonna testify [inaudible]. It could blow the whole sport.
Frankie: I agree.

That was Frankie and Betsy's story. You grow up close to Detroit you learn how to handle yourself. They had each other.

I knew they'd be okay.

16

'As a society aren't we supposed to forgive and forget and let people get back to their job? Absolutely. I'm not sure I will ever forgive you.'

Lance Armstrong to Paul Kimmage, 2009

In July 2005 Lance Armstrong won his seventh Tour de France but, unlike him, I had by then grown tired of the procession around France. It was like a dull party game: pass the yellow jersey from rider to rider until it got to the guy from Texas. He'd keep it all the way to Paris.

So, I passed on the '05 race, feeling there was nothing more I had to say, apart from three standard homilies of disapproval. Staying away denied me the privilege of hearing Lance express sympathy for the trolls of the world. *'I'm sorry that you can't dream big.'* By then, however, I suspected that even his sincerity was fake.

It wasn't supposed to end like that: Lance, on the podium, wreathed in sunshine and smiles, delivering a two-fingered salute to those of us who had tried and failed. Heist over, he was heading for the hills.

A week before, I had been covering golf at the Open Championship in St Andrews, the delightful little town on the Fife coast in Scotland. We stayed at a house not more than a mile from the Old Course and I shared a room with Paul. Two of us. Twin beds. Like Father Ted and Father Dougal.

It was the Saturday night, our work for the *Sunday Times* was done, Tiger Woods had a two-shot lead going into the final round, and we were lying in our beds not yet ready for sleep. There was something Paul needed to tell me.

'I want to talk to you about Armstrong,' he said.

'What about?' I asked.

'I think you've got to let it go. You've done great work, taken it so far and now is the time to move on.'

'Why do you think so?'

'Because it has taken over your life and I think Mary and the kids have suffered by you being so wrapped up in this.'

'Do you really believe that?'

'Yeah, I do. Do you realise that virtually every conversation we have now is about Armstrong? Every time you call me it's because of something you've heard about him, and I'm left thinking that if it wasn't for him, I wouldn't hear from you.'

'Have I been that bad?'

'Yeah. And this isn't that good for your career either. You saw what happened last year when you nearly left the paper. You have done your bit; get a bit more balance back in your working life and make sure you've got more time for your family. And remember too that Armstrong is only one guy, you don't want to forget all the others.'

I didn't argue the case. When your closest friend says something important, it is worth listening. Presume he is right and think about it. Paul was right about how much of my life Armstrong consumed.

It was once believed a man thought about sex every seven seconds, but more recent research says the true number is twenty times a day. My Armstrong thoughts were somewhere between those two figures.

'And, Mr Walsh,' the immigration officer at Chicago's O'Hare Airport would say, 'what is the purpose of your visit to the United States?'

'Business, sir.'

'And what is the nature of your business?'

'I'm a sportswriter, and I'm going to be interviewing people about Lance Armstrong.'

'Lance Armstrong, he's the cyclist, right?'

'Yeah. I'm hoping to show that actually he's a fraud, been using banned drugs to win.'

'Oh . . . you have a good day now.'

Or I'm standing in a slow-moving line to the x-ray scanner at an airport and the stranger alongside me is wearing a yellow Livestrong wristband. 'Do you support Lance?' I say to entrap him. He says, 'Yeah I do,' and I give him the full history, the overwhelming evidence, the sense that you would have to be brain dead not to see the truth. One victim has stayed in my mind: dark business suit, white shirt, clean cut, no watch, just the wristband. He looked at me, shook his head, and forfeited ten places in the line to get away.

A wet evening in Christchurch, New Zealand, 2005, getting on a media bus after the British and Irish Lions had lost a Test match to the All Blacks. I take my seat as the much-liked *Independent* rugby writer Chris Hewett offered a little light-hearted banter: 'Here comes Lance Armstrong.' It earned a few giggles but none were mine. 'Chris, what the fuck did you ever do that was worthwhile?' Chris is a fine writer and a well-rounded man, and he must have thought I had lost it completely. Possibly I had.

Despite his warning to me, Paul wasn't much better himself. In 2006 we were sharing a house in Augusta at the sportswriter's dream event, the Masters. Paul is friends with Fanny Sunesson, the caddie, and Fanny had a friend over from Sweden, a 16-year-old elite amateur keen to watch every minute of Masters play. Alas he had no pass for the final day, which Fanny mentioned to Paul, who had a spare pass.

It was arranged for Fanny's friend to come to our house early on the Sunday morning. A little after nine there was a knock on the door. He was a very impressive looking 16-year-old, over six feet tall, pencil-thin but still giving the impression of strength. And if he did make it to the pros he wouldn't have to change his wardrobe because he was dressed in creased white slacks with a bright yellow polo shirt. Blond hair and blue eyes didn't detract from the overall look. There was only one thing that didn't sit well with Paul and me. The yellow wristband. Now a pass for the final day's play at the Masters may be the hottest ticket in world sport, but if you're getting it from Paul Kimmage free, gratis, and for nothing, don't turn up with the wristband.

It wasn't my pass and not my problem. All I did was open the door and stand to one side. Paul's brain switched to overdrive.

'Hi,' he said. 'Fanny's friend, you've come for the pass?'

'Yes, that's right.'

'Okay, first though, just let me see your wristband.' The

guy stretches his right arm towards Paul. 'No, just let's see it,' says Paul, indicating that he wants him to remove it. He does that and hands it to Paul, having no idea why he's doing this. I move another step back from the action. 'Now,' says Paul, looking at Young Swede, 'watch this.'

He walks across to the drawer containing the cutlery and picks out a large pair of scissors. Then he takes the wristband and folds it over once, then a second time, then again, until it is a tightly wound coil of rubber. Young Swede is utterly perplexed but, as Paul brings scissors and rubber together, it becomes clear what is going to happen next.

The scissors slice silently through the rubber and the fragments are suddenly all over the kitchen floor. There is an embarrassed silence, broken then by Paul as he matter-of-factly points to the floor. 'That guy,' he says, 'is a fraud. You should know that.'

The young Swede remains silent. Paul then produces the pass, smiles as he's handing it over and says, 'I hope you really enjoy it out there today.'

'Thank you,' says our new friend.

Paul was right about the story consuming more of my life than it should. But because it was unresolved, it wouldn't go away.

That August *L'Équipe* journalist Damien Ressiot wrote a piece that was the culmination of an extraordinary investigation into the re-testing of urine samples from the 1999 Tour which showed Armstrong had used EPO when winning his first Tour that year. Central to the brilliance of the story was Ressiot's cleverness in getting the UCI to hand over the rider's doping-control forms so that Ressiot could check laboratory numbers against numbers on Armstrong's forms.

In the end Armstrong himself gave the go-ahead to the UCI to release the forms to Ressiot because the journalist had suggested he was investigating the rider's use of TUEs (Therapeutic Use Exemptions). Armstrong hadn't used TUEs in 1999, and thought the story would reflect well on him. With Lance's doping forms, Ressiot's job was then straightforward: compare the numbers on those forms to the numbers on the lab's 'positives'. There were six correlations.

LE MENSONGE ARMSTRONG, [The Armstrong Lie] was the giant headline on *L'Équipe*'s front page, and the story proved beyond doubt that six of the 'positives' discovered in the retro-testing of 1999 samples belonged to Armstrong. Ressiot's determination to investigate the seven-time Tour winner stemmed from disgust at the bullying of the Italian rider Filippo Simeoni in the third to last stage of the 2004 Tour. Simeoni had testified against Michele Ferrari in an Italian doping trial and that made him Lance's enemy. So when he tried to join a breakaway group in that third to last stage, Lance personally chased him down and told the other escapees they wouldn't get any leeway if Simeoni was one of their number.

But the catch was that the retrospective testing had been carried out for research purposes and the results could not be used to instigate a disciplinary action against Armstrong. Knowing he couldn't be charged on the basis of these positives, Armstrong confidently dismissed the allegations, saying it was likely the samples had been spiked. He believed it was a French witch hunt and suggested it reflected the anti-US feeling that existed in France at the time.

This wasn't an intelligent explanation because there was no way for the French laboratory to spike numbered samples and know they belonged to Armstrong; Ressiot knew they were his only because Lance had given him the reference numbers. The UCI set up an 'independent commission' under its chosen investigator Emile Vrijman, a Dutch lawyer and a friend of Hein Verbruggen's. When Vrijman delivered his report, the World Anti-Doping Agency dismissed it as unprofessional and lacking impartiality: 'Mr Vrijman's report is fallacious in many aspects and misleading.'

Though Armstrong survived the Ressiot story, it was a watershed moment because it established he had used EPO in 1999. It was easy to argue that the rules couldn't allow research testing to be the basis for a case against Armstrong, but there could be no disputing that Ressiot had demonstrated the rider cheated. Including the front page, six pages of that day's *L'Équipe* were given over to the story.

Ressiot is a journalist in the mould of Pierre: he now works the doping beat at *L'Équipe*, as Pierre had once done. 'What I can't stand is the deceit,' he says. 'We sell stories of extraordinary achievement but when we learn they are not that, we don't like to take them back. I feel I have done my job as a journalist [in producing the Armstrong story], and as a profession we need to stop building dreams on false premises.'

Many of the journalists who had been on Armstrong's side were glad to see the back of him in 2005 because it had grown harder to write about him. What more was there to say? His leaving the sport seemed an opportunity for me to let go of the story, but that wasn't possible. It kept coming back. Journalists wanting to do some more excavation on the Armstrong site, saw me as someone who could help.

Joe Lindsey came from Colorado to our house to do a piece for *Outside* magazine and wrote a balanced account of the case for and against Armstrong. Around the same time, Dan Coyle came to Cambridge and we spoke for hours in a small restaurant.[49] He was writing *Lance Armstrong's War*, his book on his year embedded with the US Postal team. As with Joe, Dan wrote fairly of the work I had done on the Armstrong story.

In the course of the interview, Dan asked about John and the impact of his loss on our family. I've never needed much encouragement to speak of our eldest son and off I went, recalling memories of a great kid and telling stories I love to tell. It is a tragedy that John's life lasted just twelve years and eight months, but he gave us so much in that time. At John's funeral my old boss at the *Sunday Tribune*, Vincent Browne, gently promised that time would help us all to cope with John's loss and get on with the rest of our lives. At the time, it didn't seem so simple. 'We will get on with the rest of our lives,' I said, 'but they will be lesser lives.'

That is as true now as it seemed then. So many times I've thought of what John would have brought to our lives: the laughs, the tears, the celebrations, the arguments, the matches that we haven't watched together. I remember too that, a few days after his accident, Emily came running into the kitchen with a joyous smile on her face, and though Mary and I were in a pit of grief we couldn't remain there.

49 Daniel Coyle is a former editor of *Outside* magazine in the US, who spent 2004 living with the US Postal team in Girona, Spain. The subsequent book *Lance Armstrong's War* became a bestseller. Since then he's collaborated with Tyler Hamilton to deliver *The Secret Race*, another bestseller.

Without Kate, Simon, Daniel, Emily, Conor and, two years later, Molly, it would have been so much tougher.

In the interview with Dan, I said I'd loved John more than any person I'd ever known. That's how it seemed at the time, but Emily says that in the same circumstances I would have said the same about any of the others. That is probably the case. Towards the end of the interview with Dan, I said that one of John's legacies to me was to have the courage to stand up to things, to ask difficult questions and not to go with the flow even if that allows you to float along. 'If I carry a little of that with me, then I'm pleased about that,' I said.

In the final chapter of his book, Dan describes taking a draft of his book to Armstrong who, he has agreed, can see it before it goes to the publishers. Without any prompting, Armstrong brings me up. 'Don't call him the award-winning world-renowned respected guy.' In an effort, presumably, to appeal to Armstrong's human side, Dan said that I seemed motivated, at least in part, by John's memory. Dan mentioned that John was my favourite, which was true only in the sense that he is my all-time favourite human being.

That mention of John unhinged Armstrong. This is how Dan described it:

Armstrong's eyes narrow. He cracks his knuckles, one by one.

'How could he have a favourite son? That guy's a scumbag. I'm a father of three . . . to say "my favourite son", that's fucked, I'm sorry. I just hate the guy. He's a little troll.'

His voice rises. I try to change the subject, but it's too late. He's going.

'Fucking Walsh,' he says. 'Fucking little troll.'

I'm sitting on the couch watching, but it's as if I'm not there. His voice echoes off the stone walls – troll, casting his spell on people, liar – and the words blur together into a single sound, and I find myself wishing he would stop.

You won, I want to tell him. You won everything.

But he won't stop; he can't stop, and I'm realising that maybe this has nothing to do with Walsh, or with guilt or innocence or ego or power or money. This isn't a game or a sport. It's a fight, and it can never end, because when Armstrong stops fighting he'll stop living.

A birdlike trill slices the air; Armstrong's eyes dart to his phone. The spell is broken.

'Listen, here's where I go,' Armstrong says after putting down the phone. 'I've won six tours. I've done everything I ever could do to prove my innocence. I have done, outside of cycling, way more than anyone in the sport. To be somebody who's spread himself out over a lot of areas, to hopefully be somebody who people in this city, in this state, in this country, this world can look up to as an example. And you know what? They don't even know who David Walsh is. And they never will. And in twenty years, nobody is going to remember him. Nobody. And there are a million cancer patients and survivors around the world, and that's what matters.'

All the stuff about me being a troll and him being a messiah, that's water off a duck's back. But it hurt that he dared to speak of my relationship with John in the terms that he did. Only Lance Armstrong would have said such a thing.

In the end, I just let it go. His time for tears would come. What's meant to be always finds a way.

17

'In a time of universal deceit – telling the truth is a revolutionary act.'

George Orwell

L.A. Confidentiel turned Pierre and me into the Serge Gainsbourg and Jane Birkin of cycling journalism. Our output scandalised English-speaking people everywhere but we went over big in France, and its pages were as toxic as *The Satanic Verses* to the church of Lance fundamentalists.[50] Few had read it but many denounced it. Sufficient unto the day was the outrage thereof.

Sufficient. And then some.

Like a stone dropped into a lake the book caused ripples which eventually reached all the way to the shore. Lance Armstrong would wind up in the boardroom of his lawyer's

---

50 Fourteen English-language publishers considered *L.A. Confidentiel* and said no. Schillings' threat to sue anyone who repeated the charges against Armstrong made in the book was enough to discourage would-be UK publishers.

Dallas office with a video camera trained on him and a stenographer poised as he prepared to be deposed under oath. Many of us involved in the case of the book would wind up in similar rooms.

It all started with a punt. Bob Hamman was once the Lionel Messi of bridge. The Michael Jordan. The Babe Ruth. He won twelve world championships but famously lost one in Bermuda to a pair of Italians who he reckoned had cheated him. He was a tough man to begin with, but being cheated brought out the Joe Pesci in him. *You think I'm funny, funny how?*

Bridge has a sedate, dusty image but Bob Hamman learned the game by playing for money. He was an excellent chess player, a fine poker and backgammon player, but in the end he was drawn to the complexity of bridge. He is a big, broad and burly man with a crown of grey hair on a glorious head.

In 1986 Bob Hamman set up a company called SCA Promotions. SCA stands for Sports Contests Associates. It was a business venture premised on Bob's greatest talent. He could calculate the odds on virtually anything. Bob has a bookie's brain and SCA, in essence, was a bookie's business with a respectable front office. The big idea? The underwriting of the risk involved in special events and promotions by other companies.

So a company sponsors the blindfold half-court overhead-throw event for audience members at an NBA game. They don't think anybody will actually sink a shot and claim the million-buck prize, but just in case somebody gets lucky they insure themselves with SCA. For a premium SCA carries the risk.

And they will carry almost any risk. Once when NASA was putting two Rover vehicles on Mars, a company called Long

John Silver approached SCA. If NASA found an ocean on Mars they wanted to give free shrimp to everybody in America. Bob came to an agreement that an ocean on Mars would have to cover the same proportion of the planet's surface as the smallest ocean on earth (the Arctic) covers.

Nothing was found. Bob didn't have to pay for a nation's shrimp.

As big ideas go it is a good one and SCA has become the world leader in guaranteeing prizes and bonuses. It seemed like grist to the very profitable mill then when Kelly Price, an insurance broker with a company called Entertainment and Sports Insurance Experts, contacted SCA in the winter of 2000.

The deal he proposed involved SCA taking on some of the risk which was at that time being carried by Tailwind Sports,[51] the owners of the US Postal team. Tailwind had

---

51 Tailwind was principally a cadre of elite businessmen who shared an enthusiasm for cycling. They funded Thomas Weisel's US Postal team and every spring got to spend a day at training camp hanging out with Armstrong and the boys. Weisel and five other investors originally put up about $2.5 million to finance what later became Tailwind Sports, the cycling-management firm that owned the Postal team. The ownership group eventually numbered at least 20 but the company remained stubbornly in deficit.

Investors also enjoyed good access to their team during the Tour de France. As the race would proceed, the businessmen, a macho bunch by all accounts, would pedal segments of the course. A following convoy of cars carried their food and water bottles. They ate well and were whisked to prime viewing spots each day. Like the team they would end the day with a massage. Having claimed to own roughly a 10 per cent stake in the company during the SCA depositions in 2005, Armstrong had changed his mind in 2010: 'I was a rider on the team. I was contracted with Tailwind Sports, I never had any dealings with the Postal Service – zero. I didn't own the company [Tailwind Sports]. I didn't have an equity stake. I didn't have a profit stake. I didn't have a seat on the board. I can't be any clearer than that.'

Tailwind had folded in 2007.

been both pleased and alarmed at the prospect of Armstrong going on to record a long sequence of Tour de France victories. Pleased because that was why they had a cycling team in the first place. Alarmed because such success was going to cost them a fortune.

So Tailwind were asking SCA to give them a quote on a deal they had come up with which would give Armstrong $1.5 million if he won in 2001 and 2002, a further $3 million if he went on to win in 2003 and then a final $5 million payment if he rolled on into the history books with a sixth successive Tour in 2004.

The SCA underwriter who dealt with the query was Chris Hamman, a son of Bob. Chris didn't much like the idea, but his father was one of life's natural dealmakers and when he took the notion to Bob he saw things differently. It was odds. Risk. Two hundred riders each year. And the same guy was going to keep on winning? Cancer guy? Bob gave the thumbs-up. In January 2001 a contract was drawn up. For a premium of $420,000 SCA would agree to pay Lance Armstrong staggered payments amounting to $9.5 million if he could win every Tour from 2001 to 2004.

After the Tours of 2002 and 2003 SCA promptly sent out the cheques to Tailwind Sports who passed the $1.5 million and $3 million cheques on to Lance Armstrong with a smile.

And then *L.A. Confidentiel* appeared. Having allowed the book to play such a large part in our lives over the previous two years, Pierre and I were delighted by sales but disappointed by how little influence the book had. All the evidence seemed to us to emphatically say something was very wrong here. We hadn't counted on the media's enduring love of an easy good news story (which Lance was) and on Lance's ability to intimidate and denigrate anybody outside his tent.

Perhaps we should have seen all that coming, but we could never have guessed that somewhere in America, a company called SCA would have a slightly unconventional lawyer by the name of John Bandy who had spent six years of his life living in France and some of those years studying at l'Université de Paris, La Sorbonne. John Bandy had fluent French and he picked up a copy of *L.A. Confidentiel* out of personal curiosity and professional duty. He read it, tapped out his own translation and paused. Hey, *attendez un peu*.

Armstrong had been due to receive his final bonus of the deal, $5 million, on 3 September 2004. Instead, the money had been placed into a custodial account with J.P. Morgan until the doping allegations detailed in *L.A. Confidentiel* were cleared up. Lance was not amused. The trolls were costing him money.

Armstrong and Tailwind duly lodged proceedings against SCA in a Dallas County District Court on 14 September. It was an odd sort of legal impasse at first. Technically, Lance's problem was with Tailwind, not with whoever Tailwind had insured the deal with. The contingent contract was between SCA and Tailwind and made it clear that the obligation to reimburse Tailwind was premised upon the fact that 'the conditions of the events scheduled herein and the sponsors' [contract with Lance Armstrong] had to comply with the terms and conditions of this contract.'

This was understood to mean more than just win the races, Armstrong had to win in a manner consistent with the requirements of the contingent contract. In other words, the question was similar in nature to the one facing journalists. It wasn't whether Lance won, but how he won. SCA were asking Tailwind the question: was Lance in compliance with all rules or was he using performance-enhancing drugs? In the end, to avoid a chain reaction of litigations, Lance was permitted to join party with Tailwind and the two sides were lined up.

Both SCA and Tailwind stated that they wanted an arbitrator to settle the matter.

The issue was simple. Tim Herman, the lawyer acting for Armstrong, claimed that SCA hadn't the right to question the Tour victories. For SCA Bob Hamman decided to do much of the investigating himself. He arrived in Europe to meet Pierre and me, he went to Auckland for a session with Stephen Swart, he spoke with Greg and Kathy LeMond, and to Emma O'Reilly. Everybody he spoke with stood over what was in the book.

I was contacted in September 2004. I immediately decided on two things: I had to protect sources; I had to protect our book. I was happy to point anybody who was interested in the truth in the direction of the truth. There followed, as I testified later, maybe twenty-five phone calls and a dozen or so emails between myself and SCA in the next year and four months. I helped with contact numbers, a few technical details and gave my opinion on the credibility of several people whom SCA were thinking of contacting.

On 19 January 2006, after a couple of false starts, I sat down in a room in a law office in Dallas to give testimony. The charm of the place is evident from the address: 12655

North Central Expressway, Suite 810, city of Dallas, County of Dallas, State of Texas. Whose bucket list is that not on?

You sit in a room waiting your turn, eating bought-in food and making small talk with other witnesses and legal people. Eventually you end up in a big room set up so that you can look across to your right and direct your answers to the three-man arbitration panel. After lawyers from both sides get to ask their questions, the three-man panel can also ask questions which, in my case, they did. Though everything is under oath, it didn't feel pressurised.

My testimony was given late in the proceedings and, unlike most of the others involved, I hadn't been deposed beforehand. It was a civil discourse limited to technical questions about the practice and ethics of journalism. Why did you call this person? Why not that person? Etc, etc. Inevitably we trawled back over a couple of greatest hits from the Lance years:

Tim Herman: Now, in testimony provided previously in these proceedings by Mr Stapleton, he testified that Ferrari was not a big story. That you, David Walsh, made it scandalous and made it into a big story by writing it. Is that a fair representation?

Walsh: It's complete nonsense.

Herman: Why?

Walsh: Because when the *Sunday Times* ran the story in early July 2001, pretty much every single newspaper across Europe, some of them on the front pages – and these were serious, quality newspapers – ran stories saying the *Sunday Times* had revealed Armstrong worked with Ferrari. I went to a local newsagent in my town and got a huge amount of newspapers from across Europe, and every one of them reported on the Armstrong–Ferrari connection, because Ferrari had that kind of reputation and, as I say, Lance was a huge figure in the sport.

At one stage, amusingly in hindsight, we had some back and forth about the admissibility of a transcript of an interview I had conducted with an unnamed source. I stuck to my right to protect the identity of the source through questioning. I was briefly dismissed and the account of what was said when I was out of the room showed the esteem in which sacred journalistic principles were held. Jeff Tillotson for SCA, the guy who was doing the friendly part of the cross-examination, explained to the arbitrators and opposing counsel while I was gone: 'There's a transcript. It's as clear as day it's Frankie Andreu, that he's an unnamed source.'

It was agreed among them that I would be permitted to proceed without naming the source and that Frankie would be recalled at a later date. Then I was readmitted and everybody politely pretended that they didn't know who I was talking about as we discussed the transcript.

A lot of evidence and a lot of hearsay got trawled through in the SCA case, and it revealed two things above all else. Firstly, anybody not still in cahoots with Lance was afraid of Lance. People had started taping conversations about Lance. And Lance had taken to calling some of those giving evidence before they could be deposed. Just saying hello! And, secondly, everybody around Lance and in the SCA was obsessed with what Betsy Andreu had heard in that hospital room in October 1996.

Most of all, what Bob Hamman and the SCA team wanted to get to was the nub of what happened in that room. The question still reverberated. The SCA hearing would spend a lot of time on who said what in Indiana. There was a small ambush during my testimony on the matter. Tim Herman for Tailwind and Lance Armstrong did the honours. Somebody had tracked down Lisa Shiels, Lance's old girl-friend. I had tried. SCA had tried. We had concluded that she had vanished in the wind. Now somebody had succeeded in finding her.

Herman: Now, you haven't seen this before, Mr Walsh, but this is an email exchange between Lisa Shiels and a lady at ESPN in 2004. And in it Ms Shiels, when asked about this hospital incident by someone totally unrelated to Mr Armstrong, indicated she had no recollection of that happening. Had you talked to Ms Shiels, or had you been in possession of this email, would that have given you some pause about the reliability of the account that was given to you by Ms Andreu?

Walsh: Absolutely not, because my information had come from three people, the two Andreus and Stephanie McIlvain, and I believed them.

Herman: All right. What if you had known there were not just six people in the room but nine people in the room, would you still have been as confident with the story from Mr and Mrs Andreu, who left the room right after the alleged statement was made?

Walsh: From my conversation with the Andreus and Stephanie McIlvain, it wouldn't have mattered if there had been one other person in the room. I thoroughly believed what they told me.

Who would have thought one line from the mouth of Lance Armstrong would be so disputed all this time later? During the taking of early depositions for the case on 25 October 2005, Betsy Andreu had gone to a small room in a Detroit hotel to be deposed on the matter. There was a surprise observer present. Armstrong showed up for the Andreus' depositions, intending to sit in on Frankie's session. The order was reversed, however, and he ended up sitting through Betsy's session instead.

Frankie is a tough man. Betsy is tougher.

When Lance turned up that day, he extended his hand to Betsy. She accepted it. 'Hey, how's it going?' he said.

'Goin' fine,' she said.

He then said, 'You wanna see some pictures of the kids,' and he pulled out some photographs of his children with his then girlfriend, Sheryl Crow.

She thought, 'He thinks I'm going to lie for him.' But that had been the point of her existence through the previous six years. She was not going to lie. Betsy was pressed again and again about what had happened once the doctors had swept in to that conference room back in 1996:

Herman: I want to focus on events that have been alleged in this case regarding certain statements Mr Armstrong made to doctors. If you can, describe for us now how these events came about. What took place?

311

Betsy: We were in his hospital room, and he was having a
scheduled meeting with his doctor. He was having a
scheduled meeting with his doctor or with a doctor, I'm
not sure. There was going to be some sort of meeting.
And there were quite a few people there, so we went
into a conference room, and there at the conference
room, people that were there were: me, and Frankie and
Lance, Stephanie McIlvain – that was the first time I
met her – Chris Carmichael, his then girlfriend now
wife, Paige.

Herman: Anyone else that you recall?

Betsy: Lisa Shiels.

Herman: Who was she?

Betsy: His girlfriend at the time.

A pivotal part of Lance's rebuttal of the Indiana hospital incident was his claim that it was impossible that it had occurred
without three other people being present: his mother Linda,
his friend Jim Ochowicz, and his lawyer/agent Bill Stapleton.
Betsy stuck to her guns.

Betsy: They began to ask him some questions – banal questions. I don't remember. All of a sudden, boom: have you
ever done any performance-enhancing drugs? And he
said, 'Yes.' And they asked what were they, and Lance said,
'EPO, growth hormone, cortisone, steroids, testosterone.'

Herman: Are you absolutely certain that's what he said?

Betsy: Yeah, I'm positive.

Herman: Now, as you recall, you were sitting there when
this conversation took place, where Mr Armstrong said

the events that you told us today he said. Who else was around you that you believe heard this same thing?

Betsy: Everybody in that room heard it. Every single person.

The fly in the ointment was Stephanie McIlvain, the Oakley sunglasses representative who had been in the hospital room that day. As previously noted, she and Betsy had met for the first time that day and had become firm friends afterwards. They had spoken many, many times since about the incident. In all those conversations since 1996, Betsy and Stephanie had chatted on the basis that they had both heard Armstrong rhyme off the substances he had taken. Betsy recalled Stephanie coming to Dearborn for a stay and the three of them – Stephanie, Betsy and Frankie – discussing the issue around the kitchen table. Now Stephanie had changed her mind and given a different account under deposition a few days earlier.

Herman: In connection with your visits to the hospital with Mr Armstrong, did there ever come a time where you were with him and with other people where there was any discussion regarding Mr Armstrong's use of performance-enhancing drugs or substances?

McIlvain: No.

Herman: Okay. There's been testimony— Let me rephrase that. Were you ever at a hospital room or other part of the hospital with Mr Armstrong where he said anything about performance-enhancing drugs?

McIlvain: No.

> Herman: Do you have any recollection of any doctor in
> your presence asking Mr Armstrong if he used in the
> past any performance-enhancing drugs or substances?
> McIlvain: No.

Poor Stephanie McIlvain. She recollected that Betsy Andreu had called her up some time afterwards and asked if she remembered an incident where two doctors came in and asked Lance Armstrong about performance-enhancing drugs, and Lance had told them what he used. Stephanie McIlvain testified that she had said no, that she didn't remember that. Yet when we had contacted her in connection with *L.A. Confidentiel* she had told us that she had been present in the room and remembered the conversation in the same way that Betsy did. She had still been willing to give that evidence when the *Sunday Times* was considering publishing the book extracts.

It would be wrong to be too judgemental about this situation. Stephanie was almost certainly feeling a lot of pressure. She had a better relationship with Armstrong than most of the other people being deposed. In 2001, when her two-year-old son Dylan was diagnosed with autism, Stephanie had decided to give up her Oakley work to be at home more. Armstrong had intervened and made it possible for her to work from home. As kindnesses go, it was no small thing and the type of gesture which Lance was capable of. More recently she had been in touch with him about a neighbour stricken with cancer. To be placed in the position she was now in was close to impossible.

It got worse. She had spoken to Greg LeMond about the

incident and he had already said in deposition that he recalled the discussion.

McIlvain: No, I told Greg LeMond I remember being in a room and I remember watching a football game and first meeting Betsy and Paige Carmichael.

Herman: Do you remember if Mr LeMond asked you if Mr Armstrong said he used drugs while you were in that room?

McIlvain: He told me what Betsy told him and asked if I remember that way.

Herman: And your response to Mr LeMond was?

McIlvain: No, I remember being in a room.

News of this development in McIlvain's evidence was deeply upsetting to the Andreus and to Greg LeMond. It left Betsy and Frankie twisting in the wind as apparently the only people who had heard the drugs exchange and it weakened SCA's case. Betsy was stunned but her world was still black and white, and when the depositions finished and the hearings took place in Dallas she was as strong as ever:

Herman: Now you know in this proceeding she [Stephanie McIlvain] has denied that she heard Mr Armstrong say such things. Is that true based upon what she has told you previously?

Betsy: She was lying.

Herman: I'm sorry, Ma'am, I didn't hear you.

Betsy: She was lying.

The hospital incident was just as much an obsession for the Armstrong team as it was for SCA. Perhaps because the details of the story are so human and believable. The science didn't seem to bother the Armstrong people. They seemed to think they could take care of Emma and of the Swarts. But the hospital incident was chewing them up.

Questioned about it by Armstrong's attorney Tim Herman during the arbitration, Bill Stapleton chipped in with some testimony of his own: 'And I was there that afternoon through the whole football game.'

However, three days later, under cross-examination, Stapleton testified: 'Lance had told me it hadn't happened . . . I wasn't in the room.'

He went on to say: 'It just defies logic that it would [happen], three days after brain surgery, that his medical history wouldn't have already been taken. But, no, it didn't happen.'

Five weeks after the Andreus had been deposed in Michigan, their old friend and nemesis Lance Armstrong had made his way to his own deposition in Austin, Texas. It was the last day of November 2005. Jeff Tillotson, lawyer for SCA, began the questioning after a brief outline of the rules. Tillotson is respectful and unaggressive but even he gets snapped at once in a while.

Still, he asks what has to be asked in his low-key way. Indiana. Hospital:

Tillotson: Okay. Do you have any recollection while these individuals were there that a doctor or doctors came into the room and discussed with you your medical treatment or your condition?

Armstrong: Absolutely not.

Tillotson: Okay. Did any medical person ask you, while you were at the Indiana University Hospital whether you had ever used any sort of performance-enhancing drugs or substances?

Armstrong: No. Absolutely not.

Tillotson: So that just never came up? No one ever, as part of your treatment, no one ever asked you that?

Armstrong: No.

Tillotson: Can you offer, or can you— can you help explain to me why Ms Andreu would make that story up?

Armstrong: Well, she said in her deposition that she hates me.

Tillotson: Do you believe she's making that story up to— to get back at you or to cause you harm?

Armstrong: Whether she's making up that she hates me?[52]

Tillotson: No. Do you believe that she's making— I mean, she's— according to you, this story where she said she specifically heard you say stuff—

Armstrong: Yeah.

Tillotson: And that when she testified she took Mr Andreu

---

52 In fact, nowhere in testimony did Betsy Andreu say that she hated Lance Armstrong. In another reference to a secret tape, Timothy Herman had asked Betsy to recall the conversation that Frankie Andreu had wired himself up for in France in 2004 when asked to meet Bill Stapleton and Bart Knaggs. Herman had asked, 'Without going through in detail, Frankie, on several occasions in that conversation with Mr Knaggs and Mr Stapleton, talks about how much you hate Lance Armstrong, doesn't he?' Betsy demurred: 'No. He just says they don't like each other but that's the extent of it.'

'Okay. So is it true that you do not like Mr Armstrong?'

'No. I don't like him.'

out and confronted him regarding whether or not he was doing the same thing. Do you recall that testimony?

Armstrong: Yeah. Vaguely. But I have no idea why she did that—

Tillotson: Okay.

Armstrong: Other than she hates me.

Tillotson: Okay. Obviously you had a relationship with them. And you knew her, and you go back some time with her. And I'm asking if —

Armstrong: I knew her very little, not very well.

Tillotson: Why would Mr Andreu say the same things?

Armstrong: Probably to support his wife, which I don't know if you're married or not, but—

Tillotson: I am.

Armstrong: Sometimes it is required.

Tillotson: And so you think . . . is it your testimony that Mr Andreu was also lying when he said that he heard you say those things regarding your prior use?

Armstrong: One hundred per cent. But I feel for him.

Tillotson: What do you mean by that?

Armstrong: Well, I think he's trying to back up his old lady.

Betsy and Frankie stuck to their guns about the hospital room. Interestingly, Lance's friend and former coach Chris Carmichael and his wife Paige, whom one might have expected to be called by the Armstrong team, did not give evidence. Neither did Lisa Shiels.

It was a traumatic experience for Stephanie McIlvain, and I'm sure there was nothing she wanted more than to be permitted to escape from the headlights. She was trapped, however. James Startt, my initial conduit to Frankie and Betsy, testified that he and McIlvain talked about the incident at the 2004 Tour de France. He had heard the story and when the opportunity presented itself in 2004, he asked McIlvain about it.

James asked, 'Is it true what happened in that hospital room . . . what Betsy told me?' And she said, 'Yes, it was.'

SCA had noted from her earlier deposition that Kathy LeMond had illustrated the stress she and Greg were feeling by telling the hearing that Greg had begun taping calls in connection with Lance. Stephanie had been taped in a thirty-three-minute call in July 2004. SCA issued a subpoena obliging LeMond to place the tape in the hands of the hearing. It made for uncomfortable listening. Greg LeMond assures McIlvain early on that he is not taping the conversation, he then goes on to talk about having been through personal issues, makes some small talk, and finally gets to the issue of the hospital room.

LeMond outlines the Betsy and Frankie version of the hospital story and asks if McIlvain would be willing to testify if he needed her support in some future lawsuit.

McIlvain: If I was subpoenaed I would.
Greg: Yeah?
McIlvain: 'Cause I'm not going to lie. You know I was in that room. I heard it.

They continue to speak about Armstrong. LeMond indulges in a little conjecture as to what might happen if the entire Armstrong myth collapsed. McIlvain is more realistic:

McIlvain: Well, the whole thing of it is, Greg, there are so
many people protecting him that it is just sickening,
you know.

Greg: But the people protecting him know.

McIlvain: I know. They all know.

Greg: Yeah?

McIlvain: Well, because I know – and this you don't
repeat – but I know for a fact then when the whole
book came out, Chris Carmichael made a call to my
friend and said, 'Oh, you know, I've been sitting here,
thinking, thinking, thinking who was in that room. If I
totally remember the incident, yes he did admit to what
he was taking. But I don't really think Stephanie and
Betsy Andreu were in there, and I don't think Lisa Shiels
was in there.' And I just laughed. I said, 'You tell him
that, yeah, I was in there because I remember him
[Chris Carmichael] looking around the room and seeing
who was in that room.' So then my friend says, 'Oh my
God, that's what he said. He said he looked around the
room to make sure everybody in that room was trust-
worthy.'

The SCA. Fun to stay at the SCA.

18

'Dude, I thought we were friends.'

Lance Armstrong

For any future biographers of Lance Armstrong, the sworn deposition available in transcript form or in video on the internet is an essential resource. *Drive-by Character Assassinations, A Compilation Album.*

Watch him. Lance sits patiently in a lilac shirt and crew cut and describes a world wherein a good man is beset at all times by a motley army of whores, drunks, addicts, cheats, liars and trolls. It is too much. He is above all this. He makes the point a few times that he has too much going on in life to have been able to familiarise himself with all this stuff he is being asked about. When Lance is not shredding somebody's reputation, he is struggling to recall some of the bigger events in his life. How much he gave. What people said. When he met key figures in his life. Lots of things were very blurry.

Armstrong also had a talent for being difficult.

Tillotson: Were you able to examine the tape that Mr Andreu made of his conversations with Mr Stapleton and Mr Knaggs?

Armstrong: No.

Tillotson: Several years later do you remember at the deposition a transcript being produced of the tape he says he made?

Armstrong: Yes.

Tillotson: Okay. If you'll turn to tab 16, which has been marked as 'Andreu Exhibit 1', I'll represent to you this is a copy of the transcript that was produced at that deposition ... I can't remember, I thought you had an opportunity to read this transcript while at the deposition. Have you had an opportunity, either at the deposition or since then, to review this transcript?

Armstrong: No, sir.

Tillotson: Okay. I'm going to turn – direct – your attention to a couple of things that are said, and if you'll turn to what's been marked as page three of the transcript ... If you'll see there at the top, Mr Andreu was reported to say, 'She won't do that. She didn't – she did not tell David Walsh about the hospital room, know that for sure ...' And then Mr Andreu says, 'Cuz I never told anybody about the hospital room, you know.' Someone says, 'Right'. 'I mean, cuz ...' and then it's inaudible. ' ... Hospital, and, you know, I don't know about [inaudible] hospital room happened, but I've never told anybody, because I – you know – David Walsh for me, what does this shit accomplish? It accomplishes nothing.' Do you see that?

Armstrong: Uh-huh. I do. It's hard to follow, but I see it.

Tillotson: Okay. If Mr Stapleton was at the hospital room watching the game, and knew that the hospital-room incident had never happened . . . do you have any reason why he wouldn't tell Mr Andreu: 'What the heck are you talking about? What do you mean you never told anyone about something that never happened?'

Armstrong: Well, I don't think he was there to take him on, but I have no idea why he wouldn't say that.

Tillotson: If you'll turn to page five of this transcript. Let me ask you this before I ask another question about some actual comments. Did you know that Mr Stapleton and Mr Knaggs were going to go meet with Mr Andreu to discuss the possibility of obtaining an affidavit or a statement from Ms Andreu regarding Mr Walsh's book?

Armstrong: No. Not that I remember.

Tillotson: So you didn't authorise them to go do it, or tell them to go do it? They just went and did it?

Armstrong: Not to my recollection.

Tillotson: Did they report back to you that they had met with Mr Andreu at the 2004 Tour de France and had talked to him about the book?

Armstrong: Not to my recollection.

Tillotson: Okay. So, until it was revealed at the deposition of Ms Andreu, did you have any idea that Mr Stapleton and Mr Knaggs had actually talked to Mr Andreu at the 2004 Tour de France regarding Mr Walsh's book and the possibility of getting a statement from Betsy?

Armstrong: Oh, I think that would be unfair to say. I mean, there's— the Tour is wide open. There are people everywhere. Frankie is somebody that was on our team. I mean, people were talking about the book, obviously, so . . . it didn't come up like that, but . . .

Tillotson: Was Mr Andreu on the team in '04?

Armstrong: No.

Tillotson: Okay. So I think it was their testimony that this conversation took place in 2004. It would have to have been because they're talking about Mr Walsh's book which wasn't published till 2004. Right?

Armstrong: Correct.

Tillotson: Okay. I don't think I fully understood what you were telling me. Do you recall if Mr Stapleton or Mr Knaggs told you that they had this conversation with Mr Andreu?

Armstrong: Not this— I mean, not this specific conversation. But they could have said that they saw Frankie in the lodge or outside the bus. I don't know.

Tillotson: Now, prior to Mr Andreu's deposition, you did call him, did you not?

Armstrong: I— yes.

Tillotson: Did you actually speak to him?

Armstrong: Yes.

Tillotson: What was your reason for calling him?

Armstrong: Well, I think I called because . . . because we— because Kathy LeMond had done her deposition, and had all kinds of crazy things to say, which were news to us.

Tillotson: Any other reason you called him?

Armstrong: Other than to say hello, no.

Tillotson: Were you trying to influence his testimony in any way?

Armstrong: Of course not.

Tillotson: Were you trying to warn him?

Armstrong: Of course not. And, in fact, he said that on the phone . . . he said, 'I totally understand.' He said, 'I haven't heard of any of this stuff either.' No. I—

Tillotson: Did you discuss with him the statements attributed to you in the Indiana University Hospital room?

As well as calling up Frankie Andreu before he testified, Lance had also been speaking to Stephanie McIlvain.

Tillotson: Did you speak with Stephanie McIlvain before her deposition?

Armstrong: Yes.

Tillotson: When did you talk to her?

Armstrong: I don't recall. She called me about her neighbour.

Tillotson: Was this a neighbour that needed some help, or was this the neighbour that has cancer?

Armstrong: Correct.

Tillotson: Okay. What did you talk with her about, other than the personal things related to her neighbour?

Armstrong: That's it.

Tillotson: Did you talk about her upcoming deposition?

Armstrong: No.

Tillotson: Did you talk about any of the testimony from Kathy LeMond, Greg LeMond or the Andreus?

Armstrong: No.

Greg LeMond had testified that he had received a series of calls from Armstrong associates. He said John Burke, president of Trek bikes, where both cyclists had contracts, told him that he was being pressured by Armstrong's associates to get LeMond to retract his words about Ferrari: 'For me, it was Lance was trying to extort me, trying to threaten me.'

As for Kathy LeMond, she had broken down during her deposition. 'Public opinion is very pro-Lance Armstrong, and we take a lot of flak if we say anything negative about him, and it's difficult for our kids.'

Now compared to so many other details in his testimony, where Lance's memory was poor to the point of being treacherous, about this one thing he was pinpoint sharp. Little wonder Kathy had broken down. Lance had news for her about her husband. Armstrong clearly recollected the call he put into Greg after I broke the Ferrari story. Poor Greg. He has big problems apparently.

> Armstrong: So I called him up and said, 'What's up with that?'
> Tillotson: What did he respond, as you recall?
> Armstrong: I've heard his recollection of the conversation, which is completely opposite from my recollection, because Greg, who I know has serious drinking and drug problems, is – was – clearly intoxicated: yelling, screaming. I had to practically keep the phone about a foot away. I then knew I was dealing with a wild man, and just— just tried to get through the conversation.
> Tillotson: Okay.
> Armstrong: But it was an assault on the other end,

which is obviously opposite of what we've all read and seen.

Tillotson: Let me ask about that. You did call him? He didn't call you? Is that right?

Armstrong: I called him.

Tillotson: Okay.

Armstrong: . . . at the Four Seasons in New York.

Tillotson: Okay. To—

Armstrong: His cell phone.

Tillotson: Okay. From your cell phone?

Armstrong: No. To his cell phone. I called from the LAN line.

Tillotson: Okay. To get some explanation for why is he saying these things? Is that fair to say?

Armstrong: I think more just to— because it came through Walsh. Obviously, I don't trust much of anything that David Walsh says. So just to . . . just to clarify that it was, in fact, what he said.

Tillotson: You said that Mr LeMond has serious drinking and drug problems?

Armstrong: I mean . . . you know, I don't go drinking with him, so I don't know for a fact, but I think that's pretty much common knowledge.

Tillotson: And is it your testimony you could tell that he was intoxicated on the phone when you talked to him?

Armstrong: Aggressive, agitated, angry, belligerent, like a drunk.

Tillotson: Okay. Were his words slurring, or was he irrational in some sense?

Armstrong: I think his words always pretty much slur.

Jeff Tillotson put it to Armstrong that in response to Greg LeMond he had said everyone dopes or everyone does it: 'Oh come on, Greg, you know we all do it.'

> Tillotson: Is that untrue?
> Armstrong: That's absolutely not true. Why would I call somebody to criticise them for saying I dope, and then say we all dope? That's ridiculous.

After a brief digression pointing out how LeMond's recollection of the conversation was entirely a drink-fuelled fantasy, Armstrong returned for another quick splash of battery acid:

> Armstrong: You know, the most interesting part of that conversation, and this is going to sound incredibly juvenile, but I said, 'Dude, I thought we were friends, you know, we've been good with each other.' And he continued to scream, and say, 'Friends, what do you mean friends? You didn't even invite me to the Ride for the Roses this year.' I'm like, 'Wait a minute. Is that the issue here?' I said, 'Well, we didn't invite you because last year you were drunk the whole time. You set up competing autograph sessions when we were trying to do good things for the fight against cancer.' I said, 'We invited you to the gala when we were going to introduce everybody that was there – Miguel Indurain, Eddy Merckx, the greatest of all time. You showed up literally sixty seconds before you were going to be introduced. Of course, we didn't invite you back.'

All this was a fascinating glimpse inside a world which we all thought was closing as we watched. If nothing came of the SCA case, and that looked to be the likely outcome, the bottom line of the contract between the insurance company and Tailwind Sports was that SCA had to pay up if Lance was the official winner of the 2004 Tour de France. If Lance didn't reverse his decision to retire then he would be riding off into a golden sunset, celebrated for ever as the man who had conquered cancer and France in that order, the guy who had made the world safe from little trolls.

It was odd to discern the various weights of his concerns. I thought Betsy's evidence was compelling but that Emma offered a more detailed forensic insight into life inside the US Postal team. And I had been hugely impressed with Stephen Swart during our time together in New Zealand in 2003.

Armstrong seemed most shaken by Betsy, though. Not that this stopped him applying the boot elsewhere.

Tillotson: She [Emma O'Reilly] has identified or said either to Mr Walsh or to others that, at one point in time during a Tour de France race, you asked her to dispose of some syringes.

Armstrong: Uh-huh.

Tillotson: Are you familiar with her statement regarding that?

Armstrong: I'm familiar with that statement.

Tillotson: Is there any truth to that statement?

Armstrong: Absolutely not.

Tillotson: Would you ever use syringes during a race – I mean, for any reason legitimate?

Armstrong: You would use IVs for, like, replenishment of fluids. Just like any – like every – sport.

Tillotson: Sure. But I've heard, for example, some professional athletes or cyclists would do injections of vitamins, hence the need for syringes.

Armstrong: Yeah, sure. Yeah. And in Europe I think that's much more accepted than the States. I mean, in Europe I think doctors are— the medical field would use a syringe, whereas here in the States, we would do it orally.

Tillotson: Okay.

Armstrong: There's not the stigma around: I mean, in America, we see a syringe, you think, 'Oh, no, is he a junkie?' Whereas in Europe that's fairly common.

Tillotson: So I guess my question is, first of all, you never asked her to dispose of any syringes?

Armstrong: Correct.

Tillotson: But would you ever have had syringes on you to be disposed [of] in connection with any race?

Armstrong: Me?

Tillotson: Yes.

Armstrong: No.

Stephen Swart's story about race-fixing was put to Lance. Was there any truth to Stephen's statements that his team was offered $50,000 in connection with attempting to fix the outcome of some races in which Lance was involved?

Tillotson: Do you know why Mr Swart would say these things?

Armstrong: As I said earlier, I have no idea why, other than perhaps, like Emma O'Reilly, he was paid for his testimony and needed the money.

Tillotson: Do you believe that's why Ms O'Reilly said these things about you?

Armstrong: Absolutely.

Tillotson: That she needed money?

Armstrong: I'm not her financial advisor, but I think—

Tillotson: Well, you have—

Armstrong: We now know that Walsh paid his sources. Which he denied in the beginning – now admits. I don't think any respected journalist would find that to be kosher.

Tillotson: But other than that, do you have any other evidence to suggest that Ms O'Reilly was making up this in exchange for money, other than the fact that—

Armstrong: I—

Tillotson: . . . she received some compensation?

Armstrong: Emma or Stephen?

Tillotson: Emma. Oh, sorry . . .

Armstrong: Pissed. Pissed at me, pissed at Johan. Really pissed at Johan. Pissed at the team. Afraid that we were going to out her as a – and all these things she said – as a whore, or whatever. I don't know. But primarily, I have to confess, I think it was a major issue with Johan . . . And it wouldn't have been a very good book if it was *J.B. Confidentiel.* There would not have been a lot of sales.

There was other stuff, of course. All fascinating. Hein Verbruggen of the UCI had furnished a letter telling us about all the drug tests which Lance had passed and how great the laboratories were. On occasion the unfortunate timelines of events threatened to ambush even Armstrong.

Dr Craig Nichols, one of the doctors who had supervised Armstrong's care and who was now chief of haematology–oncology at Oregon Health & Science University, said in a sworn affidavit that he had 'no recollection' of any statement by Armstrong while in treatment confessing to the use of performance-enhancing drugs. He added, 'Lance Armstrong never admitted, suggested or indicated that he has ever taken performance-enhancing drugs.'

Betsy and Frankie Andreu's depositions were taken on 25 October 2005 in Michigan. On 27 October, Indiana University announced that the Lance Armstrong Foundation had funded a $1.5 million endowed chair in oncology. Craig Nichols' affidavit was signed on 8 December.

Naturally, Lance Armstrong didn't like the implication when these dates were pointed out: 'It was a million and a half dollars, and I understand that's a lot of money. But to suggest that I funded that chair to get an affidavit or to get some clean medical records or some sanitised records is completely ridiculous.'

More entertaining, if you liked this sort of thing, was the issue of Lance's two unsolicited donations to the UCI, the governing body of world cycling. He had thrown $25,000 into the pot a few years previously and, according to the UCI, had recently pledged another $100,000. This seemed most generous for a man with such little respect for institutions or the blazers who run them.

Tillotson: Now, we were talking about WADA and the UCI. You have made a contribution or donation to the UCI, have you not?

Armstrong: I have, yeah.

Tillotson: Do you know when that was made?

Armstrong: Some years ago. I don't recall exactly.

Tillotson: Well, 2000, for example?

Armstrong: I don't know.

Tillotson: Was there anything that occasioned that, that you recall? Like, I'm doing it because of X or Y or Z?

Armstrong: I'm doing it to fund the fight against doping.

Tillotson: And what made you— what triggered that? I mean, was there any particular event?

Armstrong: The only event, or in support of that fight, just like I've done on other occasions.

Tillotson: Why the UCI? I mean, why give the money to UCI?

Armstrong: Because they're our governing body.

Tillotson: Okay. How much did you give?

Armstrong: I think twenty-five thousand dollars.

Tillotson: You say you think . . .

Armstrong: Yeah, I say I think because I'm not one hundred per cent sure.

Tillotson: Would it be within a range of that, though, if you're . . . I mean, it wouldn't be like—

Armstrong: Well, it wouldn't be—

Tillotson: Two hundred thousand dollars?

Armstrong: No.

Tillotson: Or one hundred and fifty thousand dollars?

Armstrong: No.

Tillotson: I mean, it could be thirty or forty, or it could be twenty, is what I'm asking.

Armstrong: It could be. I don't think it's that. But I think it's no more than thirty.

Tillotson: Was it by personal cheque?

Armstrong: I don't remember.

Tillotson: Did you tell the UCI you were going to make it before you did?

Armstrong: I don't recall, but I don't think so. I don't know.

Tillotson: You gave twenty-five thousand dollars, or approximately twenty-five thousand dollars, to the UCI, but you don't remember if you told them beforehand that you were sending them a cheque?

Armstrong: I don't recall.

Tillotson: Had you ever given any money to UCI before?

Armstrong: No.

Tillotson: Have you ever given any money since?

Armstrong: I have pledged money since, but I don't think I've done it yet.

Tillotson: When did you pledge money?

Armstrong: I don't remember. Between now and then.

Tillotson: No. I meant when did you make the pledge?

Armstrong: Between now and then. I don't recall exactly.[53]

Tillotson: Who did you give the money to?

Armstrong: Well, if you sent a cheque or a wire, I don't know who received it, but—

53 This transpired to be an even more generous pledge: $100,000.

Tillotson: I mean, like ... is it literally like one day the UCI guy comes in, opens up the mail, and there's a cheque from you for twenty-five thousand dollars?

Armstrong: I mean, I don't know. I wasn't in the mail room.

Tillotson: Okay. But did you let anyone know this is coming?

Armstrong: I told you, I don't remember.

Tillotson: Okay. Have you spoken to anyone at the UCI regarding your donation?

Armstrong: Yeah.

Tillotson: Who?

Armstrong: I have spoken to Alain Rumpf, Hein Verbruggen, perhaps others.

Tillotson: Do you know what they've done with the money?

Armstrong: I just told you, I don't know.

Tillotson: Okay. Like, they didn't buy some specific equipment or something with it that you're aware of? It wasn't earmarked—

Armstrong: Which part of 'I don't know' do you not understand?

Tillotson: So you have no idea why you gave twenty-five thousand dollars to the UCI at all. And you don't even know if you called anyone before—

Armstrong: I don't know. Personally – now, this is going to shock you – but my style is different than David Walsh's. My approach has been more of an internal one, to support clean racing, to support clean sport.

My idea of the best tactic is not to slander and defame everybody, and bite the hand that feeds you, and piss in the soup; but my fight and my commitment has always been there.

Look back and study Lance Armstrong at that time and you are looking at a man who figured that he was virtually home and clear. He was in retirement. His enemies were being quietened or smitten by lawyers. He was an icon. He had this one last inconvenience to get through and he'd collect his money and go surfing. Everything would be on the record for ever but, if he won, he won big. And for ever. So he enjoyed the entire experience.

On 8 February 2006 a settlement was reached. SCA Promotions paid Armstrong and Tailwind Sports $7.5 million – the $5 million bonus plus interest and lawyers' fees. Armstrong's statement came later, when news of the depositions began to leak: 'The allegations were rejected,' he said. 'It's over. We won. They lost. I was yet again completely vindicated.'

Not quite the case. While the 'final arbitration award' noted that the arbitrators settled after 'having considered the evidence and testimony', the panel produced no findings of fact. The business was settled without a ruling. Bob Hamman has always said, 'The panel did not rule on the case.'

The SCA business was an ending in a way. Or so it seemed. Lance Armstrong had retired. All the evidence had been put on oath. Everybody had gone in there risking perjury if they lied. It was the only time in the entire Lance saga that people got to swear under oath.[54] But nothing happened. For years the twelve volumes of depositions and questions lived in retirement, taking up a huge chunk of space on my computer. Then, like Lance, they came back to active life.

I sometimes wonder if that's what Bob Hamman had intended all along. He's a man whose life's work has been a study of chance and probability. People who have played bridge with Bob (and lost) say that what most strikes fear into them is his ability to read what is in their mind and what they have in their hand. He himself says he has what he terms 'an inferring state of mind'.

My theory is that the entire season of depositions and hearings was Bob's way of clearing the fog and getting to see what his opponent was holding. There is a manœuvre in bridge

54 In USADA's 'Reasoned Decision' on Lance Armstrong it was noted that, in an arbitration over whether Mr Armstrong used performance-enhancing drugs to win one or more of his Tour de France victories, Mr Armstrong stated words to the following effect, under oath and subject to penalties of perjury:
1. That Dr Ferrari never prescribed, administered or suggested any kind of a drug or doping programme for Lance Armstrong.
2. That there was nothing in Lance Armstrong's dealings with Dr Ferrari that would suggest that Dr Ferrari was encouraging other athletes to use performance-enhancing drugs.
3. That Lance Armstrong had not had any professional relationship with Dr Ferrari since 1 October 2004.
4. That Lance Armstrong never violated the rules of the UCI or the Tour de France in connection with the Tour de France in 2001, 2002, 2003 or 2004.
5. That Lance Armstrong had never taken any performance-enhancing drug in connection with his cycling career.
6. That Lance Armstrong never had any knowledge of Tyler Hamilton using illegal substances when he was Armstrong's teammate.
7. That Tyler Hamilton did not dope while he was on Lance Armstrong's team.
   As demonstrated by the testimony of numerous witnesses in this case, each of the above statements made under oath and subject to the penalties of perjury were materially false and misleading when made.

known as 'the psyche'. It's a complex form of bluff. A player conveys one thing while planning another. It's Bob's trademark.

He must have known from early on that once the arbitrators made up their mind about the nature of the relationship between SCA and Tailwind that all Lance had to do in order to claim his money was to prove that he was the official winner of the relevant Tours. Bob, though, pressed ahead; he let the interest mount up and the lawyers' fees mount up until the time came to settle up. He picked up his tab but by then everything, for the first and only time, was down under oath.

I think Bob created a time capsule that he could always come back to and dig up. A month after the release of the USADA report in October 2012, I read that Lance's lawyers had made an offer to SCA of $1 million to ensure that the case didn't come back to haunt them. The offer was politely turned down. SCA want more than that.

Pierre and I have looked back sometimes at *L.A. Confidentiel* and the modest waves it caused. For a while we never saw the big picture. The book gave Bob Hamman the chance to get twelve volumes of sworn testimony down.

You can say that in the end Bob Hamman got lucky. Lance came out of retirement, unexpectedly, and didn't have the emotional intelligence to appreciate the need to keep Floyd Landis on his side. You can say too that Bob's refusal to pay the $5 million bonus in 2004 simply cost him an extra $2.5 million in legal fees to Armstrong and another $1.7 million to his own lawyers.

That's a lot of money to pay for volumes of sworn testimony and Bob wasn't certain he had done the right thing when writing the cheques. So, did he just get lucky? I prefer to think that he did the right thing when refusing to pay $5 million to a man he believed to be a cheat and because he did the right thing, he earned his reward.

In the end, Bob looked down and found that he was holding a hand that he liked. *L.A. Confidentiel* was right in there, a key player in a high-stakes game.

19

'The good people sleep much better at night than the bad people. Of course, the bad people enjoy the waking hours much more.'

Woody Allen

I took 2006 as my gap year. My sabbatical, sort of. Time to go away and plug myself into a recharger, and finally write a book in English about this whole saga. It pleased me that *From Lance to Landis: Inside the American Doping Controversy at the Tour de France* was published by Ballantine Books, an imprint of Random House in New York. In the Arctic world that is home to trolls, the ice was melting.

That was also the year the SCA arbitration finished, the year the *Sunday Times* settled with Lance, the year that the Tour de France took off without its winner for the last seven years.

The Tour. No Lance. No me. I was okay with that. Paul covered the event for the *Sunday Times*. I did other things. I coached a boys' football team. I wrote my book, stayed at home and it was easier than I thought it would be.

Then Floyd Landis won the Tour de France. And a day later, as the riders would say, they popped him. Did I feel a little jealous of Paul? No. A lot jealous? Yes.

In Floyd Landis we could see the genes that would let Lance continue. More squat, more muscular, less handsome, less cunning, but Floyd was Floyd and he had a will that sometimes made Lance look like a kitten. Certain people in life you don't want to mess with.

Floyd broke his hip in 2003 on a ride just north of San Diego. He didn't just break it as normal people would understand things: there was no crack, no hairline fracture. Nope, he broke the top right off his femur.

For most people that would be the hint to go and do something else. Floyd had some titanium pins inserted, each of them four inches long, and they held the top of the bone in place. They also snagged his muscles and ligaments as they moved over the bone while he trained. So he had them replaced. Next day he headed to Europe to join the boys at training camp for the Tour. He rode the Tour all the way home. Not a problem that his hip was just rotting away like a damp fire-log.

Not normal. Nothing about Floyd Landis was normal.

He came from the most unusual of backgrounds. Lancaster County in Pennsylvania has a large congregation of devout Mennonites, which makes it a no sex, no drugs, no rock and roll type of place. Every writer wanted to write a portrait of the cyclist as a young man.

Floyd was reared in Farmersville, as a Mennonite with all the trimmings: church three times a week, no television, no sport, no exertion on Sundays, no dancing, no revealing clothing, no mingling with the unrighteous. His early races he couldn't wear shorts less the wrath of God hindered him. Finally Floyd decided that God had other things to be worrying about.

Young Floyd Landis developed a passion for mountain bike racing. Slightly sinful but he was good at it. At the age of 16, his parents had taken him aside for a little chat: 'If you continue competitive cycling, your soul will burn for eternity.' Floyd didn't believe that. Maybe Paul and Arlene Landis didn't really believe it either. They became their son's greatest fans.

Floyd moved to California at the age of 19. He'd seen one movie, *Jaws*. He'd never tried coffee, alcohol or sex. He caught up. He started road racing in 1999 and signed for US Postal just three years later. Straight in under the wing of Lance.

Landis was both odd and straight up. In Girona, where the Postal boys were living, he kept an apartment which would have been small for an impoverished student. For a pro biker it was a joke. He got about the town on a skateboard. He worked like a lunatic. He questioned everything. He made people laugh. He had the word 'winner' stamped all over him.

Nothing could stop him, not even that hip he busted up in 2003. He could only mount the bike from one side, couldn't cross his legs when sitting and was in pain most of the time. Who cared about hell for eternity when cycling was purgatory on earth?

Lance ushered Landis into the inner sanctum with unprecedented haste. Soon he and Floyd were off riding together for long stretches. Big bro. Little bro. He could see what the kid had. In 2002 and again in 2003, Landis spent five weeks before the Tour down in St Moritz in the company of Lance Armstrong and Michele Ferrari.

Floyd was inside and still he was outside. Unimpressed. When something offended his sensibilities he couldn't handle it. He could rationalise doping. Other things he couldn't tolerate.[55]

He didn't like secrecy in the team over contracts. He didn't like riders being played one off against the other. He didn't like the dumb superstitions that riders worked under. The Mennonites back in Lancaster liked to say that they lived *in* the world but were not *of* the world. That was Floyd Landis: *in* the team but not *of* the team.

The tale of his first road race is always worth retelling. Determined not to be marginalised as some sort of farm-boy hick with a religious hang-up he showed up in a helmet and visor, a dayglo jersey and a pair of argyle socks. He was wheeling a massive bike. He cleared his throat and announced: 'If there's anyone here who can stay with me, I will buy you dinner.'

That lightened the atmosphere considerably. They thought that Farmboy had made a joke. He cleared that up.

'You shouldn't laugh because that gets me angry. And if you make me angry, then I'm going to blow you all up.'

---

55 Tyler Hamilton has told the story of how, after an impressive ride up Ventoux in the Dauphiné Libéré in 2004, he got a call from Hein Verbruggen of the UCI. Verbruggen wanted to meet as soon as the race finished. At the meeting in Aigle, Switzerland, the UCI's chief medical officer, Dr Mario Zorzoli, produced data which suggested that Hamilton may have been transfused with blood from another person. Hamilton brazened it out, claiming that such a thing was impossible. Zorzoli didn't push the matter any further.

A few weeks later on the Tour de France, Floyd Landis told Tyler Hamilton that somebody had dropped a dime in a phone booth and called the UCI after the Ventoux ride. Lance Armstrong on line one.

As he cycled away from the leaders that day, he roared back at them: 'You like my socks? How'd you like them now?'

Who wouldn't want to be covering a Tour de France which had Floyd Landis among its prominent riders? Who wouldn't want a character like that to emerge as clean? Hope against hope. Paul went to the Tour de France. Wrote brilliantly. Got more to write about than he had bargained for.

All the previews called this one as a wide-open Tour. On 1 July, just before the first Tour of the post-Lance era got underway, the riders who had finished second, third, fourth and fifth in the 2005 Tour were removed from the race because of involvement by them or by their teams in an investigation into illegal blood doping. This was *Operación Puerto*, the Spanish police in full swing against blood doping. Landis was among the favourites now.

You wanted to believe in him, and it was a good sign when he said that he didn't expect to win any mountain stages, he just wanted to be in touch for the final time trial on the day before the Tour finished. He led going into the Alps but relinquished it all very tamely, giving up the lead in the Alps to Óscar Pereiro, who had started the day in 46th place some 28mins 50secs behind.

In the fifteenth stage he took back the yellow jersey which he had quietly surrendered two stages before. He came up Alpe d'Huez in fourth place. He looked strong. Then came the torture at La Toussuire. Strangely reassuring for those of us watching from afar.

Landis reached the bottom of the last climb on a day which the riders complained long and bitterly about being too hard, too tough. When he hit the bottom of the climb he had significant company. All his main rivals were there, each of them supported by two or three lieutenants. Landis had just one Phonak teammate and his support vanished at the end of the first mile of an 11-mile ride.

Landis was as vulnerable as a drunken wildebeest wandering into a barbeque afternoon for a pride of lions. Carlos Sastre, a Spaniard from the CSC team, made a break. Merciless. Landis faded. He started giving up the minutes faster than the minutes could give themselves up. One minute, two, then three, then more. The more minutes he lost the less relevant he became. He looked like death.

He reached the finish line of the 112-mile stage more than eight minutes behind Sastre and ten minutes behind the winner of the stage, Michael Rasmussen, of Rabobank. Rasmussen had ridden brilliantly, breaking away from the pack with two other riders less than a mile into a stage which included the crossing of the highest point of that year's Tour, the Col du Galibier. What a slog. The race gains nearly 1.2 miles in altitude, ascending to 8,681 feet above sea level, over the 26-mile pass.

The previous day Landis had said that he was confident that he could win the Tour. Now he was 11th, more than eight minutes behind the race leader, Óscar Pereiro. If you wanted to believe in Floyd Landis now was the time to buy your shares. When the doping machine is working well there should be no days like these. Doping, by 2006, could make the promise that it would remove the drama from your life.

'I suffered from the beginning, and I tried to hide it,' he

345

said afterwards. 'I don't expect to win the Tour at this point. It's not easy to get back eight minutes. That was the best I could do.'

Now, with six riders within four minutes of one another, the race was going to be decided before the final time trial on Saturday, the penultimate day of the Tour. That was the day Landis had marked on the calendar for his big move.

Before that, though, another killer day loomed. The final mountain stage – a 124-mile slog over four gruelling ascents and a mad seven-mile descent into the town of Morzine.

And then, having risen from the dead, Landis went out the next day and launched an 80-mile attack over three colossal Alpine passes. He won the final mountain stage of the Tour by nearly six minutes, pulling back about three quarters of the time he had lost the day before. For Jean-Marie Leblanc it was a heart-warming answer to his prayers for no more one-man tours. The Tour director called the performance, 'The best stage I have ever followed.'

Afterwards, Floyd Landis's epic climb on the road to Morzine that day was compared to that of Chiappucci on Sestriere fourteen years previously. If you knew your cycling, this was profoundly depressing, but maybe the comparison was intended to be more apt than complimentary.

On the way to Morzine, the final ascent, the epic Col de Joux Plane, is plain murderous. It measures 8.1 miles with an average slope of 8.5 per cent. Two of the last three miles of the climb have a slope of 10 per cent. Then that frightening seven-mile plunge to the end. The Col de Joux Plane was one of the few climbs where Lance Armstrong had showed mortality. He nearly collapsed there in 2000, losing two minutes to Jan Ullrich. That same day in 2000, Marco Pantani, with typical abandon, launched an attack at about the same point as Landis launched his. Pantani soon threw in his hand.

In 2006, Floyd Landis devoured it all.

Here was drama. In two days Floyd Landis had yo-yoed from first place to 11th and now, back to third. He was now just 30 seconds behind the race leader and his friend, Óscar Pereiro of Spain. Another Spaniard, Sastre, was in second, 12 seconds behind the leader. Three cyclists within 30 seconds of one another. The time trial was restored to its former prominence as the deciding factor in the race.

In a similar, earlier time trial in the Tour's first week, Landis had come in second, more than a minute ahead of the two riders now ahead of him in the standings. The only rider who bested Landis in that time trial was now more than an hour behind.

Landis finished third in the time trial on the penultimate day of the Tour. That was that, really. Tour over. He was 50 seconds ahead of Pereiro and leapt from third to first. The kid from Lancaster County went to Paris in the yellow jersey and wore it to the top of the podium.

The nightmare began the very next morning when Landis was informed of a slight problem with his urine sample from Morzine. He scrapped his lucrative racing engagements for the week, got himself to a secret location somewhere in Europe and waited for the news to break. Four days later his Phonak team announced the sad tidings to the world. Phonak had been through the Tyler Hamilton bust the year before, so they knew the ropes.

The urine sample taken from Landis immediately after his epic and unforgettable Stage 17 had come back positive, having an unusually high ratio of the hormone testosterone to the hormone epitestosterone. His T/E ratio was nearly three times the 4:1 limit allowed by World Anti-Doping Agency rules.

Landis held a short telephone conference with reporters from the US late on the Thursday evening. When Landis began declaring his own innocence it was with a heavy heart. An invisible hand seemed to be guiding him back to the fundamentals of the life he had grown up with.

'I'll say no,' he said, when first asked if he had taken drugs. 'The problem I have here again is that most of the public has an idea about cycling because of the way things have gone in the past. So I'll say no, knowing a lot of people are going to assume I'm guilty before I've had a chance to defend myself.'

He asked that the reporters cut him some slack, for everybody to take a step back. 'I don't know what your position is now and I wouldn't blame you if it was sceptical, because of what cycling has been through in the past and the way other cases have gone. All I'm asking for is that I be given a chance to prove that I'm innocent.'

Floyd Landis was a bad liar, which suggested he might not be a bad person.

In truth, if you had watched the evolution of doping it seemed a little strange that somebody who had spent so much time in the company of Michele Ferrari should be popped for something as quaint as testosterone. Maybe being done for the wrong thing fortified him as his voice grew stronger in protest against his fate. And his excuses grew more fanciful. So bad that 'The Late Show with David Letterman' created one of its famous Top Tens to mock him with:

10. High altitude in the Alps made Daddy dizzy.
9. Who can resist Balco's delicious 'spicy chipotle' flavour?
8. I was trying to impress Sheryl Crow.
7. Uh ... global warming?
6. The world hates Americans already, so does this really matter?
5. French bastards must have dosed my quiche.
4. Wanted to give *New York Post* excuse to run hilarious 'Fink Floyd' headline.
3. Hulk no need excuse.
2. Frankly, I'd rather be a disgrace than a loser.
1. Screw you – I'm Floyd ***damn Landis.

On 14 May 2007 arbitration began between USADA and Landis with regard to the Tour de France doping allegations. On 20 September 2007, the arbitrators found Landis guilty of doping. He took a two year ban. His title went to Óscar Pereiro.

I continued coaching, got the book away and continued to enjoy the break from the weekly grind of newspapers. That lasted until 2007; another phone call from Alex.

'Ready to come back?'

I was.

20

'I see in him outrageous strength, with an inscrutable malice sinewing it. That inscrutable thing is chiefly what I hate.'

Herman Melville, *Moby Dick*

Lying in a tent at Gorak Shep, 5,170m above sea level in the heart of Nepal, you don't expect Lance Armstrong to disturb the Himalayan peace. But a text message from a friend had done just that: 'Landis, sensational confession, dynamite, implicated Armstrong and others.'

It was Paul Kimmage, of course. You don't expect texts in the Himalayas. You don't expect texts from Paul written in the font 'excitement'. The serenity of the great adventure was fractured for a while.

It is a six-hour trek down through Lobuche and Dughla, a long hike criss-crossing finely made yak paths and stone walls and ancient stupas, all the way to Pheriche. There is an internet café in Pheriche. This is what cycling has done to me. I am in the most beautiful, the most remote, the most serene place on earth and I have to get to an internet connection to see what Floyd Landis is at. I am a sick man.

Finally we get to Pheriche. A collection of low-slung buildings with corrugated tin roofs mostly painted blue. The internet café is just beside the Himalayan Rescue Association Clinic and isn't hard to find. Nothing in Pheriche is.

An internet café in Pheriche. So strange. There is an odd and shiny sort of modern art installation on the stony street outside. The building is ramshackle, low at the front but extended back and upwards towards where the shoulder of a great mountain runs down toward the Tsola river and a line of washing blows in the breeze. On the gable of the extension is the sign: Pheriche Internet Café. Stay Connected – Wherever You Are. + German Bakery. Inside, it is 600 rupees for ten minutes of slow connection. This better be good.

One question recurred all the way down: why had Landis done it? He had won the 2006 Tour de France, the first Tour of the post-Lance era, having been Lance's lieutenant in the latter years. Then he had been disqualified after a positive drug test. He'd raised, it was said, about a million dollars for a Floyd Fairness Fund. Spent maybe twice that. He had also blown two years and $2 million in an unsuccessful attempt to clear his name.

He had returned to the sport after a two-year ban still preaching his innocence. And now this!

What had suddenly made him confess what he had for so long denied? D'Angelo Barksdale, a character in David Simon's iconic TV series *The Wire*, came to mind. 'The past is always with us,' D'Angelo told his fellow prison inmates. 'Where we came from, what we go through, how we go through it, all this shit matters . . . What came first is who we really are and what happened before is what really happened.'

And one other question. Was I mad?

Some time previously the phone had rung at home in Cambridge. I answered to a man with a mild South African accent. He was coming to see me. Thus it was that Lewis Pugh turned up on my doorstep. Lewis Pugh is an environmental campaigner who makes his point through swimming. He has swum in every ocean on earth. He has the ability to control his core body temperature.

The water at the North Pole was -1.7°C on the day Lewis took off his clothes and, wearing nothing but skimpy Speedo swimming shorts and a cap, jumped in and swum a kilometre. Had he drowned, which was a possibility, his unharnessed body would have dropped 4.5 kilometres into the blackness, right to the bottom of the ocean. Recovery would not have been a possibility. When people wondered what in God's name he was doing, Lewis asked a different question: what in God's name are we doing to cause so much Arctic ice to melt?

There is a lot more to Lewis Pugh than swimming in cold water, though, as I was about to find out.

At the time he phoned me, somebody else had just finished writing his autobiography. Lewis didn't like how it was going, so one day he walked into Waterstones, picked up a bundle of ghosted sports biographies and went through them one after the other until he found one that he liked. The winner was Lawrence Dallaglio, *It's in the Blood: My Life*. I had been the ghostwriter. Sometimes you win the raffle without buying a ticket.

Lewis hunted me down, and, fascinated by the man, I helped him write his book. In 2010 he came to me wanting to express his gratitude in a thoughtful way. He was going to swim across Lake Pumori on Mount Everest at an altitude of 5,200 metres and a temperature of 2°C. To get there would require an expedition complete with yaks and Sherpas through the most beautiful country on earth.

It would be life-changing. Nobody comes back from Nepal without a renewed perspective on existence. Weeks of walking, thinking and serenity are something which everybody should treat themselves to at some stage. I didn't need persuading.

It was an incredible time to be in the Himalayas. Nobody can go there without being humbled, but to be in the company of Lewis, as he attempted to bring the world's attention to our coming crisis over water, was deeply rewarding. Poignantly, the spring of 2010 had brought a strange thaw to the slopes of Everest itself, and the Nepalese were using the opportunity to remove the corpses of so many climbers who had perished there.

I thought of Yeats: 'And I shall have some peace there, for peace comes dropping slow.'

Forget that. After Paul's text came the phone call from Alex. He didn't even ask if I'd brought my laptop. My holidays at the *Sunday Times* have always been a relative experience, but that is how I've wanted it. Just as I am about to discover the secret of eternal happiness, Alex wonders if I'd like to do the Landis story. Eternal happiness can wait.

Fast forward to a middle-aged man from Slieverue in the county of Kilkenny in Ireland grabbing his laptop and a few belongings and handing these deeply spiritual things to a surprised Sherpa. Down six hours of trail to Pheriche. Find a lodging. Hit the internet café (and German bakery). Start two days' work about doped riders who live a world away. Writing with the back turned to Everest. Lewis's historical swim missed and momentarily forgotten. All concern for the watery places of the world evaporated.

Still, it was good to feel like Ahab again.

I always tell people that someday I will return to the Himalayas. And next time I'll do it without taking two days off to write about cycling, and come home in a state of eternal happiness.

Anyway to Floyd Landis. This was the story that would be the tipping point. First you had to understand the guy. What made him.

It's fair to say that there are two people out there who claim to be Floyd Landis. There is the kid who wanted to escape the strict Mennonite shackles of his rural Pennsylvania background, who defied his parents by sneaking out in darkness to train on the quiet roads around Farmersville. His father, convinced that his son was looking for alcohol or drugs, would follow. On those night pursuits he saw another side to his son. That boy would become a professional, earn a lot of money, take a lot of drugs, tell a lot of lies and live in California. But California wasn't where Landis came from. He was Floyd, son of Paul and Arlene, devout members of the Mennonite community. They were people who believed in modesty, honesty and the love of God, who didn't confuse their needs with their wants. For all that he would become, Floyd loved his parents, respected their way of life.

'What came first is who we really are,' said D'Angelo, and over the past few weeks Landis had hesitantly returned to where he came from. In his only interview since Reed Albergotti's excellent story in the *Wall Street Journal* which detailed the kind of life he led when in the Postal team, he told Bonnie Ford of ESPN that he didn't want to go on 'being part of the problem any more. I want to clear my conscience.'

Without his extraordinary backstory this would have been hard to believe. But Floyd Landis is a one-off. One person. Two versions.

The second Floyd Landis is hard and pragmatic. He surveys the landscape. He works out what is required to cross it. Away he goes. He races to win because, no matter what they tell you as a child, winning is the ultimate.

In March 2007 he had gone back home to Farmersville. He spoke to three hundred friends and neighbours and his parents in the Performing Arts Center. They gave him a long standing ovation as he rose to speak. He told them of his innocence, of the strength he took from being from this place. At the end everybody prayed. It is hard to imagine what was in Floyd Landis's mind that night as his entourage gathered up the $35 per head that the people of Farmersville had paid to help with his Fairness Fund.

At the time he was operating as the other Floyd Landis. This man who did whatever had to be done.

The email sent by Landis to cycling and anti-doping officials in Europe and the US wasn't an attack on his former teammate Lance Armstrong but a frank and heartfelt account of Landis's own grievous sins. It is not uncommon for cyclists to admit their doping, but generally they try to disconnect their actions from those around them, protecting teammates and team facilitators out of a sense of misguided loyalty.

Landis spilled everything out. The context in which he doped, the environment, the company. He was burning bridges. He told of the support and the expertise he claims he received from those around him. He offered us plenty of names. For three years, 2002–04, he rode with US Postal. The lessons began early:

FLOYD LANDIS'S LETTER TO THE UCI AND USA CYCLING

6 MAY 2010

2002: I was instructed on how to use testosterone patches by Johan Bruyneel during the Dauphiné Libéré in June, after which I flew on a helicopter with Mr Armstrong from the finish, I believe Grenoble, to St Moritz, Switzerland, at which point I was personally handed a box of 2.5mg patches in front of his wife, who witnessed the exchange. About a week later, Dr Ferrari performed an extraction of half a litre of blood to be transfused back into me during the Tour de France. Mr Armstrong was not witness to the extraction but he and I had lengthy discussions about it on our training rides during which time he also explained to me the evolution of EPO testing and how transfusions were now necessary due to the inconvenience of the new test. He also divulged to me at that time that in the first year that the EPO test was used he had been told by Mr Ferrari, who had access to the new test, that he should not use EPO any more, but he did not believe Mr Ferrari and continued to use it. He later, while winning the Tour de Suisse, the month before the Tour de France, tested positive for EPO, at which point he and Mr Bruyneel flew to the UCI headquarters and made a financial agreement with Mr Verbruggen to keep the positive test hidden.

This is just the opening section, but it certainly gets the attention. Several colourful birds smitten with one stone. Floyd implicates Armstrong, team manager Johan Bruyneel and various others. It's not done artfully. The tone is flat and resigned. The words of a man who has been crushed by his own deceit. Something inside has told him: this far and no further.

By the time I am sitting in Pheriche the allegations have, of course, been denied.

'It's just our word against theirs, and we like our word. We like where we stand,' said Armstrong, who at this point can spew out rebuttals like a ticker-tape machine.

Not for the first time, Armstrong turned his gun on the accuser. 'I remind everyone that this is a man who wrote a book for profit and now has a completely different version.'

The question is which version is to be believed? Is a man more credible when his story is told for profit or, in this case, for no material gain? Those whose careers depend on the credibility of cycling were quick to denounce Landis.

'I feel sorry for the guy because I don't accept anything he says as true,' said Pat McQuaid, the president of the UCI. There were so many rats shinning up drain pipes looking for the higher ground that a little incaution was to be expected in those less practised than Lance on that climb.

Perhaps what was worrying Pat McQuaid was the most sinister allegation tossed in near the end, about the failed test being swept under the carpet after Armstrong and Bruyneel's visit to Hein Verbruggen, UCI president at the time. In fact, Armstrong won the Tour de Suisse in 2001 and did not compete in 2002.[56]

McQuaid was insulting our intelligence here when he said that in effect he didn't believe Landis's admission of doping.

Why would any rider say he doped for five years if he didn't? It is the unadorned detail in the emails that is arresting. Instruction on how to use testosterone patches by Bruyneel. A helicopter ride with Armstrong from Grenoble to St Moritz. The gift of a box of testosterone patches by Armstrong. This exchange was witnessed by Armstrong's former wife, Kristin. You expect in these stories that every doper will have had a crossroads moment when he had to decide whether to walk away or stay and do a deal with the devil.

56 This now stands as a straightforward error rather than cause to doubt the substance of the story. In *The Secret Race*, Tyler Hamilton wrote, 'Yes, Lance tested positive for EPO at the Tour of Switzerland. I know because he told me.' Hamilton went on to quote Armstrong on the subject: '"No worries dude, we're gonna have a meeting with them. It's all taken care of."' Further on again Hamilton writes of listening to Armstrong call Hein Verbruggen from the team bus: 'He may just as well have been talking to a business partner, a friend.' UCI officials claim Armstrong's test at the 2001 Tour de Suisse was 'suspicious', not positive.

It was at this time that Armstrong made a donation of $25,000 to UCI to support their anti-doping work.

In October 2012, Pat McQuaid, president of the UCI, described Landis and Hamilton as 'scumbags'.

Poor Floyd Landis fell into a team where the culture of doping and the momentum and scale of the doping was already so well established that there was no pause for thought. He did what he did just to survive, just to keep going. The story went on skipping around Europe like a Jason Bourne movie. Spain next.

2003: After a broken hip in the winter, I flew to Girona, Spain, where this time two units [of blood, half a litre each] were extracted three weeks apart. This took place in the apartment in which Mr Armstrong lived and in which I was asked to stay and check the blood temperature every day. It was kept in a small refrigerator in the closet along with the blood of Mr Armstrong and George Hincapie, and since Mr Armstrong was planning on being gone for a few weeks to train he asked me to stay in his place and make sure the electricity didn't turn off or something go wrong with the refrigerator. Then during the Tour de France the entire team, on two different occasions, went to the room that we were told and the doctor met us there to do the transfusions. During that Tour de France I personally witnessed George Hincapie, Lance Armstrong, Chechu Rubiera and myself receiving blood transfusions. Also during that Tour de France the team doctor would give my roommate, George Hincapie, and me a small syringe of olive oil in which was dissolved Andriol, a form of ingestible testosterone, on two out of three nights throughout the duration. I was asked to ride the Vuelta a España that year in support of Roberto Heras and, in August, between the Tour and the Vuelta, was told to take EPO to raise my haematocrit back up so more blood transfusions could be performed. I was instructed to go to Lance's place by Johan Bruyneel and get some EPO from him. The first EPO I ever used was then handed to me in the entry way to his building in full view of his then wife. It was Eprex by brand and it came in six pre-measured syringes. I used it intravenously for several weeks before the next blood draw and had no problems with the tests during the Vuelta. Also during this time it was explained to me how to use Human Growth Hormone by Johan Bruyneel and I bought what I needed from Pepe the team 'trainer', who lived in Valencia along with the team doctor at that time. While training for that Vuelta I spent a good deal of time training with Matthew White and Michael Barry and shared the testosterone and EPO that we had and discussed the use thereof while training. Again, during the Vuelta we were given Andriol and blood transfusions by the team doctor and had no problems with any testing.

In my little cyber shack high in the Himalayas, the weirdness of the life of the professional doper seemed even more pronounced. Here was a Mennonite boy whose father had at one stage given him extra chores hoping that tiredness would end his infatuation with riding; a boy who'd had to struggle with and break away from so much that he loved, just so that he could ride. And he ended up in Spain, babysitting blood in the apartment of the world's most famous cancer survivor. Perhaps it was Floyd who first tweeted that little joke about Lance and how the steady drip, drip, drip of insinuation and rumour made his blood boil, which is why he kept so much chilled stuff in the fridge.

In Mennonite communities like Floyd's in Lancaster County, Pennsylvania, a gentle place with many quaint wood-covered bridges, they don't believe in infant baptism. There is no stain to cleanse. They believe that we are born innocent but with a bent toward sin. From there we grow until we reach an age of accountability. Floyd's professional life seems to follow that pattern.

Armstrong loved him. There was something different about Floyd Landis, something out there. But Lance Armstrong's greatest strength was also his greatest weakness. People. He could impress people, he could charm people, he could cajole people, he could extract love and loyalty. But when he was finished he had no feel for keeping people. He had no sense of the needs they had. Lance could change towards Floyd Landis. But Floyd would never change his view of Lance? Surely.

After the 2004 Tour, the rival Phonak team made Floyd Landis a good offer. It was more than twice what US Postal was offering. Lance Armstrong could have changed that with one phone call. He didn't. Floyd walked away. Lance branded him a traitor.

Five years later and Floyd had won a Tour de France and lost it again to a drug positive. He had served a two-year ban and done what good soldiers do, he had kept the secrets of the peloton. When he came back and pressed his nose against the window and gazed in at the world of cycling, his world, Lance Armstrong ordered that the curtains be drawn.

Floyd was one casualty too many.

It isn't his background and his sincerity which make the emails so fascinating. Here is the rider disqualified after winning the 2006 Tour, the man who looked the world in the eye and said that none of this had happened. Here is a man who has had more, way more, than his own share of troubles, the guy who wrote a book called *False Positive*. And now he not only admits to years of doping but throws out evidence which could shut the entire operation.

The truth? You can't handle the truth!

It's too easy to dismiss what he has written as the latest out-pouring in the soap opera of a proven liar. Floyd Landis has lied and cheated. He bought into that way of life but, some-where in the recent past, he has come to the crossroads and decided the deal is off. And now, same as it was when he was a rider, there are no compromises or half measures.

2004: Again the team performed two separate blood trans-fusions on me, but this time Bruyneel had become more paranoid and we did the draws by flying to Belgium and meeting at an unknown person's apartment and the blood was brought by 'Duffy', who was at that time Johan's assis-tant of sorts. The second transfusion was performed on the team bus on the ride from the finish of a stage to the hotel, during which the driver pretended to have engine trouble and stopped on a remote mountain road for an hour or so, so the entire team could have half a litre of blood added. This was the only time that I ever saw the entire team being transfused in plain view of all the other riders and bus driver. That team included Lance Armstrong, George Hincapie and me as the only Americans.

2005: I had learned at this point how to do most of the transfusion technicals and other things on my own, so I hired Allen Lim as my assistant to help with details and logistics. He helped Levi Leipheimer and me prepare the transfusions for Levi and me and made sure they were kept at the proper temperature. We both did two separate transfusions that Tour, however my haematocrit was too low at the start so I did my first one a few days before the start so as to not start with a deficit.

2006: Well, you get the idea ... One thing of great significance is that I sat down with Andy Riis and explained to him what was done in the past and what was the risk I would be taking and ask for his permission, which he granted in the form of funds to complete the operation described. John Lelangue was also informed by me, and Andy Riis consulted with Jim Ochowicz before agreeing. There are many, many more details that I have in diaries and am in the process of writing into an intelligible story but since the position of USA Cycling is that there have not been enough details shared to justify calling USADA, I am writing as many as I can reasonably put into an email and share with you so as to ascertain what is the process which USA Cycling uses to proceed with such allegations. Look forward to much more detail as soon as you can demonstrate that you can be trusted to do the right thing.

Floyd Landis

From Gorak Shep to Pheriche and for two days here in this lodge the thought has kept occurring to me that these accusations don't exist in a vacuum. They have come at a time when I thought that the entire Lance Armstrong story was dead, that pursuing Lance was a period of my life which I would have to put down to experience.

What Floyd Landis is saying, though, is interesting: it is direct evidence and it sits on the shelf with what has gone before. Seven years ago I sat in a home near Liverpool with Emma O'Reilly and listened to her tell of her five years in the shadow of Lance. She told those stories about ditching syringes and crossing borders and handing product to Armstrong in the car park of a McDonald's outside Nice. She told me about disguising the wounds from syringe punctures and about the team backdating a prescription for cortico-steroids. She'd put it all under oath back in 2006.

I sat there in the Himalayas, the room scarcely lit apart from the light from my laptop, and thought of Frankie and Betsy in Detroit. All the calls and the conversations. The stories they had from back in the days of the euro dogs, the young American cyclists on the make and on the break in the old world. They'd put all that stuff down on oath too. Armstrong said that Betsy was bitter, motivated only by her hatred of him. Frankie's team couldn't get into competitions that were sponsored by the company that owned the team.

And that night in October 2003 spent at the Auckland home of Stephen Swart, who rode with Armstrong for the Motorola team in 1994 and 1995. Armstrong, Stephen had said, was the leading pro-doping voice in the team. Swart would later repeat these allegations under oath. Armstrong said Swart was a bitter former teammate.

I thought, too, of a guy called Mike Anderson, the personal assistant employed by Armstrong for two years, 2003 and 2004. So central was Anderson to the lives of the family that Kristin Armstrong referred to him as H2: husband number two. I met Anderson in Austin, Texas, and he told of the day that changed his view of Armstrong.

It was the spring of 2004, the Armstrongs had separated. Lance had hooked up with the singer Sheryl Crow and was taking her to the Girona apartment for the first time. According to Anderson, who was in Girona ahead of his boss, Armstrong called and asked him to go through the apartment and 'de-Kik' it [Armstrong referred to his former wife as Kik]. While doing that task, Anderson claimed he found a small bottle in a medical cabinet that had the label 'Androstenone', and after looking up the list of banned products on his laptop, he was sure his boss was doping.

Their relationship was never the same after that. When Mike Anderson made public his discovery, Armstrong dismissed him as a bitter former employee.

I'd stayed in touch with O'Reilly, Swart, the Andreus and Anderson long after the interviews ended. To be slightly melodramatic about it we were like a loose group of survivors. When those around us grew weary of us speaking about Lance and the great heist, we could talk to each other. And one thing always puzzled me: why would all these good people make up vicious lies about Armstrong?

Now Floyd Landis was adding his story to the shelf.

Lying in that tent at Gorak Shep, thoughts turned to some of the forerunners. The difference with the Landis emails would be presentation. He offered them not to the public. Instead he slapped them across the face of the cycling authorities and the anti-doping world like a pair of gloves. He was asking for a duel. He was challenging their honour, having just rediscovered his. Whaddya gonna do?

Word on the yak trail was that the United States Anti-Doping Authority were interested, seriously interested, and federal investigator Jeff Novitzky was about to about to throw his net into the waters where the big fish swam.

I liked the choice of Novitzky. He lives in Burlingame outside San Francisco just a mile from the Bay Area Laboratory Co-operative. His greatest case, the BALCO case, had unfolded right on his doorstep. His work in the infamous BALCO case, involving steroids being supplied to Major League baseball players, proved one thing. You can get away with lying in lots of places but it's a bad idea to lie to federal investigators. The feds have more power than us trolls. Floyd Landis, the strangest and most unreadable dude in the entire pack, had opened a can of worms.

If Jeff Novitzky was ever to conclude that US Postal did run a doping programme, Armstrong and the others could face charges. If Jeff Novitsky was ever to conclude that through Tailwind Sports, the US Postal Service, a federal agency itself, had been defrauded, the charges would get much more serious. The penalties for misusing such funds are draconian.

Floyd Landis of Lancaster County had lit a fuse that I could see in the Himalayas. In the morning I had a shower, a treat which cost more than the room. I found my smiling $7-a-day Sherpa and set out to rejoin the group who were six hours away. Lewis, it would transpire, had swum 22 minutes across the freezing lake. He had lived and made a point.

Trekking back, though, I was in my own little world. I was

thinking of this long journey through cycling, of the happy innocence of the early days. Paul and I in rue Kléber arguing over coffees and *L'Équipe*. I was thinking of the first hints that something was wrong with this sport that we loved, the first realisation that our heroes had feet of clay and canisters of pills. We had gone so deep into that world, and in the end I had begun to think that it was inalterable.

Lewis Pugh, up there on the great mountain, had more chance of making a change than I had. He could save the world. Nobody could save cycling. And yet here, Floyd Landis had leaned into the job with us. Something was moving again.

I walked through the Himalayas having missed the very thing I had come to see but feeling happier than I'd felt in a long time. Nobody comes down from this place as the same person who went up.

Thank the gods for the gift of internet! It takes the climb out of the path to enlightenment.

21

24 July 2005

It has been a stormy love affair, but Lance Armstrong is saying goodbye to the Tour de France. After seven consecutive wins following his recovery from testicular cancer, Big Tex is leaving town. As a concession to what he has achieved and as the recognition of a sort of ceasefire with the French public, Armstrong is permitted a farewell speech. Watched by his three children he speaks in romantic terms of the race that he has made his own. He has a word for the wretched of the earth. He feels sorry, he says, for those who can't dream. He says he wants the Tour to live for ever. He has kind words for old rivals on the podium with him, Jan Ullrich and Ivan Basso. And then he is gone. You can feel the

I'm sorry you don't believe in miracles. But this is one hell of a race. This is a great sporting event and you should stand around and believe it. You should believe in these athletes, and you should believe in these people. I'll be a fan of the Tour de France for as long as I live. And there are no secrets – this is a hard sporting event and hard work wins it. **Lance Armstrong**

void, the wind blowing tumbleweeds through the ghost towns that are the sports pages. Lance Armstrong has dominated all argument, all rumour, all conjecture and all stages for seven years. He leaves behind a field which lacks a man of his stature. Love him or loathe him, the world of cycling in the age after Lance has just begun. Elvis has left the building.

27 July 2006

In France there has been intense speculation since the UCI let it be known on the morning after the Tour de France finished that that an unnamed rider has tested positive in the last week of the Tour. When Floyd Landis, crowned as champion the day before, cancels a race in the Netherlands speculation mounts. Today, four days after his triumph, it is confirmed the Tour winner has tested positive. After seven years of speculation about Lance Armstrong, his successor has been popped virtually on the winner's podium. Floyd Landis, with the farm-boy shoulders and the red hair and the piece of firewood where his hip should be, readies himself to explain to the world.

I declare convincingly and categorically that my winning the Tour de France has been exclusively due to many years of training and my complete devotion to cycling. **Floyd Landis**

In Italy, meanwhile, the Granfondo Michele Bartoli, a one-day race for medium-level pros, has finished at virtually the same time as the Tour. The Granfondo is an Italian re-creation of the Tour of Flanders, with lots of cobblestones and falls. On Sunday one rider, from the Partizan Whistle team, comes through the old arch into Montecarlo well placed. This is to be his last race. His wife Yuliet has just escaped from Cuba. One more race and he will pack away the dream and find a job that can support them both. But he falls within half a mile of the finish. A routine tumble. He thought little of it till that night in his hotel bed when he noticed that one of his buttocks had become grotesquely swollen. He went to hospital. As Floyd Landis faces his fresh hell, this Thursday morning the rider is on a surgeon's table somewhere in Tuscany. They are cutting him open in the hope of draining a haematoma and saving his life. It isn't easy. His haematocrit level is 58. His blood is one quarter sludge from the EPO. The rest is watery from thinners. They look at this mad fool who has risked his life for cycling.

He's lucky to be alive.

Like Floyd Landis he is an American from Pennsylvania. His name is Joe Papp. He is five months older than Floyd.

Late 2006

Meet Kayle. He sounds like a character lifted from an Elmore Leonard novel but Kayle Leogrande, the tattoo guy, is real and at the root of Lance's troubles.

Kayle was a good junior rider and then he gave it all up at 18. He married, had kids, divorced, became a tattoo artist. If you feel the need to get inked by a guy with a real place in sports history, he owns a shop, downstairs at a strip mall in Upland, California.

Anyway, after nine prodigal years Kayle came back to

biking. He watched Lance on the TV in 2004 and was inspired. He turned pro in 2005 with the Jelly Belly–Kenda crew. Went amateur in 2006. Turned pro again in 2007 with Rock Racing. Rock Racing was a team that seemed to understand that some guys had a past.

Leogrande bought his first EPO in late 2006 from Joe Papp. Papp was back in the US. Six weeks before his near death in Italy, he had tested positive at the Presidential Cycling Tour of Turkey. The lower you are in the food chain the grubbier doping gets. Being picked for testing on these gigs meant nothing. The team always came up with something. A bribe. Tampering with the sample by flicking in a little piece of chemical stored under the nail. Today they had something different to offer when Joe Papp said he had to take the test. The team wanted to him to catheterise somebody else's urine into his bladder. Joe said, hmmm, he'd take his chances, thanks. So now he was serving a ban from 31 July 2006 right through to 31 July 2008.

But he was dealing. The EPO he sold Kayle Leogrande didn't come with instructions. The first few times Kayle took the stuff he felt sick.

What has this to do with Lance? They have met only once, after a race in Ojai, California, in 2005. It's unlikely that Lance remembers the brief chat.

Kayle does. He was nervous, didn't know what to say.

There were cooler things which Kayle might have said. Still, no doubt Lance remembers the name these days.

When Kayle went pro again, aged 30, he suddenly began to look like a guy who'd left a great future behind him. He won the points classification at the 2007 Redlands Bicycle

classic, where he also finished second in the second-stage criterium. He took three stages at the International Cycling
Classic-Superweek in Wisconsin. He came home second
overall.

At some stage in that 2007 season he must have begun to
wonder about his dealer, because on 18 May 2007 one Joe
Papp gives testimony in
Pepperdine University,
Malibu, California, in
the case of Floyd Landis
v USADA. Papp, who is at pains to point out that he is
testifying as an expert and not testifying *against* Floyd
Landis, describes his experiences with doping, particularly
testosterone. His expertise stretches much further, though.
He once injected himself
with Pot Belge during a
race. His words punch
a modest hole in the
Landis defence position, which is that testosterone is passé
and so ineffective as to be beneath the whims of a top cyclist.

Why did they bring in Joe Papp? Who the fuck is that guy? **Floyd Landis**

I'm sure he thought, 'Who is this stupid tattooed guy?' **Kayle Leogrande**

Floyd Landis wasn't pleased.

He would be less pleased when he discovered later that
USADA had called an expert who was still in the business of
dealing performance-enhancing drugs, a vocation from
which Joe Papp was finding it hard to extract himself.

In 2007, though, Kayle Leogrande was happily amid the
pros again, this time with Rock Racing. He had more access
to knowledge. He was a good natural rider and with the EPO
in his blood he excelled. He was so good that he became paranoid that everybody must know his secret. So that summer,

on 26 July 2007, during Superweek in Wisconsin, he panicked when required to take a drug test. He was so sure that bad news was on the way that the next day he told Suzanne Sonye, the *soigneur*, about his doping. He was sure Suzanne would be okay with it.

But Suzanne wasn't okay with it.
Kyle Leogrande

As he told the *New York Times* later.

Doh!

So, in January 2008, Kayle Leogrande switched to a career in litigation. First of all, he was revealed as the hitherto anonymous rider who was suing USADA concerning his insistence that they not test his B-sample from a urine sample taken at Superweek in Wisconsin the previous year.

There was a kink in the story. Kayle Leogrande's A-sample had tested negative for any performance-enhancing drugs. USADA wanted to test the B-sample regardless. They had other reasons for believing that the rider had doped. In the end the B-sample was left untouched because without a positive result on the first, they couldn't test the second. The legal suit was dismissed.

USADA went ahead and banned Kayle on the basis of sworn testimony from Suzanne Sonye and

Joe, 2 boxes G. 100 iu; 7 boxes E. 60,000; $500. I owed you! Thanks, Kayle.

our friend Frankie Andreu, who was the team director of Rock Racing. The hearing also took into account ancillary evidence such as cell-phone records detailing calls between Leogrande and a guy called Joe Papp. They had a photo of an arm with familiar tattoos and the hand at the end brandishing vials of EPO. Plus a handwritten note from Kayle to Joe Papp.

Joe Papp provided the evidence. Kayle Leogrande still got charged with a doping violation. About now Lance Armstrong probably began paying attention. Know your *soigneur*. Treat your *soigneur* right.

There must be gold in them there tattoo parlours because now Kayle Leogrande threw in another couple of lawsuits. A defamation claim against former Rock Racing *soigneur* Suzanne Sonye, and a similar claim against former pro Matt DeCanio, who was now an anti-doping campaigner. It all wound up with a two-year ban for a non-analytical positive; that is, a doping offence based not on a lab test but on all available evidence. USADA's first non-analytical positive. The playing pitch was changed.

Then just when Kayle thought it was all over . . .

It wasn't.

Leogrande moved out of the rental he'd been living in, looking for a new start. He left a stash of EPO behind in the refrigerator in the garage. When his landlady called about it he told her to do with the drugs as she pleased.

She turned pro.

No, actually, she turned him in.

A few weeks later an FDA investigator showed up at Leogrande's door. Not just any fed either. Jeff Novitzky. He had the scalps of Marion Jones and Barry Bonds hanging from his belt, and the sky went dark when the buzzer rang. In

Novitzky: *Do ya think Lance is doing this?*

Leogrande: *If you were a rider at that level, what would you do?*

a world full of feds Novitzky is the super fed. If he is at your front door you are in more trouble than you ought to be.

This was early 2008. Leogrande spilled his heart out. Novitzky is tall, lean and handsome and smells of cordite, but he has some of the investigatory style of Lieutenant Frank Columbo about him.

Leogrande was a small fish. Joe Papp was slightly bigger. Michael Ball, the owner of Rock Racing, slightly bigger again. Ball knew the A-list guys.

Novitzky knew that the first rule of federal investigation is to never throw anything back into the river. There was a trail here which would lead to bigger names and bigger things. Leogrande's fridge had opened the door to federal involvement and the chance to have a snoop around the world of Rock Racing, a team with a reputation for being a sanctuary for cycling's born-again brigade.

Novitzky knew too that for the bigger fish most of the things that happened in France stayed in France. But many big fish came home and cycled for American teams and the law of *omerta* didn't seem to apply with the same force when they were back in a culture where the idea of doping to win a bicycle race was still novel.

Lance Armstrong and a number of other big fish had sworn oaths in America in 2006 in the SCA case. And many of those big fish had made a good living from a team sponsored by US Postal, a federal agency. There were connections, like Tyler Hamilton, once of Postal, now of Rock Racing. From Leogrande to Lance. Novitzky was in the game.

Through the investigation USADA received information about individuals who supplied Leogrande and other cyclists with illegal performance-enhancing drugs: Joe Papp's client list.

1 December 2008

Lance Armstrong announces that in 2009 he will once again compete in the Tour de France. At almost exactly the same time, USADA bans Kayle Leogrande, the stupid tattooed guy from Rock Racing, for two years. Leogrande's case will grow into the lengthy investigation that culminates in Armstrong's lifetime ban from the sport.

30 January 2009

The back-dated suspension of Floyd Landis comes to an end. Throughout 2008 Landis has been acting as an unofficial consultant for the Rock Racing crew, but now he can hit the road and do what he does best. Now that he is free to ride again, the expectation is that he will leave the

> When I see what's going on with Lance now, I have to laugh to myself a little bit. **Kayle Leogrande**

> Without Leogrande, who knows, the Armstrong investigation maybe never would have happened. **Travis Tygart**

past behind and ride the roads with happy abandon. Instead, he seems to wander deeper and deeper into his melancholic world of guilt and denial. In February he comes back to racing properly and competes in the Tour of California. He will ride for the appropriately named Ouch team.

Meanwhile, something else is brewing in the underworld.

And in the spring, *L'Express*, the French magazine, throws a fly into the ointment of Floyd's happiness. *L'Express* claims information obtained by hacking into the LNDD (Laboratoire National de Dépistage du Dopage) network was transmitted to a lab in Canada from the computer of Landis's former coach Arnie Baker. In May, Landis and Baker are summoned to France to testify before French investigators examining the hacking of LNDD data.

Pierre Bordry, the controversial head of France's anti-doping agency, knew

In January of 2009, USADA received information from a variety of sources with information about individuals who may have supplied Mr Leogrande and other cyclists with performance-enhancing drugs. Thereafter, USADA commenced an investigation into drug use and distribution within the Southern California cycling scene and began making inquiries and following up on various leads related to this issue. USADA came to understand that Floyd Landis might have information useful to this effort. **USADA**

that his lab had been breached somehow. Bordry was frequently in the wars with his superiors and with the UCI. He needed to know how confidential information from his lab, some of it detailed scientific data, was being leaked into the public domain. So he filed a legal complaint in November 2006, claiming that someone had hacked into the computers of his main laboratory. At the time, the computers were busy analysing the urine samples submitted by Floyd Landis on the Tour that year. Those samples had already tested positive for testosterone and Landis was on his way to being stripped of his Tour de France crown. But the hackers who accessed the lab's computers played with the files linked to

Landis's case. The altered data were then circulated as evidence that the lab's work was so sloppy it shouldn't be trusted as proof against Landis. Just as Landis was getting to move on with his life, the French computer scandal emerged to hobble him. In November 2011, Landis and Baker would receive one-year suspended prison sentences from the French courts. Not bad for a Mennonite raised without TV or radio.

I declare convincingly and categorically that my winning the Tour de France has been exclusively due to many years of training and my complete devotion to cycling. **Floyd Landis**

Throughout 2009 Floyd Landis was acting weird. From the first day of his disgrace he had adhered to his denial. He had not just grown in confidence about it, he had become almost messianic. There had been the book, *False Positive*, the Fairness Fund, and he'd given so many talks and done so many signings. His marriage was gone. His father-in-law had taken his own life. He took a bit of refuge in drink, but mainly he took his depression neat.

In early April of 2010 Floyd Landis decided that enough was enough. In his hearing with the anti-doping authorities he had been represented by Maurice Suh and Paul Scott. The latter was a lawyer with some experience as a research chemist. He had designed anti-doping programmes for cycling teams.

Landis put in a call to Scott, told him that he wanted to come in from the wilderness. He had information. He would hand it over. He just wanted an end to all that was happening to him. His career hadn't resumed smoothly. He felt isolated. Guys he had doped with, one guy in particular, weren't just home free, they were refusing to lend a hand.

Scott was a good choice of conduit. He had a friendship with Dr Dan Eichner, a scientist with USADA. Scott and Eichner had a telephone conversation in which Scott refused to name Landis and Eichner played along, pretending that he couldn't guess who the putative whistleblower might be.

12 April 2010

Two days after first communicating with Scott about the Landis information, Eichner meets with Scott in Scott's home office. Eichner receives additional information from Scott about the US Postal Service cycling team doping practices. Scott describes in great detail the doping programme on the US Postal Service team, including its use of blood transfusions, and the involvement of Armstrong, Dr Ferrari, Bruyneel, Jose 'Pepe' Marti, Dr Luis Garcia del Moral and a number of riders, including Landis. It is fair to say that Eichner can hardly wait to get to the office the following morning.

20 April 2010

After several direct communications with Floyd Landis, a meeting takes place between Travis Tygart of USADA and Landis to discuss his anti-doping rule violations and those of others, and whether or not USADA will handle the information appropriately. USADA assures Landis that all information will be handled as provided under its rules. Floyd Landis gives Travis Tygart the thumbs-up. Landis also says that he has information that Michael Ball, the team owner of Rock Racing, was involved in doping. The anti-doping officials suggest that Landis 'reach out' to Novitzky with this information about Ball, because a criminal investigation into Rock Racing is ensuing.

Subsequently (of his own volition as everybody is at great pains to point out – even though it was a fantastic idea), Landis sent an email to Steve Johnson, the President of USA Cycling. It was 30 April 2010. With its depiction of Johan Bruyneel's dexterity with a testosterone patch, it was almost certainly the most fascinating opening paragraph of any email that Steve Johnson had ever received.

On it went, the details of the madness sorted by chronological order, all of it unadorned with opinion or adjectives, just bald declarative statements which could bring down everybody from Lance to the UCI to the Pope.

May 2010

Due to the wrath of Landis, Armstrong, it seems, could be facing a related legal challenge. When Landis sent emails to USA Cycling accusing Armstrong and other riders of having doped, it is believed that he also launched a so-called qui

I never liked Goodfellas *till I went through this shit.* **Floyd Landis**

tam case. Qui tam suits are brought by whistleblowers who allege that government funds have been misused, fraudulently obtained or stolen. Very few are won without the intervention and support of the US Department of Justice.

Potentially at stake in the Lance Armstrong–US Postal case would be the issue of whether any of the $32 million in sponsorship contracts for the Postal team was spent on organised doping, in violation of those contracts. The civil division of the Department of Justice conducts its own, separate investigation on qui tam cases independently of any other investigations happening at the time. If Landis won, he could collect up to 30 per cent of what the government recovered. The Department of Justice was said to be thinking about it. Meanwhile Armstrong, as is his practice, has come out swinging. He has released a series of emails sent to him by Floyd Landis in the preceding weeks.

So once again I'd like to remind you that calling my close friends with allegations of alcoholism and insanity will be ineffective and – certainly threats of 'tweeting' that if I have something to say I should just say it – reflect poorly on your mental well-being. Maybe seeking help is a good idea for you. Of course, like I've stated, a legal course is preferable. **Floyd Landis email to Lance Armstrong**

Like I said the first time, it's like a carton of sour milk – one sip and you know it's bad. You don't drink the whole thing, or keep taking sips of it. **Lance on Landis**

When asked how he replied to these emails and why the replies weren't also released, Armstrong indicated that he hadn't replied. As people grew more and more fascinated with Landis's tale, Armstrong gave the definitive review.

22 October 2010

By now they are going at each other gangland style. A take-down occurs in Lance Armstrong's front garden. It is the weekend of Livestrong's Race for the Roses, an annual fundraiser for Armstrong's principal cancer charity. Yaroslav Popovych, the RadioShack rider, is in the slightly funky town of Austin, Texas, for the event. He is signing autographs down at Armstrong's bike emporium, Mellow Johnny's.

As Popovych comes out of the shop to head towards his car he is approached by an unidentified man. The man grabs the door of Popovych's car before he can close it. The rider, obviously unfamiliar with events in Dallas in November 1963, breaks the stalemate by politely suggesting that the man speak to him back at his hotel. Popovych gets into his car. The man dashes to his SUV and tails the rider's car to the hotel.

At the Hyatt Regency a man dressed all in black (according to witnesses) stands in the middle of the street and orders Popovych to stop his car. Popovych attempts to drive around the man, but two more SUVs appear, one blocking the car's front and one in the back. A woman with a badge motions the Ukrainian to the car.

When Popovych stepped out, the first guy, from the bike shop, served a subpoena for Popovych to appear in Los Angeles on 3 November to testify into the federal investigation into cycling. There were more surprises for Popovych a couple of weeks later when, as he was negotiating a round-about near his house in Quarrata, a picturesque Tuscan village, the Caribinieri sprang from everywhere, escorted him home and searched his house and computers. *Sports Illustrated* later reported that Italian police had found contemporary files linking Armstrong to Michele Ferrari.

19 November 2010

Jeff Novitzky, the thinking man's Eliot Ness, is reported to be in Europe showing the French a thing or two about how to be suave. He is, it is alleged, charming the local gendarmes into sharing the details of their investigation into the dumping of medical waste during the 2000 Tour. He is also spotted in Lyon swanning in and out of Interpol headquarters, meeting with prosecutors from all over Europe. The rumour mill insists that there could be indictments under a few Christmas trees. Several current and former pros have already been called before the Grand Jury. Is the investigation widening? Will Novitzky chase down the elusive Texan pimpernel aboard the Orient Express? Tune in next week. Or not. If you are Juan Pelota. Lance's alter ego issues a tweet baiting Novitzky. He may only have Juan Pelota – but it is made of titanium.

> *Hey, Jeff, ¿cómo están los hoteles de cuatro estrellas y la clase business del avión? ¿Qué más necesitas?*
> **Juan Pelota, aka Lance Armstrong.**
>
> *Hey, Jeff, how are the four-star hotels and the business class on the plane? Anything else you need?*

In December US newspapers would report that Floyd Landis had worn a wire and carried a small, hidden video camera to the home of Michael Ball, CEO of Rock Racing, in the spring of 2010.

16 February 2011

Citing a desire to devote himself full-time to his family, to the fight against cancer and to leading the foundation he established having survived cancer himself, Lance Armstrong retires from cycling for the second time.

It was time for him to stop. He's won everything, he had nothing left to prove to anybody. **Eddy Merckx**

So Lance puts on his slippers, and when he is not in the lab fighting cancer he is in the yard playing with the kids. All is well through the spring. Then:

20 May 2011

Tyler Hamilton announces to the world that he has been speaking to a Grand Jury. What's more, he would recommend it to anybody.

Until that moment I walked into the courtroom, I hadn't told a soul. My testimony went on for six hours. For me it was like the Hoover dam breaking. I opened up; I told the whole truth and nothing but the truth. And I felt a sense of relief I'd never felt before – all the secrets, all the weight I'd been carrying around for years, suddenly lifted. I saw that, for me personally, this was the way forward. **Tyler Hamilton**

There is a point to be made about Tyler Hamilton and doping. Namely that he is not too good at it. He suffered a two-year ban for a positive in the Vuelta a España in 2004. He had his whole doping programme exposed in the

Operación Puerto blood-doping inquiry in Spain in 2006, amid allegations that he had used a cocktail of substances

There are a lot of other cheats and liars out there too who have gotten away with it. It's not just Lance. With a little luck I would still be out there today being a cheat and a liar. **Tyler Hamilton**

including EPO, growth hormone, testosterone and cortisone. He came back to racing after a two-year ban but tested positive in 2009 for the banned steroid DHEA.

Even in retirement there is no peace.

21 September 2011

The drip of allegations takes on an Italian accent. An Italian newspaper, *Corriere della Sera*, reports that Armstrong made payments to Michele Ferrari via a third-party company in Switzerland. An investigation by Swiss and Italian authorities reportedly showed Armstrong directed funds to a company in the Neuchâtel region called Health and Performance. Ferrari had been cleared of criminal charges in 2006, but Armstrong had vowed two years previously to discontinue working with him and claimed that he had maintained only some social contact with Ferrari since then. Tick. Tick. Tick.

3 February 2012

Twenty months in the making and then the studio closed down production on its own blockbuster. Jeff Novitzky and Lance Armstrong would not be duelling on the silver screen after all. The long, seemingly inexorable, federal criminal investigation of Lance Armstrong and his former professional cycling teams ended with a whimper. In Los Angeles the United States Attorney's Office made a terse announcement that the government was ending its pursuit of the case. The FBI and the FDA were quoted as being 'shocked, surprised and angered' by the decision. Not to say ambushed.

Having assiduously rounded up witness after witness to provide confidential evidence to the Grand Jury, the FBI got thirty minutes' notice of the announcement. Still, it was two days before the Superbowl in the United States and a nation placidly accepted that Lance Armstrong had walked. Questions remained in the wake of

I am gratified to learn that the US Attorney's Office is closing its investigation. It is the right decision and I commend them for reaching it. I look forward to continuing my life as a father, a competitor, and an advocate in the fight against cancer without this distraction. **Lance Armstrong**

the abrupt ending of an investigation that had drawn on the evidence of dozens of witnesses, enough scientific and financial documents to run a mountain stage over, and multiple law-enforcement agencies in the United States and overseas. In the immediate aftermath of the cancellation of the investigation, rumours persisted that Novitzky and his team had been following new leads and were expecting indictments later in the spring. Not to be.

Why the investigation was unexpectedly closed remains a mystery. One view is that Armstrong's friends in high places applied the pressure that led to US Attorney Andre Birotte dropping the case. Another view is that Birotte decided against proceeding with the case because of the cost and the uncertainty of the outcome.

But as Novitzky rode off into the sunset he tossed the baton to Travis Tygart of USADA. For Armstrong and several of those around him, the prospect of USADA continuing a federal investigation wasn't going to cost them a lot of sleep. Surely Travis Tygart wasn't going to get his hands on the fruits of an eighteen-month long federally funded investigation just like that? USADA quietly pointed out that it had been investigating doping on the US Postal team since at least 12 April 2010. During the period from late 2010 until 3 February 2012, USADA conducted only a handful of witness interviews 'in deference to, and out of respect for' the federal investigation.

Unlike the US Attorney, USADA's job is to protect clean sport rather than enforce specific criminal laws … Our investigation into doping in the sport of cycling is continuing and we look forward to obtaining the information developed during the federal investigation. **Travis Tygart**

There has been significant evidence taken on anti-doping areas, on what may have occurred in the way of doping. It would be very, very helpful if that information was handed over. The United States anti-doping organisation is keen to get hold of that evidence and we would like to see that happen because there could well be some very relevant information there. **John Fahey, WADA**

Upon the announcement that Mr Birotte had discontinued the investigation by his office, USADA promptly proceeded to schedule interviews of potential witnesses, most of whom were interviewed between 15 March and 12 June 2012. Now the plot thickens and the pace quickens.

31 May 2012

USADA reach out. They invite Lance Armstrong to meet, to be truthful, to be part of the solution. He has other stuff on.

12 June 2012

USADA proceed to the next stage. Based on overwhelming evidence it has received during the course of its investigation, USADA notifies Lance Armstrong, Johan Bruyneel, Dr Pedro Celaya, Dr Luis Garcia del Moral, Dr Michele Ferrari and Jose 'Pepe' Marti that it is opening a formal action for anti-doping rule violations.

These charges are baseless, motivated by spite and advanced through testimony bought and paid for by promises of anonymity and immunity. Although USADA alleges a wide-ranging conspiracy extended over more than 16 years, I am the only athlete it has chosen to charge. USADA's malice, its methods, its star-chamber practices, and its decision to punish first and adjudicate later all are at odds with our ideals of fairness and fair play. **Lance Armstrong**

Calling the actions of the USADA a 'witch hunt', Armstrong takes to tweeting.

Dear @usantidoping – we have now sent you THREE letters requesting all the relevant info in order for me to respond to your 'review board'. Until now there has been no response, not even an acknowledgement of receipt. The knife cuts both ways – it's time to play by the rules.
Lance Armstrong

27 June 2012

The USADA Anti-Doping Review Board recommends that USADA proceed with its action against Armstrong, Bruyneel, Celaya, Garcia del Moral, Ferrari and Marti. A day later USADA issues a charging letter to the individuals concerned that sets forth potential sanctions and notifies them of their right to request a hearing before a panel of neutral arbitrators. Once again Armstrong is unimpressed. He litigates through the medium of tweeting.

So let me get this straight ... come in and tell @usantidoping exactly what they want to hear in exchange for immunity, anonymity, and the opportunity to continue to race the biggest event in cycling ...

This isn't about @usantidoping wanting to clean up cycling – rather it's just plain ol' selective prosecution that reeks of vendetta. **Lance Armstrong**

9 July 2012

In what appears to be one final throw of the legal dice, Armstrong gets down to the courthouse on Monday morning in Austin, Texas, and files a federal lawsuit in an attempt to halt the USADA case. He needs to derail USADA by Saturday. US District Judge Sam Sparks rejects the lawsuit, almost out of hand, calling it 'a lengthy and bitter polemic'.

This is referred to in some places as the 'talk to the hand, the face ain't listening' verdict. Sparks, however, does allow Armstrong's lawyers to file an amended lawsuit. Still, not a good day to be one of Armstrong's legal *domestiques*.

This court is not inclined to indulge Armstrong's desire for publicity, self-aggrandisement or vilification of defendants by sifting through eighty mostly unnecessary pages in search of the few kernels of material relevant to his claims. Contrary to Armstrong's apparent belief, pleadings filed in the United States District Courts are not press releases, internet blogs, or pieces of investigative journalism ... The bulk of these paragraphs contain 'allegations' that are wholly irrelevant to Armstrong's claims – and which, the Court must presume, were included solely to increase media coverage of the case, and to incite public opinion against defendants. **Judge Sam Sparks**

10 July 2012

Armstrong files the revised lawsuit. The same day, USADA announces lifetime bans against three of his former US Postal Service cycling team associates: Dr Luis Garcia del Moral, Dr Michele Ferrari and Jose 'Pepe' Marti, team trainer.

20 August 2012

Back to the courthouse for another twist of the cards. Judge Sparks dismisses Armstrong's amended complaint. The judge rules essentially that Lance Armstrong's right to due process could not be violated by USADA before any proceedings had actually occurred.

The Court concludes Armstrong agreed to arbitrate with USADA, and its arbitration rules are sufficient, if applied reasonably, to satisfy due process. **Judge Sam Sparks**

With that, the long process was virtually over.

23 August 2012

Lance Armstrong announces that he will not contest the evidence against him, understanding that this course of action will lead to the imposition of a lifetime ban and disqualification of all results since 1998, including his seven Tour de France wins. And I recalled the kid in the garden of that Grenoble hotel in 1993 telling about his love of Linda, the single mum who taught him to never quit. 'When you give up, you give in,' she used to tell him, and as he said then, his mom didn't raise a quitter. Now he had quit and announced the death of Lance Armstrong, champion cyclist. All that was left were the funeral rites.

10 October 2012

In accordance with the rules, USADA submits its 'Reasoned Decision' detailing the evidence and basis for the decision against Lance Armstrong. One commentator notes of the thousand-page document that the only people not now convinced just don't want to know.

22 October 2012

In Geneva the UCI accepts the report of USADA with remarkably poor grace. President Pat McQuaid and the spirit of the times completely fail to recognise each other.

I don't think the UCI should apologise. They didn't hold his hand when he stuck a needle in his backside. He is an adult and they know they are breaking the rules. It's not the president's responsibility if they go into a doping programme. Another thing that annoys me is that Landis and Hamilton are being made out to be heroes. They are as far from heroes as night and day. They are not heroes. They are scumbags. **Pat McQuaid**

The truth is, Lance Armstrong, on their [UCI's] watch, pulled off the greatest heist sport has ever seen. **Travis Tygart**

Kayle Leogrande went back to the tattoo game. Joe Papp served a period of time under house arrest in his mother's place back in Pennsylvania.

22

'Show me a hero, and I will write you a tragedy.'

F. Scott Fitzgerald

A grey Monday afternoon in a café off London's M25 motor-
way. I have a cappuccino that won't froth and a phone that
won't stop ringing. Its demands are ceaseless. Like a child tug-
ging my sleeve. It won't stop. Same every time.

'David? Is that David? About Lance Armstrong and today's
news, are you available to do an interview?' Canada, Australia,
New Zealand, France, the US, Ireland, Netherlands, Belgium
and so many closer to home. No, no, no, yes, no, no, no, no,
yes, no, no, no, yes, no, no, no, no.

Seven requests are from the BBC: Radio 4, Radio 5 live,
Radio 2, BBC Radio Foyle, BBC Belfast, Newsnight, World
Service. There was a time when the Armstrong story had
black circles on its body from the BBC pushing it away with
a 40ft barge pole. There was a time when to doubt Lance
Armstrong was to walk among media people wearing a bell
which warned that you were unclean.

393

But this is the day, 22 October 2012, that Lance has been officially declared an outcast, banished from the sport by his own people: cycling's governing body, the Union Cycliste Internationale (UCI). Its president, Pat McQuaid, has decreed that the former seven-time Tour de France winner 'has no place in cycling'.

This has been a squalid story from the beginning, conceived through greed and cynicism and then fuelled with the best drugs money could buy.

I wonder how Pat McQuaid can feel that he himself has a place. I've thought many times about that seminal 1999 Tour de France and the UCI's failure to protect their sport. They knew from the previous year that cycling was a mess; they knew from their '99 pre-Tour blood tests that most of the top riders were using EPO; and they knew that an EPO test was on the way.

How difficult would it have been to discreetly re-test the '99 samples in the autumn of 2000 when the test was in place? Quite a number of high-profile cheats would have been kicked out of the sport for two years, Lance included. What a statement that would have made. Instead, the UCI sat idly by as one worthless Tour de France followed another.

McQuaid wasn't president in '99 but still, listening now, I hear only brazenness.

But this is a momentous day. Armstrong himself will soon change the profile on his Twitter page, removing the five words '7-time Tour de France winner'. He's history now, another ageing story of cheating and lying and doping and bullying and sport that wasn't sport. An icon until the mask was taken away. 'The greatest heist sport has ever seen,' says

Travis Tygart, chief executive of the United States Anti-Doping Agency.

I think back to the kid I met in 1993, when I interviewed Armstrong in the first week of his debut Tour. We talked for three hours in a hotel garden outside Grenoble and got on well. He was a Texan in France, so uncool you warmed to him, and if his American gaucheness didn't win you over, his need to succeed did. Nothing was going to get in the way.

Was he always the same man? He doped before cancer, but when he came back he was harder, more focused, less tolerant of failure and, yes, less concerned by the path to victory. He'd had four shots at the Tour, his best finish was 36th. After cancer he returned a changed man: physically, psychologically and chemically enhanced. From him we learned there was a doping programme and there was an élite doping programme. He had moved up in the world.

Readers of the *Sunday Times* were mostly disgusted by what I wrote. Keith Miller's put-down touched a nerve. 'Sometimes people get a cancer of the spirit. And maybe that says a lot about them.'

You think you're impermeable, until someone says you've got cancer of the spirit.

For thirteen years, this story has been a central part of my life. Mary, my wife, has lived it more than anyone. While I have been away writing this book, she emailed her thoughts.

When Lance Armstrong first came into our lives thirteen years ago, I never dreamt he would have the impact he had. I don't think of it as good or bad, just ever present. We have six children and meal time was question time. If I had to sum up what the kids thought, it would be that they believed their dad when he said Lance was doping but they also felt it would never come out. 'You're not going to be able to prove it, Dad.'

Dave was always very passionate about the story. For the right reasons, I felt. He wanted people to see Lance for the person he really was. When people told me my husband was obsessed by Lance, I didn't feel he was. But Lance followed us everywhere; to dinner parties, weddings, gatherings in the village hall; there was always someone who had a question, often there was a line of five or six. And then there were the journalists, the TV crews who came to our house. Once, as Dave was leaving the house to play golf, he shouted back to me that there was a TV crew coming later in the day but he would be home before they arrived. They were from Canada and they got to our house two hours before Dave. What's a woman meant to do?

My friend Fiona tells me there were times when I was afraid Lance Armstrong would cost Dave his job, and I suppose I must have been at one time. When the end came for Lance, and he was finally stripped of those titles, in a strange way I felt sorry for him. I was sorry that so much of his life was spent earning the admiration of people from all over the world and then to have himself exposed . . . You might imagine our dinner table isn't as lively now but, believe it or not, there are still lots of questions from us about Lance.

My final memory is of sharing Dave for a number of years with Betsy. I'd walk into his office, he'd be on the phone and, before I'd say a word, he'd say, 'It's only Betsy.' How many times did I hear that!

Now, on this day, 22 October 2012, the game is up for Armstrong. 'Vindicated' is the word every interviewer uses. Quickly I grow to dislike 'vindicated'. It is not how I feel. I didn't need McQuaid to tell me what he and I both knew. What satisfaction there is comes from the meaning it has for a group of people that had, in one way or another, contributed to the search for truth in this story.

I thought of Christophe Bassons and how his persecution on the 1999 Tour de France was the defining moment in my reaction to Lance Armstrong. Back then, it was obvious you could not be anti-doping and anti-Bassons. Impossible. But they ran him out of town and at the head of the lynch mob, lacking only a white hood and length of rope, was Armstrong.

Bassons left pro cycling long before he should have. His trainer, Antoine Vayer, told him to go back to education. That's what he did and now he works for the French Ministry of Sport in the Bordeaux region, making sure that sport is properly organised and, where there should be doping controls, they are in place and properly executed.

Asked how he felt on 22 October, when his old nemesis went down, this is what Christophe wrote:

The news that Lance Armstrong was stripped of his Tour wins brings no great joy to me, just an appreciation that justice has been done. He cheated; it was important that this was established and that he was sanctioned. It was also

397

important to establish that the people who questioned his performances were not bitter, but true and honest.

I have no regrets about what I did in 1999. The way Armstrong treated me in that Tour was a reflection of his character and the manner in which he imposed his will on the peloton. He was the only one to say to my face what the other riders were thinking of me. If they had had the opportunity or the intelligence to create the empire he made, they would have done exactly the same. They weren't any more honest than he was, just less intelligent and courageous. They have no right to point a finger at him, like some have already done.

Having said that, I was surprised at the influence he had on his teammates in threatening and inciting them to dope. It reminded me of how things were at Festina a few years before. Richard Virenque, like Armstrong, was not easy on his teammates, especially those who disagreed with him.

For the moment I think it's probably better to stay in the present and allow Lance Armstrong to explain himself to the American justice system. The world of sport should forget him but should not destroy him psychologically. Armstrong is still a human being with an individual personality that was built during his childhood. I know he had a difficult childhood, which might explain his need to win at all costs, even if that meant not respecting other people.

Today I feel more pity than contempt for him. I always preferred to be in my position than in his. I am honest, straight and happy. I don't think he can say the same.

Contrary to what some people believe, Laurent Jalabert [the former cyclist and now television commentator] in particular, I do not consider Lance Armstrong to be a great champion. He was just someone who was prepared to abandon his morals to win at all costs. His is a story of failure and nothing else.

The spotlight now should not be on Lance Armstrong but on a sport that is still gangrenous with doping and deceit. The Tour de France 2012 did not reassure me.

Bassons showed us there were two ways of riding the Tour de France, and that you couldn't support both. And you couldn't sit on the fence. His was the side to be on, and the only cancer of the spirit in cycling was in those injecting chemicals into their veins every morning.

Once upon a time professional cycling enthralled me, tapping into my innocence and winging me off to a world that was beautifully simple and richly complex. On the same day, a stage of the Tour de France can push a man further than ever he's gone and still seem like chess on wheels. In those unsuspecting years, when EPO hadn't come with its power to distort and poison, Greg LeMond was the greatest cyclist ever I saw – so blessed with natural talent it seemed almost unfair on his rivals.

He had once been a supporter of Lance Armstrong, but the relationship turned ugly as time went on. Greg's legacy as a brilliant and clean cyclist was always greater than anything Lance could achieve. That didn't stop Lance. He hurt Greg, professionally and personally. In the three years after 2001, we talked a lot and Greg went through a lot of tough times.

Without Kathy, he mightn't have got to the other side. I asked Kathy LeMond how she felt on 22 October:

I felt some anxiety leading up to the UCI decision. I have always known that the leaders of the UCI shouldn't be trusted to make an unbiased decision, but felt that they were going to rule in the only way they could to save themselves, at least temporarily. This meant they had to find Lance guilty. He needed to be kicked out of the Tour in 1999, but the system didn't work.

When this all came out there was no joyous whooping it up at our house. This sport and our family have been through too much for that. To me this was like a criminal trial in which the accused is found guilty. The crime has happened and the victims are grieving. Yes, the accountability feels good but there is no joy, more a feeling of relief. There are others who have not yet been held accountable for their actions and I hope that those verdicts will be coming.

Greg's reputation, our business, our children's teenage years, were all consumed by a vicious vendetta against Greg and our family because we wouldn't go along with the lies. Greg and I made the decision that, even though the fall-out would be terrible, there was no other option but to be honest about what we knew. The kids were with us when we told the truth about Lance Armstrong, so it strengthened our family to be in this ordeal together. They always supported their dad.

I imagine that maybe I could feel sorry for Lance, but not after so many years of interfering in our life. No way.

He was different to others. There seemed to be no limit to his ability to insert himself into all areas of our life. It was really sick.

It is interesting that he's on Twitter and taking photos with his seven yellow jerseys. That, to me, really shows that he is different to the average person. Where is the shame? I don't see any. No apology to all those whose lives and careers were destroyed; people duped for years into believing his story – nothing for them. We all heard his speech on the podium at the Tour de France chastising people for questioning his performances: how do you get to be like that?

It is a great disappointment to me that it took so many years for ex-teammates and staff to commit to unravelling the story. All those riders that participated only told their stories with their backs against the wall. I know it will seem ungracious to ask now, but how do you keep silent when so many innocents are being destroyed?

Greg lost so much in this ordeal. He had the courage to say things that needed to be said, and it was unpopular, but he was authentic. Truly, David, as Greg and you said almost twelve years ago, it was either the greatest comeback in the history of sport or the greatest fraud. We know now.

And my oldest friend, Paul Kimmage? We have ridden side by side through all this. Innocents before this war started, we're jaded veterans now. In the war against doping in sport, you need moral certainty, and Paul has that. It fuels his courage. He once reminded me what Sam said in *Lord of the*

Rings: 'There's some good in the world, Mr Frodo, and it's worth fighting for.' Paul takes off the gloves, fights bare-knuckled, but he's always on the side of right.

I asked him how he felt on that Monday:

I lost count of the number of times I celebrated Armstrong's demise since his miraculous escape from the corticosteroid positive in 1999. There were the TV images of Del Moral dumping his syringes in 2000: That's it. He's fucked.

The revelation that he was working with Ferrari in 2001: That's it. He's fucked.

The publication of *L.A. Confidentiel* in 2004: That's it. He's fucked.

The *L'Équipe* investigation and that brilliant – sorry, I'm biased – front page: LE MENSONGE ARMSTRONG in August 2005: That's it. He's fucked.

The SCA trial in October 2005: That's it. He's fucked.

The Floyd Landis emails in April 2010: That's it. He's fucked.

The news, three months later, that he was the subject of a federal investigation being led by Jeff Novitzky: That's it. He's fucked.

Thirteen years of false dawns and wasteful swearing.

I'm not sure how I felt when he was finally nailed by USADA. I used the word 'elated' a couple of times, but it didn't feel that good; I was happy but not elated. And I didn't feel as high as I felt low, in February, when the federal investigation was dropped. That was not a good night *chez nous*, believe me: That's it. Untouchable!

I was absolutely disconsolate.

It was scant consolation that Travis Tygart picked up the baton. How would he succeed when Novitzky had failed? But succeed he most certainly did. He delivered the truth, turned the fiction into fact and the icon into a pariah.

Touchable! Take a bow, Eliot Ness.

But, Paul, what about my genteel coffee-table book about the last thirteen years? That's it. Fucked.

I think too of what this day means for Charles Pelkey, with whom I shared a car and a journey through the moral maze at the 1999 Tour. It was more fun than it should have been. When I recall Lance's endless quotes about how hard he worked, as if he'd invented the concept, I think of Charles and imagine there isn't a cyclist out there who has worked harder than Charles. Once I got a text message from him at a little after eleven o'clock in the morning, UK time. I called. 'Charles, you're up late.' It was a little after four in the morning in Laramie. 'Actually,' he said. 'I've just got up. The only way for me to combine my job while studying for a law degree is to start my day at four a.m.'

Charles would weigh the facts and come to his own conclusions. He's a lawyer now and I imagine that limber mind serves him well. Now that Lance was being excised from cycling history, I wanted to know what Charles was thinking. I could be sure that he *was* actually thinking:

I have to admit that back in 1999, getting ready for the first post-Festina Tour, I was convinced that this brash young Texan, who had battled back from stage iv cancer, could well be the vanguard of a new era in cycling. In a way, I was right, but for all the wrong reasons.

How could, one reasoned, anyone who'd faced death and suffered through cancer, surgery and chemotherapy, put his life and health at risk by taking dangerous drugs? It was a point Armstrong himself made in an interview on NPR just days before the Tour. I bought the argument. Not for long, though.

I had the privilege of spending that '99 Tour with David Walsh, along with my good friend Rupert Guinness and my boss, John Wilcockson. Four men packed into a small car for three weeks, with the topic of conversation invariably drifting to the question of doping. Walsh had arrived at the Tour with a healthy level of scepticism; scepticism that was bolstered when a sample Armstrong submitted on the day of the prologue tested positive for corticosteroids.

No, I didn't buy the back-dated prescription (but I did dutifully report Armstrong's explanation). By the time we reached Paris there were many in the press room openly asking questions about Armstrong's stellar performance, particularly the French, who'd had their national Tour nearly destroyed by drug scandal just a year earlier.

The questions led to that now infamous response from Mr Armstrong, who was clearly tiring of the 'wrong' kind of attention he was receiving: 'Monsieur Le Monde, are you calling me a liar or a doper?' Actually, Lance, 'Monsieur Le Monde' was calling you both, and the intervening thirteen years proved he had every right to do so.

For me, the Lance story pretty much ended the day USADA released its 200-page 'Reasoned Decision', bolstered by nearly 1000 pages of supporting evidence and affidavits. Now no longer a cycling journalist, I nonetheless blew off an entire day's work in my law office to read as much of that document dump as I could manage.

I've said it before and I will say it again: reading USADA's file struck me as if I was reading the unabridged version of *L.A. Confidentiel: Les Secrets de Lance Armstrong*. For McQuaid to stand there and decry Armstrong's destructive impact on the sport of cycling was akin to the madam of a bordello waxing indignant about the decline of sexual morality in her community. It lacked a certain degree of sincerity.

So, on 22 October, I didn't really think much about Lance Armstrong. I thought more about people like Betsy and Frankie Andreu, Emma O'Reilly, Greg LeMond, David Walsh, Pierre Ballester, Paul Kimmage and count-less others who were attacked, belittled and even sued by Armstrong's formidable legal team.

I thought about people like Oakley's athlete liaison, Stephanie McIlvain, who was clearly the victim of bullying and intimidation and never did talk for fear of losing a job she used to support a disabled child. I thought also of admitted dopers, like Floyd Landis and Tyler Hamilton, whose own testimony served as the thread that, once pulled, unravelled the myth much like a two-dollar sweater.

I also spent a bit of time thinking about the tenacious CEO of USADA, Travis Tygart, who actually spent time listening to those people and used his considerable resources to take down someone who, for years, thought he was somehow immune to scrutiny. He wasn't.

What's more, I spent time thinking about the cynical exploitation of a disease suffered by millions around the globe, by a man who used what could otherwise be deemed 'good works' as a shield to distract the inquisitive from raising questions about his flawed character. Having recently suffered through three surgeries and five months of chemotherapy myself, I resented the self-aggrandising attitude displayed by the man many of us in the press corps came to call 'Cancer Jesus'.

No, for me, 22 October's UCI announcement was not a milestone. It merely served as the final nail in a coffin that should have been six feet under years before.

Strange thing. When Pat McQuaid threw down the card which he hoped might be the final card in the game, it was the champion bridge player Bob Hamman who had most cause to smile. He was the man sitting on the only sworn testimonies in the entire case. Bob read *L.A. Confidentiel* and decided to withhold a $5 million bonus he owed to Lance Armstrong for winning the 2004 Tour. Everybody went into court and swore to tell the truth. Now we know that some lied.

As a player of cards, Bob is one of the best. Bridge, gin rummy, poker, it doesn't matter. 'Please,' he says, in that slow Texas drawl of his, 'don't mention the poker. I'm tired of saying no to people wanting me to play that game.' Now, eight years after deciding he shouldn't have to pay the bonus to a man he believed cheated, the man from the SCA has some good cards in his hand.

How must he have felt on 22 October?

When Pat McQuaid and the UCI cast the final stone at Lance, I was mystified. Was this the same organisation whose Honorary President Emeritus, Hein Verbruggen, had only last year loudly and publicly stated Lance Armstrong had never doped? It seemed to me that very little in USADA's report was news to the UCI. The UCI has been the fox watching the hen house. I guess it is now time for them to change uniforms.

As I further reflected on McQuaid's statement – 'I was sickened by what I read in the USADA report' – I was amazed that information disseminated by the 'Witch Hunters of USADA' would create such an expression of astonishment – such an apparently allergic reaction from the head of an organisation which, for over a decade, appeared to be very derelict in the discharge of the responsibilities to which it had given continued lip service since the Festina affair. Or perhaps McQuaid was simply having withdrawal symptoms because his supply of anti-doping medications purchased with the donations made to 'Fight Doping' had been depleted.

But still, McQuaid's words in no way removed the blight on motherhood or apple pie that was caused by SCA's unethical decision to question Saint Lance's conscientious observation of virtually every propriety known to man.

I also marvel that this unmerited criticism of the Saint has caused his previously oblivious sponsors to unjustly come to the jarring realisation that they had been hoodwinked egregiously. This shows how unfair the world can be.

In any event, since all those throwing stones seem to be having such a good time, perhaps it is time for SCA to join the party.

It sort of reminds me of a situation many years ago at a break in a high-stakes game of gin rummy, when one of the participants asked an observer what he thought of the game. The observer replied: 'Your opponent is cheating every way he can think of, but you can spot him that.' Even though the truth has been acknowledged by friend and foe alike, we did learn a painful lesson that we cannot always 'spot him that', especially if the fix is in. Hopefully, now that the last of the 'referees' has left the arena and there is no one left to provide covering fire, we can get back to somewhere within shouting distance of even.

On the day Armstrong won his first Tour de France, I wrote a piece for the *Sunday Times* suggesting the achievement of the cancer survivor should not be applauded: 'There are times when it is right to celebrate, but there are other occasions when it is equally correct to keep your hands by your sides and wonder . . . [and in this case] the need for inquiry is overwhelming.'

The paper ran the piece without question, although quietly my colleagues must have wondered what we were getting into. The years that followed were tough on my boss Alex Butler. There were times, too, when they were made tougher by my blind refusal to acknowledge that he had any duties at all except to be my shield and sword. He would say, 'When the truth comes out, you will be able to write exactly what you want.' That always seemed too far away for me.

We made several lawyers very unhappy too, but the *Sunday Times* did something that very few newspapers ever do. They ended up putting their money where my mouth had been. Lance did well out of us. But I'm still here and Alex is still there. On the legal business, the fat lady has yet to sing but our people have given her the nod. She's clearing her throat. The *Sunday Times* felt defrauded at the time and the time has come to reclaim what is justly ours.

Arbiter of the newspaper's approach to the story in 1999, Alex has seen a lot of water flow under the bridge.

I have only one regret. I didn't keep the letters. Over the years, there were scores, possibly hundreds. 'Why are you hounding this man? Can't you just marvel at his achievements? You should be ashamed.' I did keep them at first. I promised myself that I would reply to each and every one on the day he was exposed. But as the years passed, that was just another resolution that fell by the wayside. And now that the game is up, how I wish I could be replying to those letters.

When the L.A. empire finally came crashing down in October 2012 I felt glad for David. For Mary. But I can't say I felt any great emotion or surprise. Why? Easy. I'd made my mind up years ago. Did I always believe he was a doper? Maybe not. I'm a hopeless romantic. I wanted to believe. But I also wanted to believe David Walsh. And that's not been easy. Because that's not been my role. My job has been to dispute and argue with David. To doubt his conclusions.

But very early on in this thirteen-year saga, I was

convinced that David knew what he was talking about. He loved the Tour de France. He loved the sport of cycling. And he knew the sport. Much more than I did. Patiently, and methodically, he laid out his case against Armstrong in my office and in the pages of the *Sunday Times*. And I became a believer. For despite all the disquiet that David's stories created, nobody could answer me one simple question: if everyone on the Tour is taking performance-enhancing drugs, how come this American guy is leaving them for dust? I always felt that David's explanation was more plausible.

And I never warmed to Armstrong. Or his bullying. Or his people. Or his expensive lawyers. Or his chums in the media. The tame, fawning cycling correspondents. The L.A. fan club. Even the countless journalists who told me how great a job they thought the *Sunday Times* was doing while their own newspapers joined in the L.A. adulation made me cringe. And even worse, the journalists who poured scorn on Walsh's investigations because they were too damned lazy to undertake their own. They know who they are.

Even after we were forced to settle with Armstrong when he sued the *Sunday Times*, I always felt we would win in the end and get our money back. It was only a matter of time. Why? Because sooner or later, someone would talk. Americans were the leading players in this saga. I used to tell David: 'Someone will become a born-again Christian, have a costly divorce to pay for or just simply want to tell the truth and unburden themselves . . . it's the American way.' And one by one, the riders of the

US Postal team have told their story. A story that would have been told years earlier but for our stringent libel laws.

Favourite moment? Dancing around a bedroom in Holland in August 2005 after a 6.30 a.m. phone call from David informing me of *L'Équipe*'s superb exclusive report – headlined THE ARMSTRONG LIE – which revealed the Texan had used EPO in 1999.

Lowest moment? The sheer grind of litigation. And sitting in the office as Mr Justice Eady dismantled our defence while Armstrong sat smirking in Texas. The British libel laws have a lot to answer for.

Most embarrassing? When Pat McQuaid said that 'Lance Armstrong has no place in cycling', it slowly dawned on me that I had promised publicly to run around the office naked when L.A. was eventually exposed.

The reason I was able to keep reporting the Armstrong story was enough people cared about the truth. They spoke to me on and off the record. Exactly one week before Christmas Day in 2003, I sat with Jonathan Vaughters at a table in a Denver restaurant and he told me how riders were now micro-dosing EPO and how easily they were beating the new test. He also told me something that made me so mad about what the sport had become. It was the epitome of screwed-up.

When he was on the point of leaving US Postal for Crédit Agricole towards the end of the 2000 season, he showed his then *directeur sportif* Johan Bruyneel the contract being offered by the French team. It was far more money than Postal had offered, but Bruyneel had the option of upping his team's offer to keep Vaughters. Bruyneel studied the Crédit Agricole offer.

'With your haematocrit level [Vaughters has a naturally high haematocrit, 48 or 49],' he said, 'you will not be able to justify this salary.'

This was nature being turned on its head: a naturally high haematocrit should be an advantage, but on Planet Doping it's a negative.

I asked Vaughters how 22 October felt to him. He wrote:

I can't say I felt much of anything the day the UCI upheld USADA's decision regarding Lance Armstrong. I didn't feel happy or relieved. I didn't feel right or wrong. Within me, I always knew that this would come to pass, this way, if I chose to be honest about what had happened. So, the emotion was tied to the decisions that I made many years ago as to how I would behave if asked questions regarding doping and regarding Lance.

Frankly, David, it is you that convinced me to change my path. When you came to see me in 2003, writing your book and asking questions no one wanted answered, that was where there was emotion. At that point, I had decided to leave cycling and to never look back, never re-enter the sport and never be around the sport again. You said to me, 'How can a sport ever turn the corner if the good guys all leave or get pushed out?' That stuck.

I am not a good guy but it made me realise that I needed to make sure they didn't leave cycling, and it made me realise my place in cycling was to make sure they didn't get pushed out.

With that realisation, I decided that, when the right day came, I needed to be honest about my past and about the past of cycling. That moment, many years ago, contained a lot of emotion. Not many people in this world truly confront what they've done wrong. Doing so is very painful. Real emotion.

Everything from that moment forward has simply been what I've always expected to happen. A slow roll towards an inevitable conclusion. One that has no benefit, unless the good guys that haven't been driven from the sport decide to use the emotion and pain and direct it so that this process doesn't repeat itself. Maybe that gives me hope. And hope is the one and only useful feeling that should come from that day.

So I guess I did feel something: an uneasy hope. Hope that the sport can learn and can change. Change, so that this never happens again.

Pierre Ballester had a different take on cycling. He tried to be part of the solution and got fired from *L'Équipe* for his troubles. *L.A. Confidentiel* was our big roll but the dice were loaded. How can you reveal the truth if those to whom you are speaking don't want to hear? The UCI didn't want to know their sport was diseased; the Tour de France preferred to turn a blind eye to the circus the race had become, and too many of the fans couldn't bear to be told the saints were sinners.

'*Tant pis*,' thought Pierre. He did his time at the front line but ended up thinking it was a pointless war. He knew his own mind. After *L'Équipe* he got a job with the FFR, the French rugby federation, and he combines that with his

<heading level="1">David Walsh</heading>

teacher's job at the Centre de Formations des Journalistes (CFJ) on rue du Louvre in the second arrondissement of Paris. When he's not writing about rugby or inspiring France's next generation of Pierre Ballesters, he's writing books.

Early in 2013, his newest book will go on sale in France, and it is the extraordinary story of a French woman who eighteen years ago travelled deep into the Amazon, close to the Brazil–Venezuela border, to help the native Indian Yanomami people prepare for the changes that will be forced upon them. She learned their language, educated their teachers, and taught their people Portuguese.

She learned to be their nurse and doctor and she would marry a native Indian Yanomami man. So immersed did she become in life in one of the remotest parts of the world, her native French grew rusty, and when she contacted her young brother in Paris, she emailed him in English. In eighteen years she has returned to Paris just three times.

In October 2010 Pierre travelled to where this woman now lives in the Amazon. It took him nine days to get there. The last four days of the journey were in a small boat. He spent a month living among the Yanomami. 'It is a completely different world. There is no property, no notion of time, and the lives of the people are guided solely by the need to find food. They hunt and they fish and they make sure they have enough drinking water.'

The Yanomami affectionately call their Parisian 'The Lady with the Black Eye', because when she first turned up she was wearing black eyeliner. They had never seen that. Pierre called his book, *L'Amazone*, which is a play on the name of the river and the mythical warrior woman. It is the story of Anne Ballester, his sister.

So you can guess that Pierre wasn't glued to his computer on 22 October, waiting for the UCI's response to the USADA report:

I was at the CFJ that Monday. I'd forgotten it was on, but one of the students heard it and knew I had been involved in the Armstrong story. He told me about it. Later I heard the details: 'McQuaid shocked by what was in the report,' and I just laughed. What hypocrisy. Armstrong might deserve his punishment, but how can you single him out from the others? What is the difference between him and Ullrich and Basso? I feel sympathy for Lance because that night in the Oslo nightclub, after he won the world championships, you could see he was an interesting guy. You could have conversations with him about many things, not just cycling, and I thought, 'I like this guy.'

But he changed. After he came back to the sport in 1998, he was harder, like steel. Maybe the cancer experience had that effect on him. I still consider him an exceptional guy. Of course he lied, he cheated, he was a fucking bastard to a lot of people, but can you imagine what intelligence it took to create what he created? He had to take care of a lot of things.

I have no respect for the way the majority in the media have dealt with this story. When Lance was winning he was their friend the hero. They wouldn't say a bad word about him. Back then they were cowards and, as they kill him now, they're still behaving in a cowardly way. Burying Lance Armstrong now is too easy.

What disgusted me about Lance was the way he held the cancer community hostage while doing his own thing in his career.

I envy my sister a little, being part of a world where the challenge of life is just getting enough food and water. She is fighting to make life better for the Yanomami people, trying to protect the environment, and she is doing something really useful. That's what I envy her the most.

In the summer of 2004 Lance turned the heat on our witnesses: Emma O'Reilly and Stephen Swart were sued, though he did not see his cases against them go through; Armstrong called up Greg LeMond; Frankie Andreu got the persuasive charm of Bill Stapleton in Charleroi. It was a time of stress and, if Emma felt it more than anyone, Stephen was the coolest. After the book's release, he did an interview with Phil Taylor in the *New Zealand Herald* in which he reiterated everything he had said about Lance being an advocate for doping in 1995.

I remember speaking to Emma about Stephen's interview, and she drew strength from it. Stephen's like that: quietly spoken but unwavering. 'As long as you believe in the stance you are taking and why you are taking it, then you have to stay strong with it. My motivation was that the sport, when I left it [at the end of 1995], was in a very bad state. I had a young son showing interest and asking questions. What was I supposed to tell him?' he said, in a later interview with Phil Taylor in the *New Zealand Herald* on 12 October 2012.

Stephen never set out to show that Armstrong was a doper but to tell the story of his career in pro cycling. It just happened that Lance Armstrong was an influential figure in the discussions on doping taking place in the Motorola team of the mid-nineties. It would have been convenient but dishonest to have left him out. Jan Swart tagged a link to Taylor's interview onto their son Logan's Facebook page.

Logan is currently cycling the length of South America and his Facebook comment on the interview pleased his mum: 'My dad is the man,' he wrote. His friends were quick to add their comments: 'He sure is'; 'You must be proud, Logan!' etc. On the morning after the UCI's acceptance of the sanctions against Armstrong, a neighbour left a newspaper on their doorstep, because it had an article praising Stephen's courage.

It is not in Stephen's nature to see what he's done in terms of courage:

> I've received plenty of 'good on ya's', especially from people I don't even know. From family and friends, the support has always been fantastic and, when it all came out, I thought, 'This is more for them than me because they believed in what I said and why I said it.' My opinion of the UCI is they are a weak, struggling organisation with a bad culture that starts at the top. There is the need for some serious house cleaning, and promptly.
>
> I'd rather think about my plan to meet up with Logan in Puerto Montt in southern Chile at Christmas and then set off on our bikes on the Carretera Austral trail to Cochrane, which is approximately 1200 kilometres. I've

been on bike trips to New Zealand's Southern Alps and cycling around there for a week, but this is longer and very different. It will be like a race, days when you don't want to get back out there but you do it. It will be great.

And it will be good for me to spend this time with Logan. We've never been away for anything like as long and some of the nights we will be in our two-man tent. He knows his way around, as he's cycled from Holland to Istanbul and he's toured Nepal on his bike. While in Nepal he slept on a dirt floor for six months in an orphanage and looked after the kids. He's seen far more of the world than I have but this will take me out of my comfort zone. And it will be just him and me, which is good.

Lots of the people I met along the way became friends to me. And some became heroes. I had my job, the support of a paper and a sports editor and a monthly wage. I was never conflicted. I saw men and women, though, who had parts of their lives and parts of their hearts tied up in the other side of the argument. People who had lots to lose. People who grappled with their consciences every day and pushed themselves to do the right thing. As much as anything I have seen in a sporting arena, those struggles spoke of heroism and character. Emma O'Reilly would always have a special place in that list.

I was busy that Monday and don't think I really caught up on the news until the next day. I listen to Pat McQuaid and the way he's tried to distance himself and the UCI from Lance and they're just trying to distance themselves from the problem. It seems to me the cycling community is changing for the better quicker than the body that should be driving that change. As for the riders, they do what it is natural for them to do: protect their short-term interests.

I look back on the last thirteen years and see them in the light of W.B. Yeats' two poems dealing with a critical time in Irish history: 'September 1913' and 'Easter, 1916'. Back in 2003, when I decided to do that first interview, I really wanted to bring change to the sport; others felt the same and we were the revolutionaries of September 1913:

But little time had they to pray/For whom the hangman's rope was spun/And what, God help us, could they save?

We were persecuted, that's for sure, and what were we trying to save? But it is right that we spoke up, and I won't ever regret that. The fact that the USADA report got to the bottom of everything and showed us exactly what was going on is a good thing. I'm pleased for the people who had the courage to tell the truth: the witnesses and the journalists. There weren't that many, really.

In 'Easter, 1916' Yeats writes of Major John MacBride, a man he didn't like:

This other man I dreamed/A drunken vainglorious lout./He had done most bitter wrong/To some who are near to my heart.

I think of those lines and, yes, I think of Lance and Johan and the wrongs they did to so many. They weren't drunken but they were vainglorious. But it is the central theme from 'Easter, 1916' that most applies to what we've seen in cycling over the last few months. Yeats writes about the execution of the Irish patriots after the Easter rising, deaths which directly led to Ireland gaining its independence:

I write it out in verse/McDonagh and MacBride/And Connolly and Pearse/Now and in time to be/Wherever green is worn/Are changed, changed utterly:/A terrible beauty is born.

The honesty did help to bring the truth into the open and make sure that people who deserved to be punished were punished. But as Yeats thought about 1916, too much blood was spilt: I think there was too much stress and acrimony and damage in finding the truth in our little cycling story.

A terrible beauty. Then and now.

Frankie Andreu knew Lance Armstrong for so many years. I remember the closeness that grew between myself and Paul when we would talk cycling all day long on the rue Kléber back in 1984. What must it have been like for those two guys? They came to live and ride in Europe in the early nineties. Together all the time. Eating together, talking together, socialising together. And training together, those endless rides near Lake Como, then Nice; for a time Frankie was like a brother to Lance.

He married Betsy, though, a remarkable woman who held him to a higher standard of behaviour than Lance ever would. I asked Frankie to write to me about his reaction to the 22 October denouement. 'What you want?' he asked, in the straight-up tone that prompted his friends to call him

Ajax, after the abrasive little blue particles in the washing powder. Betsy asked him what he'd written about her. 'Not much,' he replied. 'Just the matter-of-fact stuff I was asked for.' She went off on one.

When Betsy lets rip, it's better to let the storm blow itself out. Frankie did that, taking the buffeting in his usual calm way. She would later say, 'Why didn't you stop me and tell me what you wrote?' and he replied, 'Why didn't you slow down or even pause, and give me the chance to speak?'

That story is so Frankie and Betsy, as close a couple as I've ever seen.

This is what Frankie actually wrote:

I don't remember where I was when the UCI upheld the decision on Armstrong. It didn't matter. To me the truth was out there with the USADA report, and whatever happened after that wasn't my problem. I was tired of defending myself, tired of Lance Armstrong, and I was ready to get his name out of my household. It had finally come to an end.

To say the last few years were stressful would be an understatement. The financial uncertainties were a stress I had to deal with. At times, I was at a complete loss at how to balance pushing for the truth yet trying to maintain my place in cycling. This led to many arguments between my wife and me. Sometimes I wanted to talk and she didn't want to; sometimes she wanted to talk and I didn't want to. I usually lost the battle. It started in 2006 with the SCA subpoena. I had left for the Tour de France, and she was left home alone to receive the brunt of the Armstrong attacks. There were many long phone calls, she shed many tears, and was angry that what was being portrayed of her was not correct. She knew the sport had a problem, that I was involved with part of that problem, and it was time to change that. Her upbringing and ethics directed her actions. She showed me that not caving in, and standing up for yourself, can set you free.

This didn't come without a price. Many times mean things were said, or we'd ignore each other; many nights we went to bed mad at each other. Over time some things became evident that I didn't realise before: Betsy was so strong-willed and determined. She stuck to her convictions like none other. We had supporters behind the scenes but we also had many detractors. The hateful messages would arrive and the fury in her would rise. She had the courage that I didn't have. As time went by I realised that her part in this was an important role – she gave a sound to our voice. No longer was the loudspeaker of lies repeatedly coming from the Lance camp the only sound that was heard. She knew the only way to reveal the truth was to defend herself at all costs. In doing so she defended me, and for that I'm thankful.

But right now, in this café off the M25, I feel no joy at Pat McQuaid's volte-face over USADA and Armstrong. Somebody once said that fate is the thing you meet on the road you took to avoid fate. Oddly, today should have been the 30th birthday of our son John, killed on his bicycle seventeen years ago.

The thing about the Armstrong scandal was that, even in

1999, the year of his first victory, you didn't need to be Woodward or Bernstein to get it. On the afternoon the American delivered his first great performance in the Alps, the stage to Sestriere, many journalists in the *salle de presse* laughed at the ease with which Armstrong ascended. He climbed with the nonchalance of the well doped.

And now on this day, as I sit in this café, Armstrong has finally gone down: 22 October, John's birthday. I ring Betsy, in whose slipstream I have travelled for almost ten years. I tell her it's John's birthday and, though she's far away in Michigan, I can feel her sadness.

'It's his birthday,' she says in a whisper. 'This is his little gift to you.'

It's a nice thought.

Acknowledgements

I don't wish to bore you any further, but some people deserve to be thanked.

I hope that those deserving the greatest credit have been properly recognised in the story. What set Emma O'Reilly, Betsy Andreu, Stephen Swart and Greg LeMond apart was their willingness to tell the truth at a time when there was nothing in it for them except vilification and other forms of bullying. They were one part of my motivation. Those riders who rode clean in the darkest days were the other. I don't know Christophe Bassons, Gilles Delion and many others, but as long as there were riders saying no to doping, we had a cause worth fighting for.

My first experience of seeing how riding clean could virtually end your pro career came from knowing and being close to Paul Kimmage. The way the sport treated him was demoralising, but through the tough times came the determination never to be another fan with a typewriter. Paul's integrity has been a constant. At the Olympics in Atlanta, we cut our teeth on the Michelle Smith story and were inspired by the work of our colleague Tom Humphries who is, by some distance, the most talented sportswriter I've ever read. A fine man, too.

There were many journalists/friends who made the journey

interesting and offered unflinching support at important moments. Tom Goldman from Northwest Public Radio was one of the first in the US to get the Armstrong story and it didn't scare him. Charles Pelkey, Gwen Knapp, Alex Wolff and the late Randy Starkman in Canada were always supportive. Pierre Ballester, co-author of *L.A. Confidentiel*, has long been a great friend.

So, too, many others. Alex Butler, my sports editor at the *Sunday Times*, has been friend and supporter. Not many sports editors would have allowed me to pursue the Armstrong story as Alex did, and for that I shall always be in his debt. Some time ago Alex described Lance as 'the story that keeps giving', and he wasn't wrong. His deputy during the most difficult days was Alan English, who did a fine job then and remains a true friend. At the *Sunday Times* we knew the truth and were determined to get it out there. Other colleagues – Hugh McIlvanney, Stephen Jones, Jonny Northcroft and Simon Ritter – were also tremendously supportive.

Along the way there were plenty who thought we were wrong, but others who backed us. I recall an evening at Veyrier-du-Lac near Annecy with Peter Zaballos and his family during a Tour de France – ordinary Americans who loved their country but wanted to know the truth behind Lance Armstrong. Enough people believed that however painful, the truth should be revealed.

My gratitude is due also to Kerr MacRae, Ian Marshall and the team at Simon & Schuster who did a terrific job in getting the book to the market place. I was introduced to Simon & Schuster by my literary agent Richard Relton, who asked for a 'ten-minute audition' and now looks like he's going to stay around for a bit. I needed time off to write the book and, as always, Alex Butler and the *Sunday Times* were generous. For solitude, I went to the south coast of Ireland where my brother Brendan and his wife Mary provided a beautiful home and excellent meals on wheels. I also thank their eldest son Brendan for the Brad Pitt quote from *Se7en* that appears in the epigraph at the front.

My own family were wonderfully supportive, not to say indulgent, through the Armstrong years. If the story hadn't been so damn interesting, I would never have got away with it. Our kids didn't always eat their vegetables, but they never did boring.